Diversity and Justice in Canada

edited by
John A. Winterdyk
and Douglas E. King

Canadian Scholars' Press Inc.　　　　　Toronto　　　　　1999

Diversity and Justice in Canada
edited by John A. Winterdyk and Douglas E. King

First published in 1999 by
Canadian Scholars' Press Inc.
180 Bloor Street West, Ste. 1202
Toronto, Ontario
M5S 2V6

We acknowledge the financial support of the Government of Canada through the Book Publishing Industry Development Programme for our publishing activities.

Canadian Cataloguing in Publication Data

Main entry under title:
    Diversity and justice in Canada

Includes bibliographical references.
ISBN 1-55130-140-7

1. Justice, Administration of – Canada. 2. Discrimination in justice administration – Canada. 3. Sex discrimination in justice administration – Canada I. Winterdyk, John. II. King, Douglas E. (Douglas Edwin).

HV9960.C2D58 1999   364.971   C98-932814-7

Page layout and cover design by Brad Horning

Table of Contents

Preface v

Unit I: Introduction 1

Unit II: Aboriginal Groups 13
Canada's Off-Reserve Aboriginal Population
Ryan J. McDonald 17
Minorities, Crime, and the Law
J. Colin Yerbury and Curt T. Griffith 26
Accommodating the Concerns of Aboriginal People
within the Existing Justice System
John Giokas 45

Unit III: Ethnicity, Immigration, and National Groups 61
Ethnic Origins of the Canadian Population
Pamela M. White 65
Visible Minorities: A Diverse Group
Karen Kelly 70
Crime, Ethnicity, and Immigration
Robert M. Gordon and Jacquelyn Nelson 82
Disproportionate Harm: Hate Crime in Canada
Julian V. Roberts 94

Unit IV: Women 117

    Women and the Criminal Justice System

        Catherine Trainor, Josee Normand, and Lisa Verdon 122

    Trends in Women's Crime

        M. Chesney-Lind 135

Unit V: Gender Orientation: Gays and Lesbians 155

    At a Glance: Violence Against Gays and Lesbians

        Infolink: National Victim Center 159

    Sexual Coercion in Gay Male and Lesbian Relationships:

    Predictors and Implications for Support Services

        Caroline K. Waterman, Lori J. Dawson,

        and Michael J. Bologna 163

Unit VI: Age: The Elderly and Youth 171

    Population Aging: Baby Boomers in the 21st Century

        Craig McKie 176

    At a Glance: Elder Abuse

        Infolink: National Victim Center 181

    Intergenerational Conflict and the Prevention of Abuse

    Against Older Persons: Final Report to Health Canada

        J.A. Tindale, J.E. Norris, R. Berman, and S. Kuiack 186

    Youth Crime in Canada: Public Perception vs.

    Statistical Information: 1997

        John Howard Society of Alberta 204

Unit VII: Mental and Physical Disabilities 213

    Profile of Canadians with Disabilities

        Katherine Nessner 217

    Sexual Abuse and Exploitation of Disabled Individuals

        Dick Sobsey and Connie Varnhagen 224

Unit VIII: Prevention and Intervention Strategies 241

    Should Victims Participate in Sentencing?

        Wayne Renke 245

    Criminal Trial and Punishment: Protection of Rights

    under the Charter

        Marilyn Pilon 252

    Human Rights and the Courts in Canada

        Susan Alter and Nancy Holmes 272

It's Time, It's Time.... Is it Time for Restorative Justice?
  John Winterdyk 287
A Balanced Approach Mission in a Restorative Framework
  Gordon Bazemore and Mark Umbreit 293

Preface

This book of readings came together as part of a major curriculum redevelopment that began in the late 1990s within our department at Mount Royal College. The redevelopment was part of our proposal to the Alberta Government to offer a Bachelor of Applied Justice Studies degree. We received permission to deliver the applied degree in May of 1999. However, the concept and need for this kind of book (i.e., reader) we suspect is shared by many criminology, criminal justice, sociology, and other programs that are interested in the issue of social diversity and social injustice. This assertion is based on the fact that we were unable to locate any single text that addressed the topic and theme with the diversity that is deemed necessary.

A course entitled "Diversity and Justice in Canada" has been included in the proposed curriculum for the department's applied degree. Representing a major shift away from an existing course called "Minorities and the Criminal Justice System." Instead of focusing on the criminal justice system's accommodations to cultural groups, the new course adopts, as stated above, a broader approach that we feel is more representative of what is happening in the social, political and demographic climate of Canada. To this end, theoretical issues relating to social diversity are considered within the context of criminal behaviour. Specifically, we wanted to look at the following questions: What groups within our society are more at risk of engaging in crime? What groups are more at risk of becoming victims of crime? What groups are less likely to have either their criminal victimization or perpetration officially reported?

Since no suitable text could be found for the redesigned course, a compendium of readings was developed. With some modifications, this book was developed from the compendium.

We would like to take this opportunity to individually express our appreciation to those involved in putting this reader together.

I, John, would like to thank my co-editor for bringing the concept and need for this book to my attention. After several discussions regarding the changes being made to the "Diversity and Justice" course, the framework for this book was established. To our department colleagues, I appreciated your continued support and sense of humour as we worked on this poignant project. And to Karen, my former partner, who is blessed with a wonderful degree of patience and understanding that is balanced with a healthy sense of reality that enabled me to juggle this and several other projects when a normal working day simply did not exist. I wish her continued health and success.

I, Doug, would like to acknowledge the important role that our students had in this book. During the fall of 1998, the redesigned course and a draft of this book was piloted. Student feedback was invaluable in the final versions of both course and text.

We are very appreciative of the fact that Canadian Scholars' Press embraced the concept of the book. Their ability to produce the book in a comparatively short period of time has enabled us to provide this reader with timely content and details. Brad Lambertus, the managing editor of Canadian Scholars' Press, was most helpful in securing permissions and nurturing the project into something we are pleased to offer (our) students. Yet, notwithstanding all his effort and support, we remain ultimately responsible for the final product.

Finally, we would both like to thank Rosemary Buck for her efforts in helping us put this book together. Rosemary helped reformat the majority of articles and track down several difficult to find sources. Her diligence and efficiency were truly remarkable.

Unit I
Introduction

With the establishment of the Canadian Charter of Rights and Freedoms, issues related to social diversity have played an increasingly pivotal role in Canadian society. Our concerns for justice are often now framed within the context of a socially diverse society. Much of the impetus towards community-based initiatives within the criminal justice system (CJS) can be found in the tensions within socially diverse communities and many traditional policies and practices within criminal justice agencies in Canada (Kazarian, 1998). These tensions are not unique to Canadian society and are mirrored in all industrialized nations (Pepitone and L'Armand, 1997).

In reviewing existing literature in Canada on the association between social diversity and justice, there is a striking uniformity in its content. The majority of published material is authored by criminal justice practitioners or individuals affiliated with a criminal justice agency. These works tend to focus on programs or policies a given police or correctional agency has instituted in response to a perceived concern. For example, since the mid-1980s, there has been a wealth of publications regarding Canadian policing initiatives and social diversity. Recruitment strategies, diversity training for officers and specialized police units are common themes in these publications (Cryderman, O'Toole, and Fleras, 1991). Corrections material with similar themes also are readily located (Moffat, 1998; Shaw, 1985).

It is much more time-consuming to locate published material that documents the basic evidence informing the changes within Canadian criminal justice agencies. Evidence such as the criminal victimization and criminal participation rates among members of minorities in Canada cannot be found in one common source. Nevertheless, separate documentation can be found on justice-related issues such as youth and crime, elder abuse, hate crime, the disabled and crime and intimate violence.

The decision to pull together this compilation of readings was the direct result of redesigning a second-year course in justice studies entitled "Minorities and the Criminal Justice System." The curriculum for the course was originally tailored towards the practitioners' model. Particular emphasis was placed on familiarizing prospective criminal justice employees with the cultural traditions of selected ethnic minority communities in Canada. A minimal amount of the curriculum was used to explore the more theoretical issues informing the dynamics of minority group status, social diversity, human rights and definitions of justice.

Before considering how issues of justice in Canadian society are influenced by its social diversity, it is important to understand what is meant by the phrase "social diversity." As will be illustrated, its current application is linked to other important concepts within the social sciences. Further, much of our practical understanding of the phrase carries with it an ideological value statement.

DEFINING DIVERSITY

Despite its increasing use within social science literature, "diversity" has yet to assume a formal definition. As such, the term is not associated with any one area of study. Its sociological usage typically infers that diversity is a characteristic of an organization, group or community. When used in a more political context, it frequently becomes an attribute of political systems and nations.

Further, the informal use of the term "diversity" within social science literature routinely carries with it an implied value statement, which suggests that diversity is a positive attribute. Organizations, communities and nations are somehow better off, it is implied, when they are more diverse. Laws, policies and procedures that protect and foster diversity are, by extension, positive (Abella, 1991). As Roberts and Clifton (1990) note, within this paradigm, the debate is not in relation to the value of diversity, but in the mechanisms to encourage and protect diversity.

An unfortunate corollary sometimes flows from the implied positive value assumption informing the term. Some of its advocates elevate diversity to a moral imperative (Abella, 1991; Burnet, 1984). To not promote diversity is falsely translated into being opposed to diversity. The Canadian Human Rights Foundation (1987) suggests that *not* to place any value on diversity (positive or negative) is frequently misunderstood as being *opposed* to diversity. For example, most criminal justice agencies in Canada have adopted the position that a diverse workforce is a positive attribute. Much of the debate in our society evolves around the mechanisms to foster this diverse workforce. Should hiring standards be changed? Should agencies actively target under-represented groups for active recruitment? Should a quota system be used in hiring? Those agencies that have not adopted any policies or procedures to actively promote a diverse workforce run the risk of being seen as being opposed to a diverse workforce. In this way, neutrality is the same as opposition.

In order to maximize its utility as a concept within the social sciences, it is important to step away from the more ideological usage of the term. Diversity is not so much a moral imperative, but a social characteristic. Therefore, it corresponds to concepts like social heterogeneity, social stratification, social inequality and minority group status. We will now take a closer look at the link between these concepts and diversity.

DIVERSITY AS HETEROGENEITY

The first necessary condition of social diversity is heterogeneity. As articulated by the American sociologist Peter Blau (1977: 9): "heterogeneity or horizontal differentiation refers to the distribution of a population among groups in terms of a nominal parameter." By nominal parameter, Blau means a socially prescribed and recognized characteristic that is used to differentiate one group from another. For example, shoe size is not considered a nominal parameter in our society, but gender, social class and sexual preference are. While individuals can be characterized in terms of possessing these nominal parameters, the *rate* that a given population exhibits these characteristics is a measure of its heterogeneity. To say that an individual is a female is different than saying that 20.6% of all police officers in Canada are female. The first is a social attribute of an individual, the second is an attribute of a group.

Independent of any social ranking along nominal parameters (e.g., "Protestants have more social status than Catholics"), the degree of heterogeneity within a group or society structures social interaction and integration. According to Blau (1977:21), "the rate of intergroup associations of the smaller group must exceed that of the larger." The relative size and mobility of the subgroups in a population will structure social interaction and integration. Assuming no other factors (such as discrimination, prejudice or personal preference) are at play, members of smaller subgroups must have more interaction with members of larger groups than vice versa.

To illustrate how heterogeneity structures social interaction, consider a hypothetical small community of one hundred people. Within that community, ten individuals are Muslim and ninety are Protestant. Assuming all other things being equal, Muslims will have a higher rate of interaction with Protestants than Protestants will have with Muslims. For example, the chances of a Muslim encountering a Protestant walking down the street is ninety out of ninety-nine other persons (nearly nine out of ten). The chances of a Protestant encountering a Muslim walking down the street is ten out of ninety-nine (nearly one out of ten).

The importance of the linkage of heterogeneity to our consideration of social diversity is in the fact that it provides us an *empirical* starting point. Given the degree of heterogeneity in a community or society at large, Denton (1998) illustrates it is possible to make objective observations about existing levels of social interaction and integration. A good example of this point is in relation to crime and crime victimization. Again, assuming all other factors are equal, Aboriginal peoples in Canada should be victimized at a higher *rate* by non-Aboriginal than by Aboriginals (see Unit II). If no other factors are at play, the *rate* of criminal activity, or incarceration for criminal activity, among Aboriginals should be the same as the *rate* among non-Aboriginals.

DIVERSITY AS SOCIAL STRATIFICATION

The fact that, in Canada, the rate of prison incarceration of Aboriginal peoples is higher in comparison to non-Aboriginals indicates that something other than the dynamics of heterogeneity are at work. In relation to their numbers in Canadian society, do Aboriginals commit more crime (and if so, why)? Perhaps their rate of criminality is the same as non-Aboriginals, but the CJS might afford Aboriginal peoples different treatment. Indeed, it could be that both processes may be at work.

Like heterogeneity, social stratification is another necessary condition of social diversity. However, social stratification introduces to our discussion the idea that socially prescribed differences often result in status distinctions. As suggested by Frideres (1991), social stratification allows use to incorporate the idea of *vertical differentiation* to the consideration of social diversity. A society is said to be stratified when its members place greater value on a particular quality or attribute. For example, it seems that a majority in Canadian society would prefer to have more formal education as opposed to less. This value preference results in increased social status for those who possess more formal education.

As first pointed out by Ralph Linton (1936), social status is a socially prescribed position in a social structure that carries with it corresponding rights and duties. Status positions, therefore, exist apart from the individuals who occupy them. To continue to use the example of formal education, increased employment income is often a consequence of the status afforded to increased education. Conversely, lower levels of formal education are commonly used to rationalize lower rates of pay.

Social stratification is also linked to the distinction between *ascribed* and *achieved status*. An ascribed status position results in vertical differentiation based on qualities or attributes over which an individual has no control. Social position based upon one's age, ethnicity and gender would fall into this category. An achieved status position is denoted by some degree of individual merit or effort in reaching the status position. The status attributed to education is customarily seen as achieved, in large measure, by the efforts of individuals who seek it.

It is the distinction between achieved versus ascribed status that is particularly significant for our consideration of social diversity. Most individuals will not express concern with the abstract idea of social diversity based on achieved status. However, debate exists as to how much achievement is actually involved in most status positions. Is access to higher education entirely up to the merits of a given individual? Is becoming a criminal a matter of achievement? Or are some people compelled into criminality?

DIVERSITY AS SOCIAL INEQUALITY

Social inequality can be said to exist when social status is reinforced through the exercise of social power. If an individual or group can restrict the claim that another individual or group has on social rewards, then social stratification moves towards social inequality. The inclusion of inequality into the definition of social diversity introduces the possibility that some expressions of diversity are not positive.

The processes by which social status is achieved or ascribed in a community or society is an important attribute in terms of social inequality. It is rare that inequality is the direct result of the open and naked expression of social power. As Lukes (1977) points out in his discussion, social power is typically expressed through more indirect means.

Oftentimes, ascribed social status (or the limit placed on achieved status) is rationalized through a group's customs and traditions. The notion of "male versus female" occupations in the 1950s was legitimated because of custom and tradition. Women were not expected to seek positions as police officers because that was "man's work." The reverse may have been even more powerful. Men did not seek positions as "homemakers" because that was "woman's work."

Control over procedural laws or standards is another mechanism through which social power can be exercised. While not overtly demonstrating bias, the application of procedures and standards can be more onerous for some groups to achieve success. The controversy surrounding the validity of I.Q. tests in assessing the intelligence of some minority groups falls within this category of social power. Some critics of current police recruit selection processes suggest that the operationalization of physical fitness in terms of some athletic standards (e.g., a standing broad jump of one metre, jumping over fences in an obstacle course run) is one mechanism that eliminates most women from competing fairly with men. Since such a standard does not accurately reflect the physical fitness demands of policing, women are being systematically discriminated against.

Recognizing that social inequality and power can be the underpinning behind some manifestations of social diversity is of critical importance. Social inequality provides those conditions that may, according to Kallen (1989), make social diversity unacceptable. As such, the ideological trap discussed at the beginning of this essay that suggests social diversity is a moral imperative that can, in some circumstances, be refuted.

DIVERSITY AS MINORITY GROUP STATUS

The linkage between the concepts of social diversity and minority group status seems intuitive. On a common-sense level, minority groups provide the content of social diversity. They often represent the visible manifestations of diversity in a community or society.

Nevertheless, some imprecision exists in the application of the concept of minority group status. A quick review of literature in the area (e.g., Li, 1990; Frideres, 1991) will find phrases such as "racial group," "ethnic group," "subculture group," "multicultural group" and "visible minority" used synonymously with that of minority group. This fact results in two inferences. First, race or ethnicity is a primary characteristic used to differentiate minority group status. Second, minority groups are necessarily smaller in numbers than the dominant group. Both of these inferences restrict the sociological import of the concept of minority group status. For example, women, young persons, the elderly, the disabled, gays and lesbians could not be characterized as minority groups given this limited operationalization of the term.

The original formulation of the concept of minority group provides for a more comprehensive application. As outlined by Louis Wirth in a 1945 article entitled "The Problem of Minority Groups," a group is considered a minority when its members are socially disadvantaged because of a common physical or socially prescribed characteristic. The social disadvantage based upon minority group status represents a form of collective discrimination against those in the minority by the dominant group.

The definition of dominant group is a corollary to the definition of a minority group. It follows that a group is considered dominant when its members are socially advantaged because of a common physical or socially prescribed characteristic. Social advantage is maintained through the group's collective discrimination against those in the minority.

This section's earlier themes of heterogeneity, social stratification and social inequality fit with the distinctive features of a minority group. The fragmentation of a society along physical or socially prescribed characteristics of its population underscores the notion of heterogeneity. When the fragmentation of society along these characteristics results in some being disadvantaged (and others being advantaged), social stratification exists. When those who are advantaged by way of their membership in the dominant group collectively work to place restrictions on those who are disadvantaged, social inequality exists.

In important ways, minority group status goes beyond heterogeneity, social stratification and social inequality. The dynamic between the dominant group and minority group is not rooted in the relative size of each group. The two groups are differentiated from one another because of their relative levels of social power (Frideres, 1991). Within a conflict perspective, dominant groups are more-or-less powerful, while minority groups are more-or-less powerless. The ability of a dominant group to create and maintain a minority group's relative disadvantage is an expression of social power. As a result, a numerically smaller dominant group can largely determine the lifestyles and life chances of a numerically larger minority group. Kallen (1989) and others point out that it is within this context that it is possible to consider women as a minority group (see Unit III).

From the perspective of the dominant group, minority group status represents the master status of those within the minority. It overshadows all relations between the two groups, thereby stigmatizing the minority in the eyes of the majority. It is also possible that the same group can be both a minority group and a dominant group. For example, all immigrants could be assigned minority group status in a society. Practices could be institutionalized (*de jure* or *de facto*) that socially disadvantage all immigrants in terms of employment. However, there could be a pecking order within the immigrant population itself. "Visible minority" immigrants may be socially disadvantaged at the hands of "white minority" immigrants.

The stigmatization of the minority group is a consequence of collective discrimination. Moving beyond the prejudicial attitudes of individuals, or the practices of an isolated individual, minority group status is reinforced in the discriminatory actions and practices that affirm the privileges of a dominant group. Collective, or systematic, discrimination can take on a variety of forms. *De jure* discrimination is codified in procedural law and statutes. Institutionalized discriminatory practices that are grounded in custom and tradition fall within the category of *de facto* discrimination.

Collective discrimination can be either direct or indirect. If the specific intent of laws, procedures or actions is to sustain the social disadvantage of a minority group, the discrimination is direct. Indirect discrimination has less to do with the specific intent of action and more to do with its consequences. For example, many times, entry-level job openings in the CJS are not publicly posted. Instead, agencies rely on word-of-mouth advertising to fill the openings. While presumably not intended to be directly discriminatory, this practice is a form of indirect discrimination in that it clearly disadvantages individuals who are not already "inside the loop."

It is not automatic that members of a minority group accept their subordinate master status. As Edwin Lemert's (1951) distinction between primary and secondary deviance points out, being labelled deviant is not necessarily the same as accepting the label of deviant. The degree to which the minority group accepts their disadvantaged master status is ultimately a measure of the relative power imbalance between the minority and dominant groups. In the long run, the greater the power imbalance between the two groups, the more likely it is that a minority group will accept their disadvantaged position as their master status.

As the power imbalance between a minority group and a dominant group becomes more equal, it is likely that the dynamics between the two groups will change. Members of the minority group may begin to openly question their relative disadvantaged circumstances. Given the right circumstances (e.g., numbers, leadership and resources), minority groups can mobilize to challenge their disadvantaged position. In response to this mobilization, a dominant group can bow to demands of the minority or exercise its established authority to suppress the challenge.

MEASURING DIVERSITY

Recognizing that diversity can be characterized in terms of heterogeneity, social stratification, social inequality and minority group status allows us to move away from the implied positive value assertion commonly associated with the term. Ideological considerations are replaced with empirical questions associated with the nature and extent of diversity in a community or society. Some of these questions are:

- Is the population of a community or society segmented according to any physical or socially prescribed characteristics (heterogeneity)?
- If the population is segmented, what is the relative size of the groups created by the division (heterogeneity)?
- Is there an applied or expressed variance in how society values or ranks these differences in terms of social status (social stratification)?
- Do differences in social status along one dimension influence an individual's array of lifestyles and life opportunities (social inequality)?
- Are institutionalized practices evident in the community or society that socially disadvantage all individuals who exhibit the lesser valued physical or socially prescribed characteristic (minority group status)?
- If collective, or systemic, discrimination is evident, what forms does it take (minority group status)?
- To what degree does the minority group accept the subordinate master status assigned to it (minority group status)?

ORGANIZATION OF THIS READER

The remaining articles in this reader are divided into seven units. Each unit focuses on the link between justice and one dimension of diversity in Canadian society. The seven units are:

- Aboriginal peoples
- Immigration, ethnicity and national groups

- Women
- Gender orientation
- Age
- Mental and physical disabilities
- Prevention and intervention strategies

Within each unit, a brief introduction provides a topical overview to the subject matter. Also, discussion questions are provided to assist the reader in linking the articles within the unit together and to the larger questions about social diversity. Finally, whenever possible, web links are identified to encourage readers to move beyond the information provided in the articles.

Within each grouping, an attempt has been made to present an array of articles that touches on diversity as heterogeneity, social status, social inequality and minority group status. The articles were not selected because they represent a particular point of view or political expression. Rather, they were selected to encourage discussion and debate about the link between social diversity and justice in Canada. In this respect, the units may be used for either class/group presentation and/or debates in a tutorial setting. Ultimately, such a decision rests with the individual instructor.

Finally, other than for the Introduction and lead-ins to each unit, we have not included the references with each article. It is our general observation that few undergraduate students access these sources. However, in providing the citation for each selected article, it is possible to locate the original article should students care to follow-up with any of the cited references.

REFERENCES

Abella, R. (1991). Equality and human rights in Canada: Coping with the new isms. *University Affairs*, June/July: 21-22.

Berry, J. (1984). Multicultural policy in Canada: A social psychological analysis. *Canadian Journal of Behavioural Science*, 164: 353-370.

Blau, P. (1977). *Inequality and heterogeneity: A primitive theory of social structure*. New York: The Free Press.

Burnet, J. (1984). Myths and multiculturalism. In R. Samuda, J. Berry and M. Laferriere (Eds.), *Multiculturalism in Canada: Social and educational perspectives*, (18-29). Toronto: Allyn and Bacon.

Canadian Human Rights Foundation (1987). *Multiculturalism and the charter*. Toronto: Carswell.

Cryderman, B., O'Toole, C., and Fleras, A. (1991). *Police, race and ethnicity: A guide for police service officers* (2nd edition). Toronto: Butterworths.

Denton, T. (1998). Social structural differentiation: Conceptualization and measurement. *Cross-Cultural Research: A Journal of Comparative Social Science*, 32(1): 37-79.

Frideres, J. (1991). Introduction. In J. Frideres (Ed.), *Multiculturalism and intergroup relations*, (vii-xii). Westport, Conn.: Greenwood Press.

Kallen, E. (1989). *Label me human: Minority rights of stigmatized Canadians*. Toronto: University of Toronto Press.

Kazarian, S. (1998). *Diversity issues in policing*. Toronto: Emond Montgomery Publications.

Lemert, E. (1951). *Social psychology*. NY: McGraw-Hill.

Li, P. (1990). Race and ethnicity. In Li, P. (Ed.), *Race and ethnic relations in Canada* (3-18). Don Mills, On.: Oxford University Press.

Linton, R. (1936). *The study of man*. New York: Appleton-Century-Crofts.

Lukes, S. (1975). *Power: A radical view*. London: The Macmillan Press.

Moffat, K. (1998). Creating choices or repeating history: Canadian female offenders and correctional reform. In Hartnagel, T. (Ed.), *Canadian crime control policy*. Toronto: Harcourt Brace Canada.

Pepitone, A. and L'Armand, K. (1997). Justice in cultural context. *Cross-Cultural Research: A Journal of Comparative Social Science*, 31(2): 83-100.

Roberts, L. and Clifton, R. (1990). Multiculuralism in Canada: A sociological perspective. In P. Li (Ed.), *Race and ethnic relations in Canada* (120-147). Don Mills, ON: Oxford University Press.

Shaw, J. (1985). Race relations training in the prison service. *Currents*, 3(2): 14-17.

Wirth, L. (1945). The problem of minority groups. In R. Linton (Ed.), *The science of man in the world crisis*. NY: Columbia University Press.

Unit II
Aboriginal Groups

In the late 1860s, a small community at the north of Salt Spring Island, British Columbia, was the scene of three brutal murders. All the victims were members of the island's Black community. Although the evidence was far from conclusive, an Aboriginal man was charged with the killings. (Who killed William Robinson?, 1998)

In 1971, the Micmac youth Donald Marshall, Jr., of Sidney, Nova Scotia was found guilty of killing a black teenager by the name of Sandy Seale. In spite of his pleas, contradicting evidence, questioned investigative work by the police, it took eleven years to clear his name. (Harris, 1986)

Although two incidents of injustice are not sufficient to make a case, our history is filled with such examples that raise serious questions about how Canadians have dealt with its Aboriginal people since first coming to the New World. In 1998, Aboriginal peoples constituted less than 5% of Canada's population. However, Aboriginal men account for approximately 15% of federal inmates while 22% of federally sentenced women are Aboriginal. Yet, the first federal prison for Aboriginal women did not open until 1995 and for men in 1997. The outspoken Albertan Judge John Reilly recently reiterated many of these sentiments in a controversial ruling when he blamed the justice system for its treatment of Aboriginal offenders. He expressed the opinion that the injustices have a long history and that it should be taken into account when sentencing native people (Dempster, 1999).

In his review of Aboriginal justice, Palys (1993) observes "there is an incredible irony concerning Canada's indigenous people." Although it is estimated that they arrived in North America between 10,000 and 40,000 years ago (compared to the Europeans who arrived around 500 years ago) their status and treatment has been marked by one tragedy after another. Their plight of injustice began with the Jesuits who forcefully tried to assimilate the Native people to embrace Christianity, the fur traders who traded cheap trinkets for valuable fur pelts, governments who took their fertile land for minimal compensation, and the North West Mounted Police who often hunted them down for the most trivial of infractions. They have been demeaned as "savages," "red skins," "drunks" and other derogatory names and have never been fully recognized as one of Canada's founding nations. Even under the first Indian Act the government tried to isolate them by revoking the legal rights of Indian women should they marry someone off reservation (ibid.).

To this day, in spite of numerous provincial and federal commissions, Aboriginal peoples continue to struggle with their diversity within the criminal justice system (CJS) and other social injustices. So while we politically espouse equality and respect individuality under the charter, the history of Canada's Aboriginal people has been marked more as one of forced assimilation rather than respect for their indigenous heritage (Chrisjohn, 1997). Why is this? Why does it continue?

In this unit, we present three articles that reflect some of the fundamental issues confronting Aboriginal groups. McDonald's article identifies some of the social, cultural and justice-related issues that confront those Aboriginals who live off reserve. Yerbury and Griffiths offer an overview of some of the major disparities in the CJS that involve the treatment and processing of Aboriginal people. The final article in this unit offers some recommendations that have been put forth to bridge the inequity of justice many Aborginal people are subjected to when they come into contact with the CJS.

DISCUSSION QUESTIONS:

1. As has happened with the Nishika people of British Columbia, should Aboriginal groups be allowed to self-govern and administer their own justice?
2. What are the advantages and disadvantages of granting diverse groups their own autonomy?
3. Conduct an in-class/department survey on people's attitudes towards Aboriginals and explore some of the issues presented in this unit.
4. We read about the conflicts and genocidal acts in Rwanda, western Asia, the former Yugoslavia and other countries, but has the Canadian CJS condoned genocide? For example, the government has not dealt with the injustices of Aboriginal children who were placed into the control of the churches and reform schools where they were regularly abused or neglected.
5. We read about the horrors of the Nazi reign, Joseph Stalin's reaction to racial minorities and political dissidents in former Russia, but why do we not speak as freely about Canada's solution to the 'Indian Problem'?

REFERENCES

Chrisjohn, R. (1997). *The circle game*. Penticton, BC: Theytus Books.

Dempster, L. (1999, January 15). Judge attacks judicial treatment of natives. *Calgary Herald*, A1, B3.

Harris, R. (1986). *Justice denied*. Toronto: Harper Row.

Palys, T. (1993). Prospects for Aboriginal justice in Canada. (On-line: www.stu.ca/~palys/prospect.htm).

Who killed William Robinson? (1998). (On-line: web/uvic.ca/history-robinson/textonly/).

Web watch: In regard to Aboriginal/Indigenous people, there are a host of interesting links that one can explore on the Internet. One source that provides numerous related links can be found at http://www.netizen.org/progressive/list/. The site includes links on Aboriginal issues ranging from human rights to the *First Nation* newspaper, prison issues and sites discussing such recent incidents as Gustafsen Lake in British Columbia and Ipperwash in Ontario.

Canada's Off-Reserve Aboriginal Population

Ryan J. McDonald

While the characteristics of Aboriginal people who live on reserve are reasonably well documented, there is a growing number who live off reserve about whom relatively little is known. An increasing proportion of Aboriginal people live in cities and towns, many of them far from an Aboriginal community. By 1986, well over half of Canada's Aboriginal population lived in communities which were not Indian reserves or settlements (as recognized under the Indian Act of Canada), and about one-third of these people lived in 11 of the larger metropolitan areas.

While Aboriginal people in general are economically disadvantaged compared to Canadians overall, those living outside of primarily native communities have lower levels of educational attainment, higher unemployment rates and lower average incomes than Canadians in general.

POPULATION DISTRIBUTION

About one-quarter of a million (220,300) single *origin* Aboriginal people lived *off* reserve in 1986. This included people whose origins were identified as

McDonald, R. (1991). Canada's off-reserve aboriginal population. *Canadian Social Trends, Catalogue No. 11-008*, (Winter): 2-7. Statistics Canada information is used with the permission of the Minister of Industry, as Minister responsible for Statistics Canada. Information on the availability of the wide range of data from Statistics Canada can be obtained from Statistics Canada's Regional Offices, its World Wide Web site at http://www.statcan.ca, and its toll-free access number 1-800-263-1136.

being only from one or more of the three major Aboriginal groups of North American Indian, Inuit and Metis. Excluding the Atlantic region and the Territories, these Aboriginal people were quite evenly distributed among the provinces, and were not heavily concentrated in Ontario and Quebec as is most of the overall Canadian population. For example, just 4% of the Canadian population (slightly over one million) lived in Saskatchewan in 1986, whereas this was the case for 13% (30,000) of Aboriginal people living off reserve (see Table 1).

The provinces in which the largest percentage of Aboriginal people lived outside of reserves and settlements were Newfoundland, where at the time of the 1986 census there were no reserves, but settlements of Innus, Inuit and Indians, and Alberta, where 65% lived off reserve. In contrast, only 26% of the Aboriginal population of Nova Scotia and New Brunswick lived off reserve.

Table 1:   Distribution of Canadian and Aboriginal population, by province, 1989

	% Total Canadian Population	% Aboriginal Population
Yukon	0.1	1.3
Northwest Territories	0.2	12.3
British Columbia	11.4	14.9
Alberta	9.3	15.3
Saskatchewan	4.0	13.4
Manitoba	4.2	13.1
Ontario	36.0	13.9
Quebec	25.8	12.8
Atlantic Provinces	9.0	3.0

Source: Statistics Canada, 1986 Census of Canada.

AGE AND MOBILITY

Off-reserve Aboriginals, like those on reserves, are on average, much younger than the Canadian population as a whole. In 1986, 45% of the off-reserve Aboriginal population were aged 19 and under, compared with 29% of all Canadians. As well, only 8% of the off-reserve Aboriginal population were aged 55 and over, compared with 20% of all Canadians. Statistics Canada has projected that because registered Indians have higher fertility rates, those living both on and off reserve will continue to have a higher population growth rate, and a younger demographic base than the overall Canadian population.

Aboriginal people living off reserve changed dwelling places more often than the overall Canadian population. In the five years preceding the 1986 Census, 61% of the off-reserve Aboriginal population aged 5 and over had moved, compared with 44% of the overall Canadian population. However, similar proportions of Aboriginal and all Canadian movers changed residences within the same community (59% and 55%, respectively).

FAMILY CHARACTERISTICS

Aboriginal people living off reserve were only slightly less likely than other Canadians to be in family households. In 1986, almost 83% of Aboriginal people living off reserves and settlements lived in family households, compared with 86% of all Canadians. Aboriginal families were, on average, larger than other families. According to Indian and Northern Affairs Canada (INAC), in 1986, when the average Canadian family had 3.1 members, the average Aboriginal family living off reserve had 3.4 people, while those living on reserve were even larger with 4.2 people.

Of Aboriginal families living off reserve, 23% were headed by lone parents, compared with 12% of all Canadian families. Women constituted 87% of off-reserve Aboriginal lone parents, whereas 83% of all Canadian lone-parent families were headed by women.

EDUCATION LEVELS

In general, Aboriginal people in Canada have much lower levels of educational attainment than the overall Canadian population. In 1986, 41% of off-reserve Aboriginals aged 15 and over had less than a Grade 9 education, and only 2% had completed university. In contrast, 17% of Canadians aged 15 and over had less than a Grade 9 education, and 10% were university graduates. That same year, 17% of Aboriginal people had some non-university postsecondary education, close to the overall Canadian figure of 21 %.

Levels of educational attainment also varied by province (see Table 2). Newfoundland had the highest percentage of Aboriginal people with less than a Grade 9 education (52%), whereas Ontario had the lowest at 23%. This compared with 27% and 15% of the respective overall population. Among those whose highest level of educational attainment was a high school diploma, the rates were highest in the province of Quebec for both off-reserve

Table 2:   Percentage of Aboriginal and Canadian populations with less
            than Grade 9 education

	% Aboriginal Population < Grade 9	% Total Canadian Population < Grade 9
Yukon	37	11
Northwest Territories	60	33
British Columbia	25	11
Alberta	31	11
Saskatchewan	38	19
Manitoba	34	18
Ontario	23	15
Quebec	31	24
New Brunswick	27	24
Nova Scotia	31	17
Prince Edward Island	13	17
Newfoundland	52	27

Source: Statistics Canada, Catalogue 93-110 and Employment Equity Program.

Aboriginals (12%) and for provincial residents (16%). Nova Scotia and New
Brunswick had the highest percentages of Aboriginal university graduates
(3%), while this was the case for 9% and 7% of the respective provincial
populations (see Table 3).

LABOUR FORCE CHARACTERISTICS

Aboriginal people living off reserve were less likely to participate in the
labour force than were Canadians overall. In 1986, 66% of Aboriginal men
participated in the labour force, compared with 77% of all Canadian men.
Aboriginal women also participated less in the labour force (45%), compared
with 55% of all Canadian women.

Those who did participate in the labour force were more likely than
Canadians overall to be unemployed. In 1986, the unemployment rate for
Aboriginal people living off reserve (28%) was almost triple the rate for all
Canadians (10%). The unemployment rate for Aboriginal women (27%) was

Table 3: Percentage of Aboriginal and Canadian populations with university degree/diploma

	% Aboriginal Population With Degree/Diploma	% Total Canadian Population With Degree/Diploma
Yukon	0	10
Northwest Territories	0	8
British Columbia	1	10
Alberta	1	11
Saskatchewan	2	7
Manitoba	2	9
Ontario	2	11
Quebec	2	9
New Brunswick	3	7
Nova Scotia	3	9
Prince Edward Island	0	7
Newfoundland	0	6

Source: Statistics Canada, Catalogue 93-110 and Employment Equity Program.

slightly lower than the rate for Aboriginal men (29%). This contrasts sharply with rates for the entire Canadian population where unemployment was lower for men (9.6%) than it was for women (11.2%).

Unemployment rates were highest for Aboriginal people living off reserve in Prince Edward Island, Newfoundland, and British Columbia at about 40%. The lowest rates (18%) were found in both Quebec and Ontario. The Prairie provinces showed the greatest discrepancies between the unemployment rate for provincial residents and the rate for Aboriginals. Aboriginal people living off reserve in Manitoba, Saskatchewan, and Alberta had unemployment rates of over 30%, while in each of the three provinces, the overall unemployment rate for all provincial residents was less than 10%.

While unemployment and participation rates reveal activity in the labour force, they do not reflect those who are discouraged and stop looking for work. A higher proportion of the male and female Aboriginal population was not in the labour force (34% and 55% respectively), than was the case among

Canadians overall (23% for men and 44% for women). However, Aboriginal people living a traditional lifestyle also would be included with those not in the labour force.

Aboriginal people who were employed in the labour force were concentrated in different industries than Canadians overall. Off-reserve Aboriginals were twice as likely as the entire Canadian population to be employed in government services (15% compared with 8%), and were less likely than the overall Canadian population to be employed in the retail and finance sectors (10% compared with 17%). The Aboriginal population living off reserve also showed a notably lower participation rate in manufacturing (12%), where 17% of the Canadian labour force was employed.

INCOME CHARACTERISTICS

Aboriginal Canadians had much lower incomes than the overall Canadian population. In 1985, the average income of Aboriginal men living off reserve was $14,300, while the average income of all Canadian men was $23,200. Aboriginal women earned $9,000 on average, compared with $12,900 for all Canadian women.

An even greater inequality is revealed when median incomes are compared. In 1985, 50% of Aboriginal men living off reserve were earning less than $9,800, while for all Canadian men, 50% earned less than $20,800. The median income for Aboriginal women living off reserve was $7,200, while for Canadian women overall, the figure was $10,800. This suggests that Aboriginal incomes are more concentrated at lower levels compared to the whole population.

Comparisons of income within the off-reserve population reveal substantial provincial differences. Aboriginal men living in Newfoundland had the lowest average income ($10,800), followed by Saskatchewan ($11,200). Incomes were highest for Aboriginal men living off reserve in Quebec and Ontario, where average income was $18,300 and $16,500, respectively. Similarly, the incomes of Aboriginal women were highest in Quebec and Ontario and lowest in Newfoundland.

Like most Canadians, Aboriginal people living off reserve derive most of their income from employment. However, Aboriginals rely more on income from government transfer payments (welfare and unemployment insurance), and less on employment income and income from investments and retirement funds than do Canadians overall. In 1985, employment earnings accounted for 73% of Aboriginal people's income, compared with 79% for all Canadians. Transfer payments to Aboriginal people living off reserve amounted to 24% of their total income, more than double the percentage for the entire Canadian population. Only 3% of the income of off-reserve Aboriginals was derived from investment and retirement funds, compared with 10% of the total income of all Canadians.

Aboriginals living off reserve in Ontario had the largest proportion of income from employment (79%), while those in Saskatchewan had the lowest (61%).

URBAN ABORIGINAL POPULATION

Table 4:   Unemployment rates of Aboriginal people living off reserve and total population, 1986

Selected Census Metropolitan Areas	Aboriginal Population Unemployment Rate	Total Population Unemployment Rate
Halifax	17.6	9.5
Montreal	13.6	11.7
Ottawa-Hull	14.5	8.3
Toronto	12.4	6.7
Hamilton	19.6	8.8
Winnipeg	30.3	8.7
Regina	35.7	9.8
Saskatoon	35.6	10.0
Calgary	30.6	10.2
Edmonton	34.9	12.0
Vancouver	36.2	13.2

Source: Statistics Canada, Catalogue 71-529 and Employment Equity Program.

In 1986, 31% of the off-reserve population lived in 11 of Canada's largest census metropolitan areas (CMAs). These CMAs —Halifax, Montreal, Ottawa-Hull, Toronto, Hamilton, Winnipeg, Regina, Saskatoon, Calgary, Edmonton, and Vancouver —together accounted for 47% of the Canadian population. The off-reserve Aboriginal population was more heavily concentrated in large urban areas of western Canada than in eastern CMAs.

Winnipeg had the largest number of Aboriginal people of all CMAs (13,500), or 6% of the entire off-reserve population. Vancouver ranked second with 11,100 (5%), and Edmonton third with 10,900 (5%). Toronto and Montreal, the two largest CMAs in Canada had only 3% and 4%, respectively, of the off-reserve population.

In 1986, 3% of the populations of Regina and Saskatoon were Aboriginal people living off reserve. In Winnipeg, Aboriginal people constituted 2.1% of the city's population, compared with just 0.2% of Toronto's and 0.3% of Montreal's populations.

Aboriginals in major urban areas had somewhat lower unemployment rates and higher incomes than the overall off-reserve population. In 1986, the unemployment rate for Aboriginals living off reserve in the CMAs averaged 26%, compared with the national average of 28% (see Table 4). From Halifax to Hamilton, their unemployment rates ranged from 12% to 20%, compared with 30% to 36% from Winnipeg to Vancouver where more of the urban Aboriginal population is concentrated. Aboriginal people living in Toronto had the lowest unemployment rate at 12%, while those in Vancouver had the highest at 36%.

The average income for Aboriginal men was approximately $1,000 higher in the 11 CMAs than the national average for Aboriginal men living off reserve. Aboriginal men living off reserve in Montreal had the highest incomes, averaging $22,700, Montreal was also the only city examined in which Aboriginal men with single origins earned more on average, than those with a mixed Aboriginal and non-Aboriginal background. Aboriginal people in Winnipeg had the lowest average incomes, $11,700 for men, and $8,500 for women. Women's incomes were greatest in the National Capital Region of Ottawa-Hull, where average income exceeded $14,000.

PROSPERITY AND ATTITUDES VARY BY PROVINCE

The single origin Aboriginal population (those with a purely Aboriginal ancestry) were more economically disadvantaged than were those of mixed Aboriginal and non-Aboriginal descent. Aboriginal people living off reserves and settlements experienced a greater degree of economic disparity by province than did the Canadian population overall. On average, Aboriginal people living off reserve in western Canada had lower incomes and higher unemployment rates than did those living in the east.

Along with economic disparity, public attitudes toward native issues also varied by province. According to opinion polls conducted in 1986, people in western provinces were best informed of native issues; however, they were least supportive of them. People in Quebec, on the other hand, tended to be least knowledgeable, but were most supportive.

Minorities, Crime, and the Law

J. Colin Yerbury and Curt T. Griffiths

One of the major considerations in studying crime and criminality in Canada is recognizing that Canada is a multicultural society with myriad cultural and ethnic groups. In this chapter, we explore the issues surrounding minorities and the law, focussing on the patterns of crime and the nature and extent of contact with the legal system of two groups: Canada's indigenous people and the Doukhobors. Both are characterized by a lack of political, social and, in some cases, legal and economic power. In this, these minority groups share much with women, the topic of Chapter 11. We will see that the application of a national *Criminal Code* to indigenous peoples, and to religious sects, historically and in contemporary times, has often been characterized by discrimination and conflict. There remain many unanswered questions about crime among minorities and how to effectively administer justice in a country as geographically and ethnically diverse as Canada.

SOME IMPORTANT DEFINITIONS

At the outset of our discussion, it is important to define a number of terms that are widely, albeit often incorrectly, used. First, what is a minority?

Dictionaries generally define a minority as "a racial, religious, political, national or other group regarded as being different from the larger group of which it is a part." For purposes of our discussion, we will use the term *minority group* to refer to one whose members are relegated to a subordinate position in society and thus experience lack of prestige, privilege, and power. As a result, the minority group members may be subjected to a wide range of discriminatory treatment by societal institutions, including schools, the employment sector, and the law.

Race has been used in a variety of ways—to categorize linguistic groupings (Aryan, English-speaking), to categorize religious groupings (Moslem, Hindu, Jewish), to denote a national grouping (Portuguese, Italian, German), and to categorize mystical, quasi-scientific groupings (Teutonic). The definition of race has largely been a societal definition. A scientific definition, however, would require us to be able to isolate the physical or biologically transmitted characteristics of a group and to show how their differentiating factors influence their behaviour and way of life. For example, the adherents of **biological determinism** might seek to show how members of certain racial groups displayed greater propensities for criminal behaviour. This is not possible, nor of interest to most social scientists. As a matter of fact, race has become a "four-letter word" to serious researchers.

Many groups referred to as "racial" by laymen are what social scientists define as *ethnic*. Most scientists have rejected the notion that human behavioural limits are transmitted genetically; rather, such traits are acquired through learning during the socialization and education process in a society. *Culture*, rather than biological makeup, is the primary determinant of behaviour, and an ethnic group is identifiable by its distinctive cultural characteristics. Ethnicity, then, suggests the existence of a distinct culture or subculture within which group members feel themselves bound together by common ties that are recognized by other members of the society. Nationality, language, religion, and tribal identity are ethnic categories that can be used to distinguish groups. Ethnic groups are inherently *ethnocentric*. Members of the group look upon their cultural characteristics such as religious values, sexual behaviours, eating and drinking habits, political conceptions, economic structures, laws, and customs and other cultural elements as natural, correct, and superior to those of other ethnic groups: the cultural characteristics of other groups are considered bizarre, inferior, strange, and, perhaps, immoral.

Prejudice is a manifestation of ethnocentrism. This is an aversive or hostile attitude toward an individual because he or she belongs to a particular group and is assumed to share the objectionable qualities ascribed to the group. This is often called stereotyping. Discrimination, however, is the acting out of prejudice. Prejudice is an attitude; discrimination is behaviour.

When one ethnic group has political power, that group's views are reflected in criminal law; so, laws and the administration of justice can be ethnocentric, even discriminatory. In our discussion, we will see that Canadian indigenous peoples and religious minorities have been subjected to prejudiced and discriminatory laws.

Further, we will see that members of some minority groups are involved with the criminal justice system to a greater extent than are members of the dominant Euro-Canadian society, both historically and in contemporary times. This involvement is manifested in three ways:

1. Behaviours accepted in one culture may clash with the standards and laws of the dominant culture. For example, laws were passed criminalizing opium use; and, existing laws against arson were used to prosecute Sons of Freedom Doukhobors.
2. Rebellion against dominant authority or political dissent can be responded to as a crime. This was the case with the Métis leader Louis David Riel who in the late 1880s led a political rebellion calling for the rights of his people. The selling of cigarettes on some Native Indian reserves is interpreted variously as a crime or as a legitimate expression of native sovereignty.
3. The high rate of conventional crime, such as assault and theft, can be seen as a consequence of a disadvantaged position in Canadian society and the treatment of minority group members by successive generations of Euro-Canadians.

When minority groups such as Canada's indigenous peoples and the Freedomite Doukhobors are perceived to have problems or are acknowledged to be problems by Euro-Canadian society, these problems are inevitably ascribed to the inherent characteristics of the minority group, rather than to defects in the larger social system. For example, Canadians often attribute the high school dropout rate of indigenous students, their chronic poverty, and their overrepresentation in correctional institutions to deficiencies inherent in native persons themselves.

And, in the following discussion, we will see that, while Canada's indigenous people have made initial attempts to develop their own community-based justice services such as police forces, the strong, centralized government in Canada and the national *Criminal Code* have mitigated the potential effectiveness of such initiatives in reducing native conflict with the law. In fact, it could be argued that, despite Canada's self-identification as a multicultural society, this diversity has not extended into the legal realm, and that such a label eschews the socio-structural disparities that exist between the dominant Euro-Canadian majority and indigenous, religious, and immigrant groups, which, in turn, increases their likelihood of conflict with the law and involvement in the legal system.

CANADIAN INDIGENOUS PEOPLES AND THE LAW

In the following discussion, we will consider the socio-structural position of indigenous peoples in Canadian society, including the relations between Euro-Canadians and indigenous peoples and the plight of indigenous communities, as well as the nature and extent of indigenous contact with and conflict with the criminal law.

Indigenous peoples in Canada are distinguished by their cultural and linguistic attributes as well as by their legal status. Status Indians are indigenous people who are registered under the federal Indian Act. Non-Status Indians are those who identify themselves as indigenous people but who are not registered under the Indian Act. Métis are the descendants of mixed Indian and European ancestry, while Inuit are a distinct cultural group who reside primarily in the Northwest Territories, Labrador, and in Arctic Quebec.

Indigenous peoples comprise approximately 2% of the total Canadian population and are distributed, albeit unevenly, across the country. It is apparent that, in the northern territories, indigenous peoples comprise the greatest proportion of the population.

Statistics from the 1981 Census of Canada indicate that these groups are distributed as follows: Status Indians (59.9%); Métis (20%); non-Status Indians (15.3%); and Inuit (5.2%). In the following discussion, we often use the term "indigenous peoples" to include all of these groups, but we do make reference to specific groups where the distinction is significant. A discussion of these groups is hindered by the lack of published materials. Statistical information is collected in a systematic manner only on Status or registered Indians. In 1987, there were 415,898 Status Indians in Canada.

There is considerable diversity among the 573 recognized Indian bands in Canada in terms of their culture, social, and political organizations, and in the attributes of individual Indian communities. The majority of the Indian bands in Canada—nearly 65% of the registered Indian population—are situated in rural and remote areas of the country, compared to 25% of the national population. The remoteness is a key factor in Indian involvement with the law and the delivery of justice services to Indian people.

The majority of registered Indians live on reserves, although the growth rate for off-reserve Indians is higher than the on-reserve growth rate. In recent years, an increasingly larger number of Indians has migrated to urban areas of the country and the proportion of off-reserve Indians has increased in all regions.

EXPLAINING INDIGENOUS CRIMINALITY

In the published literature, there are a number of perspectives that have been developed in an attempt to explain crime among indigenous peoples and their involvement in the criminal justice system (May, 1982). These approaches are not mutually exclusive and, as we will see in the following discussion, they are closely connected with the process and consequences of colonization.

The five dominant explanations for indigenous crime are as follows:

1. *Adjustment/acculturation*: Criminality and conflict with the law are consequences of colonization and the difficulty that indigenous peoples have in relating to the dominant society and its institutions.
2. *Social disorganization*: Crime among indigenous peoples is the result of conflict between the indigenous culture and that of the dominant Euro-Canadian society. This results in a breakdown of community and leadership structures and the internal mechanisms of social control that traditionally served to maintain order and prevent crime.
3. *Traditional social organization*: Crime among indigenous peoples is an extension of traditional cultural behaviour. The patterns of crime and deviance vary across cultural groups, based on the types of behaviours encouraged by the group. Such behaviours may conflict with the dominant, nonindigenous law and legal systems.
4. *Overt and covert discrimination*: Indigenous peoples are more visible to agents of the criminal-justice system, such as the police, and, once detected, are more likely to become involved in the criminal justice process. Once in the criminal-justice system, indigenous peoples have less ability to "escape" from conviction and incarceration. The likelihood of discrimination is increased when an alien system of law and justice are imposed on a colonized people and when criminal justice practitioners have little or no understanding of the culture and lifeways of indigenous peoples.

5. *Indigenous peoples as victims of socio-structural deprivation*: The likelihood of conflict with the criminal law and involvement in the criminal justice process is increased by the pervasive socio-structural deprivation and economic and psychological dependency of indigenous peoples.

In the following discussion, we will consider the various dimensions of these explanations.

INDIGENOUS PEOPLES IN CANADIAN SOCIETY

The law and the criminal-justice system are only two of several primary societal institutions (others being health care, education, etc.). We must first consider the larger societal context within which Canada's indigenous population lives before narrowing our focus to contact and conflict with the law. If Canada's indigenous peoples are in conflict with the law and with the criminal-justice system, it is highly likely that they will also be expecting conflict in other areas, be they economic, educational, or cultural.

We must, therefore, not lose sight of the larger structural factors that may be related to the nature and extent of crime among indigenous peoples and that contribute to high rates of violent crime, alcohol and solvent abuse, domestic violence, and property offences that are present among indigenous bands and communities in many jurisdictions across the country.

Many observers argue that the subordinate political and economic position of indigenous peoples in Canada is a consequence of the colonization by Europeans and by Canadian government policies that have exerted control over virtually every aspect of indigenous life. As noted in the introduction to this unit, the indigenous population was exploited by early entrepreneurs to extract resources, principally furs, for European markets. As settlement, and therefore agriculture, moved from east to west, Indians were forced out, gradually being contained in nonviable reserves, reliant upon government support to survive. The federal Indian Act enshrined in law a paternalistic policy that denied them any legal, political, or economic autonomy or self-determination.

A major consequence of this subordinate, minority status is the "victimization" of indigenous people, which is evidenced by pervasive poverty, high rates of unemployment and reliance upon public assistance, low levels of education, high death rates from accidents and violence, and increasing rates of family and community breakdown. Particularly vulnerable are youth, aged

15 to 24, who are most susceptible to violent and accidental death, suicide, and alcohol and solvent abuse (Griffiths, Yerbury & Weafer, 1987; Siggner, 1979). An example of the consequences of the socio-structural condition of indigenous peoples is evidenced when one compares the suicide rate of Status Indians with the Canadian suicide rate.

Throughout Canada's Arctic, there are high rates of violent and property-related offences, widespread alcohol and drug abuse, an increasing incidence of suicide and family breakdown, and other symptoms of community and cultural disintegration. Sociological and anthropological studies have documented the decline of Inuit from a proud, independent, and self-determinant people to wards of the Canadian state (see Irwin, 1988; Mayes, 1982).

While there is a paucity of published material on the socio-economic condition of non-Status Indians, Métis, and Inuit, data on registered Indians presented by Siggner (1986) and Lithwick, Schiff, and Vernon (1986) indicate that:

- in 1984, 47% of Indian housing was in poor physical condition, 36% was overcrowded, and 38% lacked running water and/or indoor plumbing;
- in 1981, the unemployment rate for Indians was two and one-half times that for the Canadian workforce; twice as many members of the experienced Indian labour force did not work in 1980, as compared to the non-Indian experienced labour force;
- in 1980, the average annual income for Indians was 60% of that of the general Canadian population; one-fourth of the Indians had no income;
- in 1981, 19% of Indians had completed some post-secondary education, compared with 36% of the total Canadian population; in 1978-79 and 1982-83, nearly one-half of the Indian students in the fourteen-to-fifteen age range were in grade levels below those appropriate for their ages.

These data indicate that on-reserve Indians fare far worse in terms of "social conditions" than do their off-reserve counterparts, although the socio-economic disparities between Indians and non-Indians extend to urban areas of the country. In Winnipeg, Clatworthy (1980) found that the unemployment rate among Indians was four times higher than that for non-Indians, while household income for Indians was about one-half that of the total population. Among the Indian population, there was a high percentage of single-parent families, and Indian youth and women experienced particular hardships. Similar findings have been reported in Edmonton (see Native Counselling Services of Alberta and Native Affairs Secretariat, 1985).

There does appear to have been some improvement in the socio-structural position of some indigenous peoples over the past three decades. In a recent study of registered Indians, Indian and Northern Affairs Canada (1988) reported:

- the mortality rate per 1,000 had declined from 10.5 in 1955 to 5.3 in 1986;
- the infant mortality rate per 1,000 had declined from 80.2 in 1960 to 16.5 in 1986;
- the number of Indian children who are in grade twelve or thirteen after consecutive years of schooling has in creased from 3.4% in 1980-81 to 33.9% in 1985-86;
- the number of Indians enrolled in university has increased from 50 in 1960-61 to 5,800 in 1985-86;
- since 1977, there has been a steady decline in the number of children in the care of child-welfare authorities;
- during the period 1963-86, the percentage of houses with running water increased from under 14% to 75%.

This report also provides some evidence of the increasing involvement of indigenous peoples in assuming control over key institutions in their communities and in self-government:

- the number of band operated schools has increased from 53 in 1975-76 to 243 in 1986-87;
- in 1971, Status Indians administered 20% of Department of Indian Affairs and Northern Development program expenditures, a figure that had risen to 64.1% in 1986-87.

Such figures should be viewed with caution, however, as they relate only to Status Indians on an aggregate level. There are wide disparities between Status Indians across the country, and there is no systematic information gathered on non-Status, Metis, and Inuit peoples. Further, even among Status Indians, there are signs of continuing dependency. Over the period 1981-82 to 1986-87, the number of dependants on social assistance steadily increased, and total social assistance expenditures to Status Indians increased twofold from 1973 to 1986.

There are also concerns about the relations between indigenous peoples and nonindigenous Canadians, particularly in terms of the stereotyping of indigenous people as "lazy drunks". There are several excellent studies that examine patterns of interaction between "whites" and indigenous peoples at the community level including one by Niels Braroe (1975). More recently, the sensitivities surrounding white-indigenous relationships have been highlighted by the publicity and inquiry into the death of a young Indian woman, Helen Osborne, in the northern Manitoba community of The Pas.

INDIGENOUS PEOPLES AND THE EURO-CANADIANS: COLONIZATION AND CONFLICT

The relationships between the federal government of Canada and indigenous peoples, both historically and recently, are best understood from a majority/minority or colonial perspective (see Havemann, 1989; Kellough, 1980; Morrison, 1986; Ponting, 1986). For purposes of our discussion, *colonialism* is defined as a set of processes whereby the resources and destiny of a satellite region are controlled by an imperial, metropolitan region.

In Canada, colonization has been an intentional, long-term process and has involved replacing the traditional, self-determinant lifestyle of indigenous people with a dependent and subordinate status. Historically, the whalers, missionaries, fur traders, and government officials have been the primary agents of change in the Westernization process (Coates, 1985; Crowe, 1974; Swiderski, 1985).

In the Canadian North and in other areas of the country, coerced resettlement was used by the federal government to establish sovereignty over indigenous peoples. This involved moving people from their traditional camps and villages to newly created, "artificial" communities, ostensibly for humanitarian and administrative reasons. These settlements were based on Euro-Canadian notions of community: streets rather than the traditional Indian and Inuit cluster groups of families, and single-family housing units that did not accommodate the traditional extended-family arrangement of the indigenous people.

The traditional hunting-and-gathering, subsistence lifestyle was gradually replaced by one based on a wage economy. The consequence of this process was the transformation of the social, cultural, and political life of the residents. The experience of the Grassy Narrows reserve, as documented by Shkilnyk (1984), illustrates the consequence of these processes for an indigenous community.

Over time, the indigenous culture was increasingly displaced, and many Indian and Inuit communities were swept into resignation and feelings of hopelessness. The introduction of Euro-Canadian culture resulted in rapid and overwhelming change in the culture of Indians and Inuit. This, in turn, created widespread culture shock and anomie on both the community and individual levels.

One of the major consequences of the colonization and the attendant government policies has been the destruction of indigenous communities and of the very foundations of indigenous culture and traditions. The high rates of death and conflict with the law are, in many instances, a manifestation of this loss of community. In the preface to the book *A Poison Stronger than Love* (Shkilnyk, 1984), Kai T. Erikson used the term "collective trauma" to describe the destruction of indigenous communities:

> the community no longer exists as an effective source of support and . . . an important part of their world has disappeared without even so much as a sound. As people begin to emerge hesitantly from the protective shells into which they had reflexively shrunk at the time of the assault, they learn that they are isolated and alone, living in a kind of social wasteland with no one to turn to. They have lost both the physical and spiritual health that comes from being m communion with kinsmen and neighbors who can be counted on to care (p. xvi).

The imposition of Euro-Canadian culture also had an impact on the traditional Indian and Inuit systems of social control. Morse (1983) identifies four possible outcomes when the legal system of a dominant, colonizing government comes into contact with the traditional system of social control of an indigenous minority:

1. *total avoidance*: the two systems of law function separately, with neither assuming jurisdiction over the other,
2. *co-operation*: the two systems of law function side by side, with clearly defined jurisdictional boundaries;
3. *incorporation*: one society dominates the other to the extent that certain elements of the other's law that do not fundamentally conflict with its own are adopted; and
4. *rejection*: there is outright rejection of the indigenous legal system by the dominant group, in this case Euro-Canadian society.

Historically, the position of the Canadian federal government in relation to indigenous peoples can be characterized as one of "total rejection." Keon-Cohen (1982, pp. 191-92) notes that, while American Indian tribes in the United States have enjoyed a unique constitutional position that provides them with legal sovereignty over the administration of criminal justice on reservations, the Canadian government has traditionally resisted attempts by indigenous peoples to assume jurisdiction in this area: "tribal governments and justice systems based on inherent powers have not, to date, developed in Canada.... Canadian natives, like their [Australian] Aboriginal counterparts, and unlike their American Indian brethren, are thus totally subject to, and processed by the Anglo-Canadian legal system, as compared to separate tribal justice systems." The reluctance of the federal government in Canada to encourage or recognize the development of "autonomous" or separate indigenous justice systems continues to the present, although in recent years several indigenous-controlled police forces and court-worker and social service programs have been created (see Griffiths & Verdun-Jones, 1989).

A major dimension of the involvement of indigenous peoples in crime and with the Canadian legal system is the conflict between the traditional Indian and Inuit "law" and Euro-Canadian laws. One of the more infamous cases involved two Inuit men who in 1917 were tried for murdering two priests. Little attempt was made to accommodate Aboriginal culture and traditions during the trial (see original article – Box 12.2 - for further details about the trial and injustice).

There are key distinctions between the Euro-Canadian and Indian/Inuit concepts of crime. For example, the general components of a criminal offence in Euro-Canadian law are *actus reus* and *mens rea*: in order for a criminal offence to have occurred, there must have been a prohibited act and a guilty mind. Such is not the case within traditional Indian and Inuit culture. To the Inuit, for example, an offence is completely subjective and situational: the *actus reus* may have occurred in conjunction with the *mens rea*, yet the act may be considered a "nonoffence" by Indian or Inuit standards if:

- the act occurred, such as theft, and the offender intended to return the property or pay restitution at a later date;
- the act occurred, and the offender apologizes to the victim;
- the act occurred, and it was done for prestige gathering; or
- the act was attempted, such as a break-and-enter, with the intent to steal an item that was then not taken, and the actor did not complete the act as intended; therefore, nothing wrong was done.

Law was closely intertwined with the natural environment, and personal offences were viewed as transgressions against the individual rather than the community. Sanctions were on an individual-to-individual basis, rather than emanating from the collective. This system of dispute resolution, in which a primary objective was the restoration of order in the community, was in stark contrast to the adversarial Euro-Canadian system of law, which places an emphasis on deterrence and punishment, and the notion that the response to offensive behaviour should come from the collective or from those in positions of authority acting on behalf of the collective.

INDIGENOUS PEOPLES AND THE LAW: A HISTORICAL VIEW

The whalers, missionaries, and fur traders who had initial contact with the indigenous peoples brought with them Euro-Canadian concepts of law and justice. The Hudson's Bay Company, with its monopoly over the fur trade, imposed Euro-Canadian laws in order to maintain order and ensure a steady flow of commerce. The officials in charge of the Hudson's Bay Company trading posts acted in the roles of police officer, prosecutor, and judge (Morrison, 1985). In addition, once settlement of the prairies began, the criminal justice system was used to isolate the Indians on reserves and enforce dependence upon the federal government.

With the westward pattern of settlement, Indians were pushed out of their homelands to somewhat marginal land reserves. In the Arctic, the Inuit had remained largely isolated from Western culture, until the beginning of the twentieth century. Even today, there are very few people who claim Indian ancestry living in the Atlantic provinces, while indigenous peoples constitute a majority of the population in the Northwest Territories and almost 20% in the Yukon.

The North-West Mounted Police (NWMP) had first ventured north in the late nineteenth century, and became well established in the Yukon during the Klondike gold rush. The maintenance of Canadian sovereignty, in the face of a dispute over the Alaska/Canada border, occupied much of their attention until the discovery of gold in Alaska ended the massive migration into the Yukon. It was during the early 1900s that the first attempts to enforce the Queen's law on the indigenous peoples of the Canadian North occurred, and this provides us with an illustration of the conflict between the indigenous and Euro-Canadian culture and legal systems as well as the policy of rejection of the indigenous culture by the federal government in its attempt to colonize indigenous people and establish sovereignty over the vast areas of the North and West.

Early patrols of the NWMP often visited the Inuit and Indian communities of the Northwest Territories to "show the flag" and assist the government in establishing sovereignty over more remote areas of the country. Among the duties of the police were census taking, surveying, the collection of taxes from the fur traders and whalers, acting as customs officers, and enforcing the peace between indigenous peoples and Euro-Canadians. Company officers also acted in the role of police magistrates and justices of the peace.

PATTERNS OF INDIGENOUS CRIME

Our consideration of the nature and extent of crime among indigenous peoples is hindered by a lack of published research. Official statistics generally include only Status or registered Indians, and there are few data on the crime patterns of Metis, Inuit, and non-Status Indians. Still unexplained are the data from the Uniform Crime Reporting System (Canadian Centre for Justice Statistics, 1989, (p. 30) that reveal that the Northwest Territories (22,199 Criminal Code offences per 100,000 population) is second only to the Yukon Territory (22,648 per 100,000) in the number of Criminal Code offences per 100,000 population. In 1987, the rate of violent crime in the Northwest Territories (4,410 per 100,000 population) and the rate of property offences (9,841 per 100,000 population) were the highest reported rates in the country. Others have noted that the same pattern is found in other Arctic countries. Given the high concentration of indigenous peoples in the territories, it is difficult to examine crime in the North without a consideration of crime by indigenous peoples.

Despite these rough indicators, there have been very few empirical studies on crime among indigenous youth, adults, women, and the elderly, or their involvement in the criminal justice system. Neither do we have a clear understanding of the crime patterns in the various jurisdictions—"northern" and "southern", rural, and urban—across the country.

As a consequence of this, we are able to present only a general overview of the patterns of indigenous crime in Canada, with the caveat that there are wide variations across the country, between rural and urban areas, and across the different cultural and linguistic groups. From the materials that have been produced, we can distil the following attributes of indigenous crime:

- indigenous peoples tend to commit less serious crimes than do their nonindigenous counterparts, with the exception that, in many jurisdictions, indigenous peoples are involved in a large number of violent crimes against persons;

- the socio-economic condition of indigenous peoples plays a significant role in their involvement in criminal behaviour;
- alcohol use is present in a high percentage (up to 90% in some jurisdictions) of crimes committed by indigenous peoples;
- in comparison with their nonindigenous counterparts, indigenous offenders were first identified by the criminal justice system at an earlier age; and
- in many jurisdictions, indigenous youth evidence rates of arrest are up to three times that of their nonindigenous counterparts.

INDIGENOUS PEOPLES IN THE CRIMINAL JUSTICE SYSTEM

There has also been increasing concern about the extensive involvement of Inuit peoples in the criminal justice system and, in particular, the conflict experienced by Inuit with the Euro-Canadian systems of law and justice. To date, there have been no comprehensive, cross-national studies of indigenous peoples in the Canadian criminal justice system. From the research that has been conducted to date, however, we can make the following general statements:

- while indigenous peoples tend, on average, to commit less serious crimes than do their nonindigenous counterparts, they are more frequently arrested, found guilty, and incarcerated;
- indigenous peoples, both adults and youths, are overrepresented (in proportion to their representation in the general population) in arrest statistics, court conviction statistics, and correctional institution populations in many areas of the country;
- indigenous peoples comprise about 7% of the total federal inmate population; in provincial institutions, they often constitute 60 to 70% of the inmate population;
- on average, the sentences received by indigenous peoples were shorter than those given to nonindigenous peoples, accounting for their overrepresentation in provincial corrections-institutions populations;
- in many jurisdictions, indigenous youth are overrepresented in arrest statistics, in youth court systems, in detention facilities, and in child care systems;
- indigenous women are overrepresented in the criminal justice system in many jurisdictions, particularly in the Prairie provinces, where, in 1982, indigenous women constituted up to 40% of the admissions to

provincial correctional facilities in Alberta and more than 70% in the Northwest Territories, Yukon, and Manitoba.

More specifically, Hylton (1980) found, in Saskatchewan, that male Status Indians were 37 times more likely to be incarcerated, while Métis and non-Status Indians were 12 times more likely to be confined than were non-Indians. Compared to their non-Indian counterparts, Indian women were 118 times more likely to be incarcerated, and Métis and non-Status Indian women 25 times more likely to be incarcerated than non-Indian women.

During the period 1985-90, several events forced Canadians to face the possibility of discrimination and prejudice in the administration of justice for indigenous peoples. These include the case of Donald Marshall, a Nova Scotia Micmac Indian; the shooting of Indian leader J.J. Harper by police in Winnipeg in 1987; and the inquiry into the 1977 killing of Helen Osborne in The Pas, Manitoba.

The circumstances surrounding the shooting of J.J. Harper by a Winnipeg police officer and the inquiry into the murder of Helen Osborne were examined as part of the work of the Manitoba Aboriginal Justice Inquiry, co-chaired by Mr. Justice A.C. Hamilton and Judge Murray Sinclair of the Provincial Court of Manitoba. This inquiry was perhaps the highest-profile examination of the issues surrounding indigenous peoples and the law, and involved extensive hearings in Indian communities throughout Manitoba as well as submissions and testimony from criminal justice personnel, Indian leaders, and community residents.

While the police are the "front line" and point of first contact between indigenous peoples and the criminal-justice system, the relationships between police and Canadian Indians and Inuit in rural and urban areas are often characterized by mutual hostility and distrust. This situation increases the likelihood of conflict between the two groups and may be a contributory factor in the high arrest rates experienced by indigenous peoples in many areas of the country.

In a study of police-Indian relations in the Prairie provinces of Alberta, Saskatchewan, and Manitoba, Donald Loree (1985) surveyed regular RCMP members as well as Indian Special Constables. Loree found that nearly 43% of the regular members described the general state of Indian-non-Indian relations in their detachment area as "fair," while almost 34% defined them as "good" and only 3.7% as "very good." According to the regular members interviewed by Loree, the greatest areas of difficulty in policing Indian communities were "differences in cultural values and outlook on life," "problems linked to high unemployment," and "dealing with young people."

Two of the more significant findings from the Loree (1985) study are: (1) for regular members, alcohol-related incidents are the most common context within which police officers come into official contact with Indian people, and (2) a primary determinant of the quality of Indian-police relations appears to be the age, experience, and personal policing style of the individual police officer.

Police officers' knowledge of the communities and people they are policing is also important, although Loree (1985) found that a significant proportion of the officers he interviewed described themselves as having only a "fair" level of general knowledge about Indians. And, as importantly, most of the knowledge the officers did have had been acquired after they had arrived in the community. A high percentage of the officers surveyed felt that the police-Indians relations could be improved through an increased emphasis on police-community relations and more active involvement of officers in sports and social activities in the community.

Conflict between indigenous peoples and agents of the Canadian criminal justice system may also be precipitated by a lack of knowledge on the part of Indians and Inuit peoples about the law and the legal system. Many observers have argued that indigenous peoples in rural, urban, and northern areas of the country have only a cursory understanding of the law, their legal rights, and the criminal justice process and that this contributes to the high rates of arrest, guilty pleas, and confinement. In a study of police-Indian relations in the Yukon, for example, Pamell (1979) found that nearly 90% of the Indians interviewed stated that they required more information about the law, and 55% desired information on their legal rights.

Conflict between indigenous peoples and the police may also occur in urban areas. In a study of police officers in Regina in the 1970s, Hylton and his colleagues found that a large percentage of the officers viewed Indians as "lazy" and as "drunks". Perhaps no one event, however, has served to focus attention on police-Indian relations in urban centres more than the death of Indian leader J.J. Harper in Winnipeg in winter 1987.

Concerns have also been voiced that indigenous peoples in the Canadian North, many of whom do not speak English, have little understanding of the principles of Canadian law and the functioning of the adversarial system of criminal justice. This may also be true of indigenous peoples in other remote areas of the country.

While police officers are posted to northern communities, judicial services are provided via the circuit court, which has been the subject of increasing attention (and criticism) in recent years. Circuit court parties —comprised of a provincial or territorial court judge, court clerk, defense lawyer, and Crown counsel— travel to communities (generally, by air) on a regular basis to hold court.

While many communities are served monthly, others are visited every three months, or more infrequently if there are no cases to be heard or if the weather prevents a scheduled visit. The most extensive circuit-court systems are in the Northwest Territories, where Territorial and Supreme Court justices travel on 6 circuits to the 62 communities, and in northern Quebec, where the circuit criminal courts cover the James Bay and Ungava Bay regions.

Indigenous organizations and communities have argued that many of the defendants who appear before the circuit courts do not understand the adversarial proceedings of the court nor the legal terminology that is used. A major dilemma that often confronts the sentencing judge is whether to impose a disposition that results in the removal of the indigenous offender to a correctional facility many miles from the community or to utilize community-based programs and services. Further, it is argued that the dispositions available under the *Criminal Code* do not address the unique needs of the specific community, offenders, and victims.

GOVERNMENT-SPONSORED AND INDIGENOUS-CONTROLLED INITIATIVES TO REDUCE CONFLICT WITH THE LAW

The conflict with the law experienced by indigenous peoples and their extensive involvement in the criminal-justice system has placed pressure on the federal, provincial, and territorial governments to develop policies and implement programs to address these problems.

A close examination of the response of the federal government provides key insights into how the dominant majority has approached the task of addressing indigenous crime and conflict with the law. The basis of government initiatives was the National Conference on Native Peoples and the Criminal Justice System, held in Edmonton in 1975. This conference was attended by federal, provincial, and territorial, as well as Indian and Inuit leaders, and was the first attempt to identify and discuss the major areas of conflict that indigenous peoples experienced with the law.

A major recommendation of the conference participants was that programs and services for indigenous peoples in conflict with the law be developed and that indigenous communities become more extensively involved in the design and delivery of justice services. During the years following the conference, a number of program initiatives were undertaken, including the deployment of Indian Special Constables who assist regular RCMP officers in policing indigenous communities and reserves (a program that is now being phased out), and the creation of native court-worker programs to provide assistance to indigenous offenders during the court process (Griffiths & Yerbury, 1984; Hathaway, 1986).

Despite the proliferation of government-sponsored programs and services, there has not been, in the two decades since the 1975 Edmonton conference, a significant decrease in the numbers of indigenous persons in conflict with the law and, in most areas of the country, the rates of arrest, conviction, arid (*sic*) incarceration are higher than they were prior to the conference. Many observers have argued that the failure of government-sponsored initiatives to reduce indigenous conflict with the law is the result of the failure to address the causal factors related to indigenous crime, including the socio-structural position of indigenous peoples in Canadian society.

Critics such as Havemann (1989) also point to the reluctance of the federal government to encourage the development of "autonomous" or separate justice systems for indigenous peoples, and contend that the federal government has pursued a policy of "indigenization," whereby indigenous people are recruited to fill such positions as Special Constable and court-worker, within the criminal justice system, and that such policies ensure that the federal government retains power over indigenous peoples.

Despite the preference of the federal government for developing programs and services for indigenous peoples within the framework of established criminal justice and social service delivery systems, many bands and communities have taken the initiative to create autonomous, community-based programs. There are several indigenous-controlled police forces operating in Canada, including the Amerindian Police Force in Quebec, the Dakota-Ojibway Tribal Council Police in Manitoba, and several reserve-based police forces in Alberta.

There has been an increased involvement of Indian and Inuit communities in developing community-based alternatives to the formal justice system and, in many instances, these alternative programs and services incorporate customary law and traditional methods of social control. In the province of Quebec and in the Northwest Territories, for example, "traditional" Inuit adoption, whereby an Inuit mother may "give" a child to a member of the extended family or to another community resident for upbringing, has been recognized in provincial law. In many Inuit and Indian communities, elders are playing an increasingly larger and more influential role in addressing problems relating to youth and adult crime.

There are other examples of community-based initiatives designed to address crime problems and conflict with the criminal-justice system. Often these initiatives occur in conjunction with the revitalization of the community— the assertion of independence and individual and community confidence to confront and resolve problems. One of the more widely publicized "success" stories was the transformation of the Alkali Lake Indian Band in British Columbia from nearly 100% alcoholic to over 95% abstinent.

Such initiatives have an opportunity to work where government policies and programs have failed. There is an emerging consensus that indigenous communities must play the primary role in addressing problems of crime, and that they should be given the necessary resources and jurisdictional authority to do so. For it is the indigenous communities that can best identify the problems and needs of the people and mobilize community-based resources to address them.

The failure of the Canadian federal government to give indigenous peoples the legal sovereignty and jurisdiction over the administration of justice, however, means that the development of community-based, indigenous-controlled programs and services will continue to be uneven. And, even with increased autonomy of reserve-based peoples, this leaves large numbers of non-Status, Métis, and Inuit peoples, as well as Status Indians residing off reserves, who will continue to come into contact (and conflict) with the criminal-justice system.

Accommodating the Concerns of Aboriginal People within the Existing Justice System

John Giokas

INTRODUCTION: AN EMERGING NEW RELATIONSHIP

It is clear in 1992 that the relationship between Aboriginal and non-Aboriginal Canadians has changed irrevocably. The general nature of the Aboriginal political mobilization since 1945 that has seen Aboriginal peoples move from being the object of national debate in Canada to participants in that debate is proof enough of that. It cannot be forgotten that when Canadian status Indians first advanced the idea of being direct participants at the negotiating table in the constitutional renewal process in the 1970s it was initially considered by the federal government to be a non-starter. In essence, Aboriginal organizations entered the constitutional debate in the 1970s as citizens groups of a special type and came out of it at the 1992 Charlottetown meeting as full participants on a par with the federal and provincial governments in most respects.

This is not an isolated Canadian phenomenon. Throughout the world there are growing political movements among indigenous peoples for new power sharing arrangements within their respective states. The collective force of these movements is such that 1993 has been declared by the United Nations

Giokas, J. (1993). Accommodating the concerns of aboriginal people within the existing justice system. In *Royal Commission on Aboriginal People, Aboriginal peoples and the justice system*. (pp. 184-206). From Privy Council Office. Reproduced with the permission of the Minister of Public Works and Government Services Canada, 1998.

to be the international year of the indigenous people. Indigenous political movements since 1945 have been supported by the international expansion of human rights consciousness over the past several decades that finds expression in a worldwide intellectual trend toward "ethnic pluralism and a global ideology of racial and cultural equality".

The domestic Canadian counterparts of the international rights expansion include the *Canadian Bill of Rights*, under which the first modern human rights challenges to Canadian Indian legislation were brought, the Charter and the various federal and provincial human rights acts and codes.

But the international movement has gone beyond the protection of individual human rights to the protection of the right of self-determination of "peoples", largely under the auspices of the United Nations. The Canadian parallel is the demand of Aboriginal peoples for self-determination in the form of a constitutionally protected right to self-government that has resulted in the various first ministers conferences on the subject and which will likely continue to dominate the national debate around Aboriginal issues generally for some time to come.

This paper has been written against the backdrop of this national and international drive of Aboriginal peoples for a greater degree of control over their own affairs. The basic theme of this paper can be summarized in one word: emergence. A new order is emerging in Canada that will cover most important aspects of the new relationship between Aboriginal and non-Aboriginal Canadians. Its shape is not yet entirely visible. The Aboriginal peoples, however, are ahead of most Canadians in that they can sense the general contours of the new relationship, and have been pressing in a number of areas to permit it to be fleshed out in an orderly way. Justice administration is one of those areas.

Many voices are now heard to argue for particular solutions to the Aboriginal justice problem such as a parallel or separate Aboriginal justice system. Given the thesis set out here, however, the final form the new relationship will take in the justice field is of marginal relevance. The real issue from this perspective is whether government can play a useful role to facilitate change within the current constitutional framework. During this period of transition to a new relationship, it will be important to lay the groundwork for the coming changes to the power sharing relationship between Aboriginal peoples and the federal and provincial governments.

It will be equally important, however, to lay this groundwork in such a way that the overall relationship between Aboriginal and non-Aboriginal Canadians can be maintained in the face of the challenges that will inevitably test that relationship. The essential quality required to perform both tasks will be a renewed commitment to an equal partnership between the Aboriginal peoples and the federal and provincial governments. The approach set out in this paper is an attempt to provide a way to foster such a renewed commitment. As in so many other areas of national life of late, however, the proof will be in the actual doing.

The Current Debate About Aboriginal Justice in Canada

One of the starting features of the present debate around Aboriginal justice issues is that there is so much disagreement while at the same time there is such a remarkable degree of consensus. The various provincial inquiry reports, academic studies, research papers, government documents and even public opinion coalesce around four broadly shared conclusions:

- the current justice system has failed Aboriginal people;
- the solution is increased Aboriginal responsibility for defining and resolving Aboriginal justice problems;
- given the diversity of Aboriginal peoples and communities across the country, those definitions and solutions will not be identical; and
- those Aboriginal definitions and solutions cannot exist apart from the current justice system, at least at the outset.

Disagreement is in the details of the problem and in the nature of the solutions; i.e., whether the failure is primarily with respect to more traditional, reserve-based Aboriginal peoples or whether it applies equally to urban residents; whether the causes are socio-economic or whether they lie in cultural differences or a combination of the two; or whether we start our analysis and efforts from the current justice system, or whether we start from the position of a more generalized right to a parallel or separate system, etc.

In many ways, these differences reflect, on the one hand, the disagreements over the nature and causes of crime generally, for which there is no singular explanation, and, on the other hand, the merging of Aboriginal justice issues with the broader political debate around Aboriginal self-government. Thus it may be expecting too much to have a higher degree of agreement regarding Aboriginal crime than exists in the scientific community regarding crime theory generally. And it may also be naive to expect easily to disentangle justice issues from the wider self-government debate.

But, as general as the four points of consensus may be, they nonetheless provide a framework for approaching the problem while the particular points of difference are investigated and debated in scientific and even in political and constitutional forums. For whatever may be the ultimate explanation for these problems, the one common element in all the reports is that there are simply too many Aboriginal people being processed and incarcerated by the current justice system. At this point, and after around thirty reports and studies, it is hard to disagree with the trenchant observation of Patricia Monture-OKanee and Mary Ellen Turpel that "the era of collecting data about the over-representation of Aboriginal people in the criminal justice system must end. It is now time to begin to focus on meaningful change."

JUSTICE SYSTEM FAILURE

Three themes have consistently emerged in the various provincial Aboriginal justice inquiries and studies over the past decades. Aboriginal over-representation is affirmed by report after report documenting the high contact rates of Aboriginal people with police and their disproportionately high rates of arrest, conviction and imprisonment. Over-representation in prisons and jails is now an acknowledged fact, and there is every indication that the problem may be worsening, given that the federal Aboriginal inmate population is increasing at more than twice the national rate. In 1991, Aboriginal persons generally were around 11% and 15% of the populations of federal and provincial carceral institutions respectively. Rates are even higher for Aboriginal women. In addition, Aboriginal offenders are less likely to be paroled early in their sentences. Aboriginal youth are also disproportionately represented in juvenile detention facilities. General Aboriginal over-representation is particularly acute in the prairies.

A second common theme is the existence of discrimination against Aboriginal people at all levels of the existing justice system. The reports and studies conclude that it is largely systemic and have made numerous recommendations to correct it. Aboriginal people have indicated through their testimony before the various inquiries that they believe they are dealt with more harshly by the justice system. In court they often do not understand the trial process, the sentence hearing or the sentence itself. Many assert that police and prison staff are racially prejudiced in their treatment of them. The various inquiry reports and studies are careful about accusing anyone of overt racism, but their conclusions also support the existence of some degree of overt discrimination in the system.

These factors have fuelled a third common problem: the perception among Aboriginal people that "the criminal justice system is an alien one, imposed by the dominant white society." In short, it is not "theirs" in a way that would command their respect and has come to be seen as their enemy, a view too often derived from first-hand experiences with the systems of child welfare, youth justice, family court and criminal justice. Every indication is that the alienation of Aboriginal people is pervasive and growing. Increasingly it finds academic support in the continued emphasis on cultural differences between Aboriginal and non-Aboriginal approaches to justice issues.

It also finds political legitimacy in the statements of national Aboriginal leaders and the acknowledgements and apologies of Canadian churches and politicians regarding past and present injustices in all areas of the relationship between Canadian society and Aboriginal peoples. This apparently profound sense of alienation may itself be the most serious aspect of the overall Aboriginal criminal justice problem since it is intimately tied to the political struggle being waged by Aboriginal peoples for new power sharing arrangements in Canada as well as abroad.

One thing preventing a concerted focus on meaningful change is the lack of general agreement on the causes of these problems. From the publication of *Indians and the Law* in 1967 the inquiry reports and studies are of one voice regarding the relationship between Aboriginal justice problems and underlying social and economic problems. But beyond that observation, there remain quite different ways of explaining the connection between Aboriginal socio-economic conditions and criminal justice problems. In a recent article, Michael Jackson refers to the "larger pattern of social disorganization and economic deprivation that characterizes life in many Aboriginal communities" and goes on to discuss the diverse explanations for over-representation and the pattern of Aboriginal social and economic disruption. His analysis crystallizes the explanations into three main camps.

The first, cultural difference between Aboriginal and non-Aboriginal Canadians, holds that the gap between Aboriginal and non-Aboriginal cultures is so great that Aboriginal societies have not been able to adapt to non-Aboriginal values and conceptions. This has led to their marginalization from mainstream culture and the modern Canadian economy. The second explanation sees Aboriginal criminal justice problems in structural terms, as problems grounded in economic and social disparities that are not necessarily related to cultural factors. From this perspective, age and socio-economic status, for example, are more reliable indicators than culture in explaining why Aboriginal persons are disproportionately represented in the prison population. A third view reconciles these two explanations. It focuses on the process of colonization "which has made native peoples poor beyond poverty" and strikes a responsive chord in the experience of other indigenous peoples worldwide.

All three explanations have independent merit and should be explored further. But that exploration should not delay action. From these explanations it seems possible to derive working hypotheses to underpin that action while that exploration goes on:

- The unique history and current socio-economic circumstances of Aboriginal peoples and communities create equally unique pressures on them; behaviours designated as criminal are but one symptom of deeper inequities.
- The justice system has historically functioned, and continues to varying degrees to function, in ways that discriminate against Aboriginal people, whether through racial prejudice, insensitivity or lack of knowledge or some combination of these factors.
- The very process of defining crime and of setting justice priorities reflects a Euro-Canadian conceptual framework and continues to dominate in ways that exclude and perhaps even threaten Aboriginal culture.

INCREASED ABORIGINAL RESPONSIBILITY FOR JUSTICE

That the solution to Aboriginal justice problems is increased Aboriginal responsibility hardly seems arguable in 1992. This theme emerges from virtually every provincial Aboriginal justice report, as well as the only federal government document to address Aboriginal justice from a conceptual framework.

The theme of increased Aboriginal responsibility for defining and resolving Aboriginal problems is also a political commitment. It underpins federal government Aboriginal policy as set out in the Prime Minister's "four pillars" speech to the House of Commons on September 25, 1990 where he promised that "this government will find practical ways to ensure that Aboriginal communities can exercise greater control over the administration of justice." He reaffirmed this in his speech of April 23, 1991 to the First Nations Congress in Victoria, B.C., adding that "Aboriginal leaders have sought reform in the justice system as a necessary step towards the realization of their wider aspirations."

As already mentioned, a global human rights revolution is going on that has assisted Aboriginal peoples worldwide in their drive for new power sharing arrangements in the states in which they are found. Since 1982 and the renewed emphasis on rights under the Constitution, it seems inevitable that a new relationship based on new political and constitutional rules that will recognize the right of Aboriginal peoples in Canada to self-government is just around the corner. It is important to note that the rights revolution has changed not only the rules of the game, but also the language through those rules will be debated. Maxwell Cohen, writing nearly twenty-five years ago, noted the burgeoning Canadian interest in human rights and commented that human rights had become "an important piece of debating language" and a "part of the political dialogue, part of the debating experience of peoples in all parts of the world, even those in affluent societies." This helps to explain the curious dominance of the debate by lawyers, and the generally enhanced policy role of the Supreme Court in national policy-making.

In addition to these larger trends, in the justice area there has been a general turning away in Canadian society from notions of reactive policing and aggressive criminal justice processing to one of community crime prevention. A recurrent theme in the literature and submissions to various task forces has been the importance of empowering communities to identify and solve their own crime problems. Given this, and the international and domestic movement toward the empowerment of Aboriginal peoples and communities and the recent political commitment to the same principle, what is it that impedes Aboriginal peoples and communities from assuming greater responsibility for their justice processes and problems?

One impediment is the merging of the more abstract human rights rhetoric around self-government issues with the concrete and day-to-day crime and justice problems experienced at the community level. The international and domestic human rights expansion and accompanying political mobilization of Aboriginal people has, in effect, created a new process or "track" for resolving Aboriginal issues. This track is oriented towards global solutions, necessarily operates at a higher level of abstraction and uses the language of legal rights. This is the track sometimes referred to as the "political agenda" of Aboriginal peoples.

There are now two tracks for action regarding Aboriginal issues: the pragmatic, community level empirical approach; and the global human rights/self-determination approach. In the self-government debate these tracks appear as the Department of Indian Affairs-led community-based self-government program and the more recent Indian Act alternatives approach versus the constitutional entrenchment of the inherent right to self-government. In the justice area, these tracks appear as the pragmatic approach of working with Aboriginal communities and of repairing the existing system versus the rights/self-determination approach of establishing a parallel or separate Aboriginal justice system.

The terms in which the debate has been cast have created something of a false dichotomy between the two tracks as if they were mutually exclusive. The entire process seems to have been hijacked by this dichotomy and all action has been arrested while the debate plays itself out. At the risk of stretching a metaphor, the debate boils down to the following question: Should we provide the right to an Aboriginal justice system first and then build the remedy in the form of Aboriginal processes and institutions, or should we build the remedy first and then provide the right to them?

From this perspective, the real debate seems to be less incremental adaptation of the existing system versus a global right to create parallel or separate systems, but whether there is any kind of blueprint for action to address Aboriginal justice problems. The tendency has sometimes been to see a right to a parallel or separate system as such a blueprint. But it is not; it is merely a rights framework for the realization of Aboriginal responsibility for justice processes. In many ways justice issues, like constitutional issues, have become a lawyers debate that discounts the fact that on either track the actual assumption of greater responsibility begins in the same way — at the community level on the basis of community needs and desires.

Of course, the advantage of the rights track is that it establishes a framework of rough equality from the outset. This is the ideal way to proceed. But the starting point for action will be the same whether the rights framework is there or not: it will be the community, and the terms upon which it is willing and able to begin to take responsibility for its own processes in the justice area, and the degree of political will on the side of government to assist the community to take responsibility. The rights track merely provides a lever in the form of the threat of court action if political will is lacking on the government side.

The tendency has been to cast this as an either/or issue: either we deal with the rights track or we focus exclusively on pragmatic community matters. Few voices are heard to argue that both efforts proceed simultaneously. But at the community level the question has in many cases been rendered moot. Many communities are not standing still waiting for their national leaders to resolve the issue with national non-Aboriginal leaders. They are simply going ahead in practical, community-oriented ways to deal with local community issues, including justice problems. The federal Justice Department knows of well over a hundred such community justice projects that are seeking federal funding assistance. There are in all likelihood more local initiatives going ahead with provincial funding or with no financial assistance at all.

Two things are evident at this stage of the debate. The first is that we cannot await the outcome of the larger debate about rights and self-determination before taking action: the justice system has failed Aboriginal people and there is danger in delay. Further delay risks rupturing what is left of the partnership between Aboriginal people and government upon which action on Aboriginal justice issues depends. As will be discussed below, the need for partnership between Aboriginal peoples and government will in all probability extend well into the future whether or not a constitutionally entrenched right of self-government or separate systems come into being tomorrow.

Second, we cannot ignore the rights debate and the broader political aspirations of Aboriginal peoples. Patricia Monture-OKanee and Mary Ellen Turpel express it well:

> An additional but related factor required for reform is an appreciation and sensitivity towards aboriginal political objectives..., an idea of what type of criminal justice system aboriginal peoples can respect can be facilitated only by respecting aboriginal political authority, not only the authority of non-aboriginal politicians. An appreciation of aboriginal political objectives is only possible through extensive consultation and review of aboriginal generated literature.

Other students of Aboriginal issues such as Sally Weaver seem to agree that we have passed beyond the point where Aboriginal political aspirations can be discounted in formulating policy in other areas. She argues that Canada is currently experiencing a "paradigm shift" in Indian (and by extension, Aboriginal) policy development as we move from a paradigm or perspective that focuses on legal formalism and state control to one that focuses on justice more broadly defined and emphasizes mutual adaptation and ongoing inter-cultural relations. This paradigm shift would thus correspond with the shift in role of Aboriginal peoples in Canada—from objects of debate in the 1940s to full participants in that debate in 1992.

While the thinking in many government circles still has not caught up to the permanent change in the federal landscape of the country, the thinking in other circles seems to have gotten well ahead of the real pace of change in Canada. This, it is submitted, is one of the reasons for frustration on all sides of these complex issues. During the shift from one paradigm to the other, Sally

Weaver argues that "we should expect to see erratic policy experiments, unfocused initiatives and false starts until the new mode of thinking settles into acceptance." From this perspective, the current round of inquiries and studies may be seen as a form of judicially led and somewhat erratic experiments in policy thinking that are still seeking focus. This Royal Commission National Round Table on Aboriginal Justice Issues is one way of trying to develop that focus so that false starts may be avoided.

Importantly, the essential characteristic of the new paradigm is the permanency and flexibility of the relationship between Aboriginal peoples and the state:

> The first and perhaps most basic idea in the new paradigm is the notion that the relationship between the First Nations and the state (Canada) is a *permanent organic relationship*, one that will prevail into the distant future. The relationship is an ongoing and growing one, not a convergent one where the two political entities are expected to meld into a unitary form. Rather it is cast as parallel political forces flowing down through time, the key feature being that each force adjusts to the other and the environment in which they both operate. Hence there is no concept of termination of First Nations' relations with the state.... In sum, new paradigm thinking holds that finality is neither empirically achievable nor politically desirable.

Two important elements of new paradigm thinking will be joint policy-making and the transformation of some government departments into service providers to assist Aboriginal people rather than to direct them. The permanency of the relationship is crucial, as is the openness and partnership that this paradigm implies.

DIVERSE PEOPLES: DIVERSE SOLUTIONS

One reason why there cannot be a global blueprint for action is the sheer diversity of the Aboriginal peoples of Canada themselves. Patricia Monture-OKanee and Mary Ellen Turpel seem to agree that not only must the Aboriginal justice challenge be faced in partnership, but that there can be no singular answers for diverse peoples:

> What must be remembered as we begin to face this new challenge together is that the shape of the answer is not singular. There is not

a single answer that will speak to the diversity of experience, geography, and culture of aboriginal people and our communities. To give but one example, the problems and solutions will be different for aboriginal people living on reserves or Inuit or Métis communities, as compared to those living in urban centres. Any reasoned response must be tailored to answer both the internal dimension of criminal justice problems (i.e., for aboriginal communities) and the external dimensions (i.e., for aboriginal individuals living away from their communities.)

Projections from available census data reflect some of this diversity. Canada's population includes 958,500 Aboriginal people: 490,178 status Indians, 33,000 Inuit, and 435,322 non-status Indians or Métis. Most experts would probably agree that the figures for non-status Indians and Métis are highly approximate, given that self-identification is the major tool for identifying these groups. The Native Council of Canada, for example, has repeatedly asserted that it represents 750,000 people (status Indians off-reserve, non-status Indians and Métis). The Manitoba Métis alone are claimed to number 111,000 people.

Of the status Indians, only around 60% (less than 300,000) live on reserve. Of those living on reserve, 40% live in or near larger urban centres. The rest, nearly 180,000, live in rural or in isolated areas. Of the 603 bands and the 617 registry groups (discrete groups contained within a single band listing), 40 have less than 100 people, 265 have between 100 and 499 people, 259 have from 500 to 1999 people, and 53 have populations of over 2000. The effects of Bill C-31 on the overall population of status Indians are still unknown. Projections for 1991 for all status Indians indicate a potential population of just over 521,000.

Aboriginal peoples inhabit all regions of Canada, with 84% living west of Quebec. Aboriginal cultures are often as or more different from each other as those of the countries of Europe are from each other. There are over 50 Aboriginal languages in Canada falling within 11 different linguistic groups. Moreover, Aboriginal peoples have different historical experiences of contact with non-Aboriginal settlers, and have different legal and constitutional relationships with the federal, provincial and territorial governments, depending on that history of contact and their status under Canadian law.

In short, the notion of Aboriginal "people" as such appears to be an illusory abstraction, as does the notion of a singular and global "Aboriginal" solution to problems in an area as broad as justice administration. Large numbers of Aboriginal people now live in urban centres. Of those Aboriginal people who continue to live in Aboriginal communities, many move back and forth to urban centres, often on a seasonal basis. Many exclusively Aboriginal communities are themselves in close proximity to non-Aboriginal centres, with their residents of necessity following lifestyles reflecting a mix of cultural values. Many Aboriginal traditions have been wholly or partially lost, and some communities are now engaging in the difficult task of reconstructing traditional approaches and in adapting them to the modern reality of Canada. Thus, the Indigenous Bar Association makes a point which is often lost when non-Aboriginal commentators discuss Aboriginal people and Aboriginal culture as a unitary phenomenon:

> All of the foregoing, of course, must be qualified by the observation that traditional values are more likely to be found in Aboriginal people who have had a traditional upbringing and less likely to be observed in Aboriginal people who have prior exposure to a contemporary urban lifestyle or to the criminal justice system. Moreover, it should also be kept in mind that the behaviour of individuals varies widely. Nevertheless, traditional values exist and have been the subject of frequent comment....

But this is not to say that there are not common values or commonalities of approach among the widely different Aboriginal peoples. The Alberta Task Force Report sets out in broad terms the different underlying cultural values of Aboriginal and non-Aboriginal societies in terms that are reflected in much of the inquiry testimony of Aboriginal people across Canada. There is an identity of culture in the broad sense among the otherwise diverse Aboriginal peoples that is real and undeniable.

There is also an identity of aspiration in the broad sense that has been called the Aboriginal political agenda and which expresses itself in the language of rights. It coalesces around the issue of self-determination and has been discussed earlier as one of the two tracks on which Aboriginal issues are being advanced. Thus, at the level of international debate and domestic constitutional discussions there is a tendency for Aboriginal peoples to speak as if they were one, as if their aspirations were identical or nearly so. This is natural given the high level of abstraction of human rights and self-determination terminology. It is also natural given the political imperatives that demand from Aboriginal peoples a high degree of cooperation in advancing such issues. But even on this track the particular forms that the right will take will reflect cultural and political diversity as well as shared cultural and political aspirations.

In short, on one track there may be exaggerated similarities, while on the other there may be exaggerated differences, depending on the focus of the inquiry. The truth will lie somewhere in the range between them and will be discoverable only through action at the community level in accordance with the will of that particular community. But there increasingly appears to be little possibility of a universal blueprint to be followed in the area of Aboriginal justice, even to repair problems about which there is consensus.

ABORIGINAL JUSTICE SOLUTIONS AND THE JUSTICE SYSTEM

Thus, even if the political agenda of Aboriginal peoples on the rights track succeeds in bringing about constitutionally protected forms of self-government satisfactory to Aboriginal peoples, the relationship with Canada will continue. Hence the requirement in the Charlottetown Accord constitutional package that inherent sovereignty was to be exercised within Canada, federal and provincial laws apply until displaced by Aboriginal laws, and that federal and provincial laws "essential to the preservation of peace, order and good government" will trump Aboriginal laws.

Similarly with regard to Aboriginal justice, it cannot be expected that parallel or separate systems will have no linkage with the existing system, even in their most developed forms. The starting point for their creation will be what now exists; they will of necessity evolve in stages from what now exists, and they will in all likelihood retain substantial links with what now exists because they will still be within Canada. In any event, even if a separate system were created tomorrow, it is highly unlikely Aboriginal communities would wish to take on the full range of *Criminal Code* matters, for example, even if such a thing were contemplated by government.

The establishment of parallel or separate systems will change the terms of that relationship, but not the fact of a relationship. In other words, parallel or separate systems of Aboriginal justice would not spring full blown from the void and they would not exist in a void even in their most fully developed form. The necessity of proceeding in stages is recognized by the authors of the Manitoba Inquiry. They propose a process based on trilateral negotiations as a way of acquiring gradual Aboriginal jurisdiction over different areas:

> It seems logical to us that one of the concerns which Aboriginal groups will want to address in particular is the question of having the provincial justice system withdraw from particular areas of jurisdiction at the same pace as they are being assumed by Aboriginal justice systems.

This is a vision that is apparently shared by the national chief of the Assembly of First Nations. In an extensive interview, Ovide Mercredi described his vision of an Aboriginal justice system in terms that indicate a similar phased approach, the absence of an authoritative blueprint and continuing linkage with the existing system as a matter of practical necessity:

> The basic approach we want to take in the creation of our own systems of justice is flexibility, allowing for the evolution of systems of justice rather than a universal plan. For example, if one community wants to proceed on the basis of a juvenile court system and that is all they want, then that is all they should have until they want more in the future. If a group of First Nations wants to join together to create a family court, or a child welfare court, let them do it in their own way. If that is the only system of justice they want to administer, so be it. If they want to keep the *Criminal Code* for the other system, that's their decision. Flexibility is important.

> Consensual development is equally important. If a native group wants to adopt parts of the white system and create other parts of an indigenous court system where the two work in tandem, that's their business. Those are things that can be worked out. It really depends on each First Nation and what their needs are. The Manitoba Report presented one model of how to proceed. They have studied the situation in Manitoba, and the model they present is probably workable in that area. The idea of Indian tribal courts is a very plausible option, provided the people want it that way. The key is consent — the people's consent.

> Right now, there is a feeling that the white system of justice is not serving the interests of native people, so we're looking to alternatives. But the alternatives that are developed have to be developed by us. And they have to be accepted by the community, otherwise they're not going to work. It would be another imposition by people like myself, or chiefs. If the people consent to it, they will respect the system and they will work within it. The native system doesn't have to be a mirror of the institutions of justice that are presently in place.

> We don't have to have courts, we can set up grievance procedures or mediation panels. The important thing is to restore harmony in the community and to provide some form of recovery or healing.

Leaving aside this conceptual debate about linkage between the Canadian system of justice generally and whatever variations may emerge in Aboriginal communities, there are also practical reasons why specifically Aboriginal definitions of and solutions for Aboriginal justice problems cannot exist apart from the existing system: economies of scale, human and financial resources, the needs and desires of communities themselves, etc. In short, it cannot be expected that Aboriginal systems within or outside the formal structure of the existing system of justice will not be linked. Thus, from this perspective the more useful question is not whether there should be a move to separate systems. Rather, it is how to move to Aboriginal control over and responsibility for Aboriginal justice processes under present conditions in a way that will provide the basis for their continued evolution should the momentum of the Aboriginal political agenda result in some sort of parallel or separate status for them.

Unit III

Ethnicity, Immigration, and National Groups

The Japanese, Chinese, Dukabors, Sikhs, and Armenians are among the many diverse groups who have been treated less than fairly within the CJS. A number of years ago, Sikhs were not allowed to wear their ceremonial headdress in the RCMP, a Royal Legion branch in Red Deer banned Sikhs from entering their establishment. As recently as January 1999, upon visiting North America, the Pope was still calling upon Americans to rid the continent of racism. (Pope calls..., 1999)

In 1996, former Canadian Ambassador to the United Nations, Stephen Lewis prepared a report in the aftermath to the 1991 racial riot that took place in Halifax. Among his findings, Lewis found that the police, prosecutors, and judges are largely responsible for the lack of confidence in the injustices of our CJS. For example, police had released 29% Caucasians after being as compared to 18% of blacks for similar offences. Similarly, blacks were less likely to receive bail than Caucasians. (Letdown..., 1996)

The great American civil rights anthem reminds us, "We shall overcome, some day." However, if truth is found repetitively throughout recorded history, then Canada has had a long history of racism against different religious, ethnic and non-white people. And while time may be the supposed ally in the struggle against such groups, we have been slow to educate ourselves. For example, in 1996 Justice Jean Bienvenue of Quebec Superior Court retired before becoming the first superior court judge to run the risk of removal from the bench after uttering insensitive "comments about women and about Jews who died in the Holocaust" (Blanchfield, 1997).

Section 15 of the charter states that all Canadians are guaranteed the same rights and protections regardless of race, class or ethnicity. Yet, why is it that certain diverse groups, within this general classification, continue to experience injustices at the hands of our criminal justice system (CJS)? The CJS has prided itself in trying to "accommodate" religious, ethnic and racial differences. In fact, one of the guiding principles of Correctional Service Canada's (CSC) mission reads: "The Correctional Service of Canada, as part of the criminal justice system and respecting the rule of law, contributes to the protection of society by actively encouraging and assisting offenders to become law-abiding citizens, while exercising reasonable, safe, secure and humane control" (*Corrections in Canada*, 1998:8). However, as the commissioner of CSC, Ole Ingstrup (1998) observed, in order to accommodate such diversity we must first understand the backgrounds of these groups. This does not mean treating them all the same but treating them with equity.

As Bruce Shepard (1997) notes in his accounting of blacks who moved to the Prairies in the early 1900s, we must research and understand our past racist heritage so that we can better deal with the issues that confront us today. In 1999, B.C. columnist, Doug Collins was fined $2000 for promoting hatred against Jews in the Vancouver suburban *North Shore News*. At the time of the ruling, Collins's expressed no intention of paying the fine and the paper's editor voiced outrage that the government could assume it has the right to act as "public watchdogs" on such issues (Moore, 1999).

In this unit we present three articles that cover a broad spectrum of how different minority groups have been dealt with by the justice system in Canada. Collectively they point to the fact that laws alone cannot eradicate discrimination and racist attitudes. Rather the strategy lies in education and research and perhaps more poignantly the realization that we are all souls who have a common mission in this life and it behooves us all to recognize this.

The article by White presents statistics on the British and French origins of Canada. Kelly's work highlights recent immigration patterns. The link between immigration, ethnicity and crime is explored by Gordon and Nelson, challenging a commonly held belief that immigrant groups are often over-represented in the CJS. Section 718 of the Criminal Code of Canada was introduced in 1995 to recognize that crimes motivated by racial hatred, ethnicity, gender or sexual orientation are of special concern to society. Roberts's research provides some of the first documentation of the extent of hate crimes across Canada.

DISCUSSION QUESTIONS:

1. How can the justice system ensure that all religions be treated equally in Canadian society?
2. Why does the CJS continue to use arrest, legal processing and correctional classification practices that discriminate on the basis of class, gender and race?
3. Given the range of groups represented in this unit, how might we begin to respond to such diversity in a plural sense?
4. To what extent might our era of political correctness be co-opted by interest groups and minority groups and added to the complex issues confronting these groups within the criminal justice system?
5. How can we begin to respond politically in such a way that we administer justice in a fair and equitable manner?
6. Consider: George Washington grew marijuana while Bill Clinton admitted to smoking it; neither was ever arrested. Even though he bludgeoned and

shot his wife in 1983, former Saskatchewan premier Colin Thatcher, in late 1998, was moved to a minimum-security facility and allowed to bring his horse to the prison (Corrections Canada..., 1999). To what extent do politicians represent a privileged group?

REFERENCES

Blanchfield, M. (1997, November 26). Judge says justice is victim of political correctness. *Ottawa Citizen*. (Online).

Corrections Canada probes Thatcher horse play. (1999, February 6). *Calgary Herald*, A12.

Corrections in Canada: 1997 Edition. (1998). Ottawa: Solicitor General.

Ingstrup, O. (1998, Nov.). Respect and human rights. *Let's Talk*, 24(4):1.

Let down by the system. (1996, April). *Canada and the World Backgrounder*, 18-21.

Moore, D. (1999, February 4). Columnist guilty of promoting hatred. *Calgary Herald*, A20.

Pope calls on Americas to rid continents of racism, drug-trafficking and abortion. (1999, January, 24). *Calgary Herald*, A3.

Shepard, B. (1997). *Deemed unsuitable*. Toronto: Umbrella Press.

Web watch: http://www.mtps.on.ca/int/haterpt.html. Compiled by the Toronto Metropolitan Police in 1998, this site presents a wide range of hate related injustice directed at a wide range of groups and organizations in Ontario— includes statistics and charts.

www.gillianguess.com/socal.html An interesting site that uses the Gillian Guess case to illustrate how social injustice can still be found in the Canadian criminal justice system—includes comments from experts and media excerpts.

Ethnic Origins
of the Canadian Population

Pamela M. White

At the turn of the century, the Canadian population was made up largely of people representing two major ethnic groupings: British and French. However, successive waves of immigrants from many different countries have resulted in a much more ethnically diverse country. During the first decades of this century and after the Second World War, large numbers of immigrants came to Canada from Western and Eastern Europe, as well as from Scandinavia. In the 1960s, a growing proportion of immigrants came from Southern Europe and the United States; in the 1970s and 1980s, immigrants have come primarily from Asia, Africa, the Caribbean, and Central and South America.

The current ethnic composition of the population represents a combination of the Canadian-born descendents of the various waves of immigrants, recent arrivals, and the Aboriginal population. By 1986, people with British or French backgrounds still made up the largest ethnic communities; however, neither group accounted for a majority of the population. At the same time, nearly one in four Canadians reported an ethnic background that did not include British or French origins.

White, P.M. (1989). Ethnic origins of the Canadian population. *Canadian Social Trends, Catalogue No. 11-008*, (Summer): 13-16. Statistics Canada information is used with the permission of the Minister of Industry, as Minister responsible for Statistics Canada. Information on the availability of the wide range of data from Statistics Canada can be obtained from Statistics Canada's Regional Offices, its World Wide Web site at http://www.statcan.ca, and its toll-free access number 1-800-263-1136.

Most Canadians British or French

In 1986, people with British and French ethnic backgrounds were the largest ethnic groupings in Canada (see Figure 1). People with British backgrounds, that is, those who reported either English, Irish, Scottish, Welsh, or some combination of British origins, made up 34% of the population. Those who reported a French background made up 24% of all Canadians. In addition, another 5% of people reported a combination of British and French ethnic backgrounds, while 13% reported some combination of British and/or French and other origins.

Figure 1: Ethnic Origins of Canadians, 1986

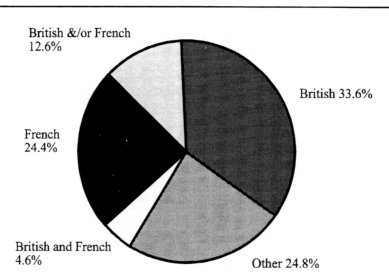

British &/or French
12.6%

British 33.6%

French
24.4%

British and French
4.6%

Other 24.8%

Source: Statistics Canada, 1986 Census of Canada

Many with Non-British, Non-French Roots

People whose ethnic backgrounds do not include either British or French roots also make up a major component of the population. In 1986, 25% of all Canadians reported that they had neither British nor French ethnic origins.

People with European backgrounds have traditionally comprised the largest groups having neither British nor French origins. Overall, in 1986, people reporting a single European background other than British or French made up 16% of the total population. Those reporting German, Italian, and Ukrainian ancestry were the largest of these groups, accounting for 3.6%, 2.8%, and 1.7%, respectively, of all Canadians.

However, as a result of increasing levels of non-European immigration in the 1970s and 1980s, a significant proportion of the population now reports non-European, particularly Asian, backgrounds (see Figure 2).

People reporting a single Asian background made up 4% of the overall Canadian population in 1986. Of these, 1.4% reported Chinese origins, while people with South Asian backgrounds, primarily Asian Indians, made up another 1.1 %.

The largest single non-European ethnic group, however, are North American Aboriginals. In 1986, over 3/4 of a million people, 3% of the total population, reported some Indian, Inuit, or Métis ancestry. Of these, about half reported a mix of Aboriginal and non-Aboriginal origins.

Figure 2: Ethnic Origins of Non-British, Non-French Population, 1986

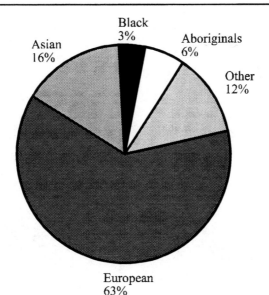

Source: Statistics Canada, 1986 Census of Canada

WIDE REGIONAL VARIATION IN ETHNICITY

The ethnic make-up of the population varies considerably across Canada. While people with British origins made up the largest proportion of the population in all provinces except Quebec, the size of this group ranged from almost 90% of the population in Newfoundland to only 30% in Manitoba and Saskatchewan.

Not surprisingly, most of the population in Quebec, almost 80% in 1986, reported French as their ethnic origin. People with French ancestry also represented about a third of the population of New Brunswick. The proportion of the population reporting French origins was much smaller in the other provinces, ranging from 9% in Prince Edward Island to just 2% in British Columbia and Newfoundland (see Figure 3).

There was also wide variation in the proportion of the provincial populations with origins other than British or French. This grouping made up over 40% of the population in Manitoba and Saskatchewan, over 35% in Alberta, and over 30% in Ontario and British Columbia. By contrast, just 11% of people

Figure 3: Proportion of the Population with Non-British, Non-French Ethnic Origins, by Province, 1986

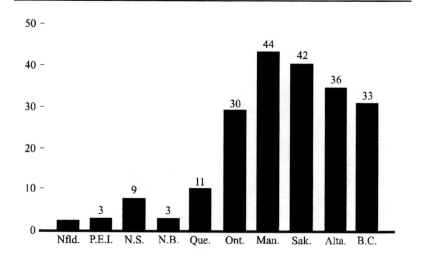

Source: Statistics Canada, 1986 Census of Canada

in Quebec, 9% in Nova Scotia, 3% in New Brunswick and Prince Edward Island, and 2% in Newfoundland reported other ethnic affiliation.

The composition of the population with neither British nor French ethnic origins also varies considerably by province. In the Prairie provinces, people of German and Ukrainian ancestry were the largest of these ethnic groups. In fact, people giving a single ethnic origin of either German or Ukrainian represented 19% of the population in Saskatchewan, 17% in Manitoba, and 12% in Alberta.

People of German ancestry were also the second largest ethnic group in British Columbia. People of Asian descent, however, made up the next largest ethnic group in this province: 4.0% of British Columbia residents said they had Chinese roots and 2.4% were South Asian in origin.

The western provinces also have relatively large Aboriginal populations. People reporting native ancestry as their only ethnic origin made up 6% of Saskatchewan residents, 5% in Manitoba, and 2% in Alberta and British Columbia. People of Italian descent were the largest non-British, non-French ethnic group in both Ontario and Quebec. Those reporting Jewish ancestry and Aboriginals made up the next largest ethnic groups in Quebec, while in Ontario, people of German and Dutch ancestry were the next most numerous groups.

People giving German ancestry as a single ethnic response made up just under 3% of Nova Scotia residents, while those of Dutch descent represented about 1% of residents of both Nova Scotia and Prince Edward Island. As well, just under 1% of Nova Scotia residents reported they were black, the highest provincial figure for this group.

People of Aboriginal descent were the largest ethnic group other than British or French in both Newfoundland and New Brunswick. However, at just over 0.5% of the population, they made up only a small proportion of the residents in each province.

Visible Minorities:
A Diverse Group

Karen Kelly

Recent changes in immigration patterns have increased the size of Canada's visible minority population and have also changed its composition. In 1991, the 1.9 million adults in a visible minority in Canada represented 9% of the population aged 15 and over, doubling the 1981 proportion. More than three-quarters (78%) were immigrants, 15% were born in Canada and the remainder (7%) were nonpermanent residents. As was the case during the 1980s, Chinese, Blacks and South Asians accounted for two-thirds of adults in a visible minority in 1991. During the past decade, however, there have been large increases in some of the smaller visible minority groups such as South East Asians and Latin Americans.

People in a visible minority in Canada have much in common. Most, for example, live and work in Canada's larger cities. Nonetheless, the visible minority population comprises groups that are, in many ways, very diverse. It includes not only recent immigrants but also those who have lived in Canada for a long time or who were born here. Although some recent immigrants quickly adjust to their new life in this country, others may have a more difficult time accessing

Kelly, K. (1995). Visible minorities: A diverse group. *Canadian Social Trends, Catalogue No. 11-008*, (Summer): 2-8. Statistics Canada information is used with the permission of the Minister of Industry, as Minister responsible for Statistics Canada. Information on the availability of the wide range of data from Statistics Canada can be obtained from Statistics Canada'a Regional Offices, its World Wide Web site at http://www.statcan.ca, and its toll-free access number 1-800-263-1136.

services or participating in the labour force because they lack the necessary language skills in English or French.

Visible minority groups also differ in their age structures, levels of educational attainment and the types of jobs they have. For example, South East Asians and Latin Americans, more than half of whom immigrated to Canada during the 1980s, are among the youngest of all visible minorities. They tend to have less formal education and have both the lowest rates of labour force participation and the highest rates of unemployment. In addition, over half of their populations are employed as clerical, service or manual workers. In contrast, those in the Japanese community, two-thirds of whom were born in Canada, are older than members of other visible minority groups. They are also among the most highly educated, have the lowest unemployment rate and are among those most likely to hold professional or managerial positions.

Despite educational diversity among the various groups, visible minorities are generally more highly educated than are other adults. And yet, even among those aged 25 to 44 with a university degree, adults in a visible minority are less likely than others to be employed in professional or managerial occupations. Rather, many are concentrated in lower-paying clerical, service and manual labour jobs.

TWO-THIRDS OF VISIBLE MINORITIES ARE RECENT IMMIGRANTS

Almost two-thirds of adults in a visible minority have come to Canada since 1972, with 35% having arrived between 1982 and 1991. With the exception of the Japanese, most adults in all visible minority groups were born outside the country. Nonetheless, immigration patterns vary across individual groups.

More than one-half of South East Asian and Latin American adults living in Canada immigrated between 1982 and 1991 (see Table 1). Over one-third of West Asian and Arab, Chinese, Filipino, Korean, and South Asian adults also arrived during this period, while this was the case for about one-quarter of Blacks. In contrast, relatively few Japanese (6%) and Pacific Islanders (15%) came to Canada during the 1980s.

Despite large increases in certain visible minority groups in recent years, Chinese adults still accounted for the largest share of those in a visible minority in 1991 (26%), followed by South Asians and Blacks (each accounting for 20%). The next largest groups were West Asians and Arabs (11%), Filipinos (7%), and Latin Americans and South East Asians (each 5%).

Table 1: Distribution of adults in visible minority groups, 1991

Visible Minority Group	% All Visible Minorities	% Aged 15-44	% Immigrants	% Arrived 1982-1991
Chinese	26%	69	81	39
South Asians	20%	71	85	34
Blacks	20%	73	72	23
West Asians and Arabs	11%	71	74	40
Filipinos	7%	72	83	37
Latin Americans	5%	82	79	52
South East Asians	5%	81	94	52
Japanese	3%	60	23	6
Koreans	2%	66	86	34
Multiple Visible Minorities	2%	77	73	25
Pacific Islanders	.02%	79	63	15

Source: Statistics Canada, Census of Canada.

INDIVIDUAL VISIBLE MINORITY GROUPS CONCENTRATED IN DIFFERENT CITIES

Almost all visible minority adults live in urban areas. In 1991, 93% of all adults aged 15 and over in a visible minority lived in one of Canada's census metropolitan areas (CMAs), compared with only 59% of other adults. Visible minorities were also much more likely to live in one of Canada's three largest CMAs. More than two-thirds of the adult visible minority population lived in either Toronto (40%), Vancouver (15%) or Montreal (14%). In contrast, less than one-third of other adults lived in these urban areas.

As a result of the concentration of visible minorities in these three areas, large proportions of the populations in each of these CMAs are now visible minorities. In 1991, the adult visible minority population accounted for 24% of the adult population in Toronto, 23% in Vancouver and 10% in Montreal.

Visible minority groups, however, do not all settle in the same cities. Blacks and Koreans (each 50%), South Asians (48%) and Filipinos (42%) were concentrated in the Toronto CMA in 1991. The Vancouver CMA, on the other hand, was home to almost half (49%) of Pacific Islander adults. The Chinese and Japanese communities were split between these two cities: 39% of Chinese and 27% of Japanese adults lived in Toronto, while 28% of the Chinese and 31% of the Japanese lived in Vancouver.

Many West Asians and Arabs (35%), Latin Americans (24%) and Blacks (20%) lived in the Montreal CMA in 1991. With the exception of South East Asians, only a small proportion (less than 8%) of all other visible minority groups lived in this CMA.

South East Asians, 8% of whom arrived in Canada between 1972 and 1991, were more dispersed across the country than any other visible minority group. In 1991, Toronto and Montreal were each home to 24% of adult South East Asians, while another 10% lived in Vancouver.

LATIN AMERICANS, SOUTH EAST ASIANS AND PACIFIC ISLANDERS ARE YOUNGEST GROUPS

In 1991, almost three-quarters of the adult visible minority population were under age 45 (22% were aged 15 to 24 and 50% were aged 25 to 44). Among non-visible minority adults in Canada, less than two-thirds were that young (18% were aged 15 to 24 and 43% were aged 25 to 44). In addition, seniors accounted for only 7% of the adult visible minority population, while they represented 14% of all other adults in Canada.

Latin Americans, South East Asians and Pacific Islanders were the youngest visible minorities, with about 80% of each of their adult populations aged 15 to 44 in 1991. Blacks, South Asians, Filipinos, and West Asians and Arabs each had between 70% and 75% of their adult populations that age. Chinese and Koreans tended to be older, with 69% and 66% of their adult populations, respectively, aged 15 to 44 in 1991. The Japanese were the oldest visible minority community in Canada that year: only 60% of adults were under age 45 and 14% were seniors.

KOREANS, FILIPINOS, JAPANESE, AND WEST ASIANS AND ARABS MOST EDUCATED

Visible minority adults are much more likely to have a university degree and less likely not to have completed high school than are other adults. In 1991, 18% of the visible minority population aged 15 and over had a university degree, compared with 11% of other adults. Also, 33% of visible minorities had less than a high school level of education, while this was the case for 39% of other adults.

Part of the reason for these differences may be that visible minority adults are generally younger than others adults, and educational attainment tends to be higher among younger than among older people. The different age structures of the two populations, however, do not fully explain differences in educational levels. The proportion of visible minority adults with a university degree did not change after age standardizing the visible minority population so that it had the same age structure as the non-visible minority population. The proportion of visible minority adults with less than a high school education was slightly higher after age standardization (36%), but remained lower than for other adults.

Educational attainment among individual visible minority groups varied considerably and, again, could not be explained by differences in age structures. Among men: Koreans (36%), Japanese and West Asians and Arabs (each 28%), and Filipinos (26%) were the most likely to have a university degree (after standardizing for age). In contrast, only 9% of Pacific Islander, 13% of Black, 14% of Latin American, and 16% of South East Asian men were university educated. Among women, the pattern was similar, with Filipinos (25%), Koreans (21%), Japanese (20%), and West Asians and Arabs (17%) the most likely to have a university degree. Black (7%), South East Asian (8%), and Latin American and Pacific Islander (each 9%) women were the least likely to have that level of education.

LABOUR FORCE PARTICIPATION HIGHEST AMONG FILIPINOS, BLACKS, SOUTH ASIANS AND PACIFIC ISLANDERS

Visible minority adults (70%) were somewhat more likely than other adults (68%) to have been in the labour force (that is, either working or looking for work) in the week before the 1991 Census (see Figure 1). This was largely because proportionately fewer people in visible minorities than in the rest of the population were seniors. Once the labour force participation rate of the visible minority population was age standardized, the rate—66%—was lower than that of the non-visible minority population.

After standardizing for age differences, four visible minority groups had higher labour force participation rates than non-visible minorities: Filipinos (75%), and Blacks, South Asians and Pacific Islanders (each 69%). Participation rates were lowest among South East Asians (60%), and Latin Americans (61%).

Overall, after standardizing for age, visible minority men (74%) were slightly less likely than other men (76%) to be in the labour force. Filipino men (79%) were the most likely to be in the labour force, followed by Pacific Islander (78%)

Figure 1: Age-standardized labour force participation rates of visible minorities, 1991

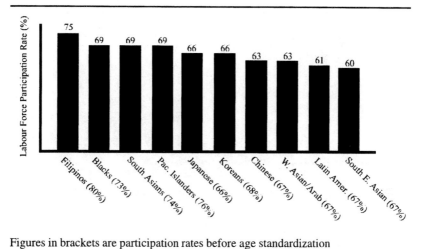

Figures in brackets are participation rates before age standardization

Source: Statistics Canada, Census of Canada

and South Asian (77%) men. In contrast, only about 70% of South East Asian, Chinese and Latin American men were in the labour force in 1991.

Among women, the participation rate for visible minorities and others was the same (59%). Filipino women (72%) were the most likely to be in the labour force, followed by Blacks (64%) and Pacific Islanders (62%). Participation rates were lowest among West Asian and Arab (50%), and South East Asian and Latin American (each 52%) women.

LATIN AMERICANS AND SOUTH EAST ASIANS HAVE HIGHEST UNEMPLOYMENT RATES

The unemployment rate of visible minorities overall (13% before and after age standardization) was higher than that of other adults (10%) in the week prior to the 1991 Census (see Figure 2).

Latin Americans and South East Asians, who had the lowest labour force participation rates, also had the highest age-standardized unemployment rates (19% and 17%, respectively). Unemployment was also high among West Asians and Arabs, and South Asians (each 16%). The low participation rates and high unemployment rates for Latin Americans and South East Asians may relate to

Figure 2: Age-standardized unemployment rates of visible minority groups

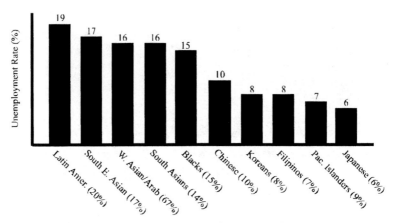

Figures in brackets are unemployment rates before age standardization

Source: Statistics Canada, Census of Canada

their recent arrival in Canada: over half of their populations arrived during the 1980s. In addition, many Latin Americans and South East Asians, as well as West Asians and Arabs, lived in the Montreal CMA in 1991, where unemployment was higher than in Canada's other two largest CMAs. In the week before the 1991 Census, 11% of the non-visible minority population living in Montreal were unemployed, compared with 9% of those in Vancouver and 7% of those in Toronto. Japanese (6%) and Pacific Islander (7%) adults had the lowest unemployment rates after standardizing for age. Koreans and Filipinos also had unemployment rates (each 8% after age standardization) that were lower than those of both visible minorities in general and other adults.

SOUTH EAST ASIANS AND LATIN AMERICANS MOST LIKELY TO BE MANUAL LABOURERS, AND FILIPINOS TO BE SERVICE WORKERS

According to the 1991 Census, 1.4 million adults in a visible minority had worked sometime during the 18 months prior to the census. Of those who worked during this period, visible minority adults were as likely as other adults to be employed as clerical workers (17%). They were, however, more likely than other adults to be manual labourers (16% compared with 13%) or service workers (13% compared with 10%). South East Asians (32%) and Latin Americans (29%) were by far the most likely to be manual labourers, whereas this was the case for only 8% of Koreans and Japanese, and 10% of West Asians and Arabs. Filipinos, on the other hand, were especially likely to be in service jobs (25%), compared with only 8% of Koreans and 9% of South Asians and Japanese (see Figure 3). While some differences existed by gender, these patterns were similar for both men and women. In addition, although the proportions of visible minority adults in all occupations are age standardized, there are almost no differences between these figures and the proportions before age standardization.

KOREANS, JAPANESE, AND WEST ASIANS AND ARABS MOST LIKELY TO BE MANAGERS

Of those who worked in the 18 months before the 1991 Census, visible minorities were less likely to be employed in managerial occupations (8%) than were other adults (10%). This was true for both men and women. Among visible minorities, 10% of men and 6% of women were in such positions, compared with 12% of other men and 8% of other women. Adults in a visible minority were, however, as likely as others to be in professional occupations (13% after standardizing for age). Visible minority men were actually more likely (14%) than other men (11%) to have professional jobs, whereas the opposite was true among women (13% compared with 16%).

The proportion of visible minority adults holding either managerial or professional positions varies considerably by group. After standardizing for age, Koreans (17%), Japanese (13%), and West Asians and Arabs (12%) were most likely to be in managerial occupations, while less than 5% of Filipinos and South East Asians were in such positions. Japanese were the most likely to have professional jobs (19%), followed by Chinese and West Asians and Arabs (each 15%). Only 8% of Latin Americans, 9% of Pacific Islanders and 10% of South East Asians were in professional occupations (see Figure 4).

UNDEREMPLOYMENT AMONG VISIBLE MINORITIES WITH POST-SECONDARY EDUCATION

Visible minorities aged 25 to 44 are as likely as other adults that age to have at least some education or training beyond high school. Among adults aged 25

Figure 3: Age-standardized proportion of visible minority groups in selected occupations, 1991

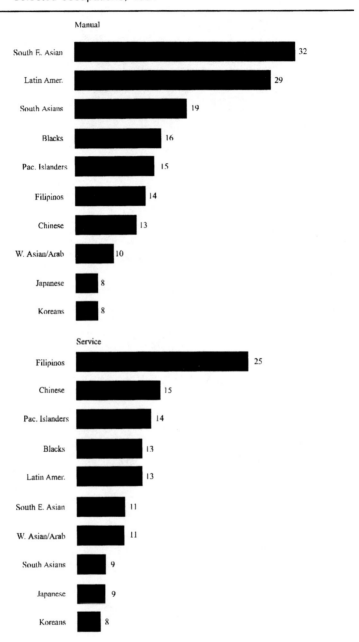

Manual

South E. Asian	32
Latin Amer.	29
South Asians	19
Blacks	16
Pac. Islanders	15
Filipinos	14
Chinese	13
W. Asian/Arab	10
Japanese	8
Koreans	8

Service

Filipinos	25
Chinese	15
Pac. Islanders	14
Blacks	13
Latin Amer.	13
South E. Asian	11
W. Asian/Arab	11
South Asians	9
Japanese	9
Koreans	8

Diversity and Justice in Canada

Figure 4: Age-standardized proportion of visible minority groups in selected occupations, 1991

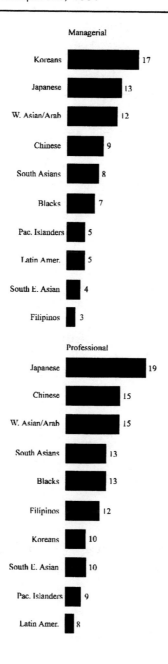

Managerial

Koreans	17
Japanese	13
W. Asian/Arab	12
Chinese	9
South Asians	8
Blacks	7
Pac. Islanders	5
Latin Amer.	5
South E. Asian	4
Filipinos	3

Professional

Japanese	19
Chinese	15
W. Asian/Arab	15
South Asians	13
Blacks	13
Filipinos	12
Koreans	10
South E. Asian	10
Pac. Islanders	9
Latin Amer.	8

to 44 who worked in the 18 months before the 1991 Census, visible minorities were more likely (25%) to have a university degree than were other adults (17%). They were, however, somewhat less likely to have some other post-secondary education (41% compared with 45%).

Nonetheless, visible minorities with a university education are not as likely as others with the same level of education to be employed in the higher-paying professional or managerial occupations. Among those aged 25 to 44 with a university degree who worked in the 18 months before the 1991 Census, just over one-half of visible minorities had either a professional (39%) or managerial (13%) job, compared with 70% of other adults (52% in professional and 18% in managerial positions). University-educated Japanese aged 25 to 44 were the most likely to be in professional or managerial occupations (65%), followed by Chinese adults in that age group (61%). In contrast, only 27% of university-educated Filipinos aged 25 to 44 were in these occupations, as were 42% of Latin Americans.

Similarly, among those aged 25 to 44 with other types of post-secondary education, 26% of visible minorities were in professional, semi-professional or managerial occupations, compared with 32% of other adults. The proportion in these occupations ranged from highs of 36% among Japanese and 33% among Koreans, to lows of 17% among Latin Americans and 20% among South East Asians and Filipinos.

A disproportionate share of Filipino adults with at least some education beyond high school worked in service jobs in the 18 months before the 1991 Census. Among adults aged 25 to 44 with a university degree, 17% of Filipinos were service workers, compared with 5% of visible minorities overall and 2% of other adults. Similarly, among those aged 25 to 44 with some other post-secondary education, 29% of Filipinos had service jobs, compared with 12% of visible minorities and 8% of other adults.

Manual labour jobs were relatively common among highly educated South East Asians and Latin Americans who worked in the 18 months before the 1991 Census. Among those aged 25 to 44, about 25% of South East Asians and Latin Americans with some post-secondary education were in manual labour jobs, as were 11% of Latin Americans with a university degree. Overall, 12% of visible minorities aged 25 to 44 with a post-secondary education, and 4% of those with a university degree had such jobs. Among other adults that age, 8% of those with some post-secondary education and 2% of university graduates were manual labourers.

A Look to the Future—The Visible Minority Population is Expected to Increase

As was the case during the 1980s, the visible minority population is expected to continue to increase faster than the total population. The number of visible minority adults is projected to triple between now and 2016 to just over six million. Canada's non-visible minority adult population, on the other hand, is projected to increase by about one-quarter. As a result of such different growth rates, adults in a visible minority could account for about 20% of all adults by 2016, more than double the proportion in 1991 (9%).

The number of adults in a visible minority is projected to increase during each of the five-year periods between 1991 and 2016. The growth rate, however, is expected to decline in each successive period, from a high of 42% between 1991 and 1996 to 17% between 2011 and 2016.

Individual visible minority groups are expected to increase at different rates. The West Asian and Arab adult community is expected to be the fastest growing, with the population in 2016 projected to be four times higher than in 1991. The Filipino and other Pacific Islander, Latin American, Chinese and most other Asian communities are expected to more than triple in size over the same period. Growth in the size of the adult populations of Blacks (2.9 times greater in 2016 than in 1991) and South Asians (2.5 times greater) will be somewhat slower. These differences in growth rates among individual groups could contribute to a further diversification of Canada's visible minority population.

Crime, Ethnicity, and Immigration

Robert M. Gordon and Jacquelyn Nelson

INTRODUCTION

The relationships among factors such as crime, ethnicity, and immigration have been of sporadic interest to policy-makers and academics in North America for at least 60 years, beginning with the work of the Chicago School of sociology. Of late, however, the connections between these variables have received renewed attention in Canada due, in part, to a vigorous politicization of crime and punishment by conservative politicians, media reports that immigrants and particular ethnic groups are responsible for a disproportionate amount of crime (especially "gang-related" crime and welfare fraud), commissions and committees of inquiry into systemic racism in the criminal justice systems of several provinces (and especially in police departments), and a heated debate among policy-makers, practitioners, and academics over the ethics of recording and using crime, ethnicity (or race), and immigration statistics.

Discussions of crime, ethnicity, and immigration tend to centre around two main issues: criminal justice system bias; and the causal connections (if any) among the variables. In Canada, the United States, and Britain, allegations of ethnocultural bias in the criminal justice system are not uncommon. These allegations may be directed toward any point in the criminal justice process:

police arrests or practices (Jefferson and Walker, 1992); bail and remand hearings (Brown and Hullin, 1993); jury selection (O'Connell, 1991); the activities of court personnel, prosecutors, and judges (Frazier, Bishop, and Hennelly, 1992; Johnson, 1988); sentencing including, in the United States, the differential use of the death penalty (Gross and Mauro, 1984; Johnson, 1988); and parole and other alternatives to incarceration (LaPrairie, 1992).

Charges of justice system bias range from allegations of overt racism to more subtle evidence of so-called "adverse effects" discrimination: policies that are appropriate for one group (usually white, non-immigrant males) but that have adverse effects on others. Archibald (1989) has explored the rise in the importance of "adverse impacts" or systemic discrimination in the Canadian courts, noting that there is an increasing demand to determine whether discrimination exists based on evidence of social patterns or legal practices, rather than simply stereotypes and attitudes.

Suggestions of bias may be countered by claims that certain ethnocultural groups, or immigrant groups, are simply more disposed to commit crimes than others. This may be supported by evidence of the overrepresentation of ethnic minorities or immigrant groups in prisons (see, for example, Walmsley, Howard, and White, 1993) coupled with media reports of the crimes of ethnic minorities such as "Asian gangs", Hispanic drug traffickers, and the involvement of blacks in prostitution. Criminologists and sociologists tend either to debunk such claims by pointing to the effects of justice system bias on the police exercise of discretion and court sentencing practices, or to point the finger of blame at social structural variables such as systemic racism, class, and gender (Etherington et al., 1991). Some search for causality in the oppression of particular groups, in the barriers blocking access to society's material rewards and other symbols of success, and in the way the criminal law maintains differential power relations and maintains the traditional hierarchies of race, class, and gender (Reiman, 1989; Burtch, 1992). Other criminologists have invoked concepts such as culture conflict, friction between old and new world moralities (especially in the case of immigrants); social environmental factors such as the ecology of cities; and the strains of integration (see, for example, Thomas, 1992).

Unfortunately, as Etherington et al. (1991) note, there has been little empirical research in Canada on systemic ethnocultural bias at discretion points in the criminal justice system. The exception is the work on aboriginal peoples in the justice system, which tends to point to the overrepresentation of such peoples in, for example, prisons and the various systemic and social structural biases that may account for this phenomenon (Jackson, 1989; Archibald, 1989;

LaPrairie, 1990). Similarly, the causal relationships among crime, ethnicity, and immigration remain largely unexplored possibly because of concerns that the results of a singular focus upon such variables would be misused and undermine multicultural policies (see, for example, Roberts, 1994). There is little information about crime and criminality among ethnic and immigrant groups in Canada even though such information could be supportive, rather than destructive, of multicultural policies. The exceptions are two recent and important studies of the ethnocultural composition of the correctional populations in Canada, both of which contain "good news" for advocates of multiculturalism.

RECENT STUDIES OF CORRECTIONS POPULATIONS IN CANADA

Prior to examining these studies of the correctional populations, it is necessary both to define some key terms and to provide an important caveat with respect to the limitations of the data. The authors of both studies (Thomas, 1992; Gordon and Nelson, 1993) focused upon three overlapping groups: offenders who were members of visible ethnic minorities; offenders who, regardless of ethnicity, were not born in Canada (i.e., "immigrants or "foreign-born"); and offenders who fell into both groups—those from visible ethnic minorities who were immigrants. In both studies, an offender was considered to be a member of a visible ethnic minority if he or she differed in physical appearance from the dominant ethnic (or racial) group in Canada, namely, fair skinned, Euro-Canadians commonly referred to as "Caucasians".

Gordon and Nelson (1993) divided their prisoner population into six major ethnic groups: aboriginal, Caucasian, Indo-Canadian, Hispanic, black, and Asian. Each group was further divided into subgroups according to the prisoner's region or country of origin. Thus, for example, the Hispanic group included those of Spanish-American ethnic origin from regions such as the Caribbean and Central America. The Asian group included inmates of Chinese ethnic origin from Hong Kong and from China and those from Vietnam and the Philippines. The ethnic categorization of prisoners was an open-ended process, the outcome of which was ultimately determined by the data rather than by predetermined and rigid categories, and the authors ended up with 32 different subgroups.

The caveat with respect to the two corrections studies concerns the representativeness of such populations: Is it valid to generalize on the basis of research conducted with the inmates of provincial and federal correctional facilities? This is an important question because prison populations can be either over- or under-representative of the population at large, and of subgroups within that population such as all immigrants or all offenders. Overrepresentation could occur as a result of the kinds of systemic biases outlined at the beginning of this chapter (e.g., the police may pursue and prosecute individuals from particular ethnic groups with greater enthusiasm because of entrenched racist attitudes). Underrepresentation could occur as a result of reverse discrimination or, where discrimination is not a factor, as a result of routine practices within the criminal justice system. Even if an offender is caught, and then prosecuted, and then convicted—each step containing a filter that excludes subject— terms of imprisonment are not the first choice for most courts in most cases. And even fewer offenders are sentenced to terms of imprisonment for two years or more that must be served in a federal facility. All of this means that prison populations are a select sample of the offenders found in, for example, a particular ethnic group, and may not represent the total offender "population" of such groups in society as a whole. At the same time, the inmates of provincial and federal facilities can be considered to be the more serious and persistent of offenders and, arguably, are interesting and important individuals for the purposes of both general criminological inquiry and government policy-making.

The two corrections studies proceeded with similar research questions and assumptions. If the rate of incarceration of visible ethnic minorities or of immigrants reflects the proportion of such groups in the population as a whole, it is probably safe to argue that ethnicity and immigration either are not significant factors in explaining crime among these groups or that any negative experiences associated with ethnicity or immigrant status (e.g., persistent and blatant discrimination) are counterbalanced by powerful contrary influences. These influences can include the resources of a particular community, the presence of strong supportive networks within it (Goldenberg and Haines, 1992), or its "institutional completeness" (Breton, 1964). These kinds of assets can protect the group from the damaging effects of racist stereotypes and non-inclusive practices.

Thomas's study (1992) of the population of the federal correctional system in Canada is especially helpful in determining the extent to which the members of visible ethnic minorities and immigrants—two separable although not always separate groups—are over- or underrepresented. Thomas's work began with the assumption that if there is no systemic bias and if the members of ethnic minorities and immigrants are equally predisposed to commit crimes, then the percentage of these individuals who are charged, convicted, or incarcerated would equal the proportions of those from ethnic minorities and those who are immigrants in the population as a whole. An overrepresentation in the correctional system could suggest either systemic bias or a higher disposition to commit crimes, phenomena that would then need to be explored further. In fact, his study found an underrepresentation.

Using data from the Correctional Services of Canada and from the 1986 national census, Thomas found that offenders from non-aboriginal, visible ethnic minorities, and regardless of whether they were foreign-born or not, were underrepresented in the population of the federal correctional system. In 1989, only 5.2% of the federal corrections' population were from an ethnic minority, compared with approximately 6.3% in the national population (1986 Census). By 1991, these proportions had increased to 6.3% and a projected 8.5% respectively. According to Thomas, the most common region of birth among those from visible ethnic minorities was the West Indies (especially Jamaica) followed by South and Central America. These particular ethnic groups were both overrepresented and the fastest growing visible minorities in the federal system. The numbers of those of West Indian ethnic origin had increased from 265 in 1989 to 420 in 1991, while the numbers of those from South and Central America had increased from 157 to 238 in the same time period.

Thomas (1992) also explored the representation of immigrants in the federal correctional system, regardless of their ethnic origin. He found immigrants were very significantly underrepresented in the population of those incarcerated for serious crimes in 1989 and 1991. The underrepresentation appeared to be most pronounced in British Columbia and the Prairies. In British Columbia, 13.5% of the federal corrections' population in 1989 were foreign-born, and by 1991, this had remained reasonably stable at 13.2%. The 1986 national census data showed that 26.6% of the general population of the province were foreign-born. Of particular interest, given the high level of immigration to the area, is the fact that between 1989 and 1991, the representation of foreign-born people in the Pacific region actually declined slightly whereas in all other regions there was a noticeable increase.

These data represent the more than 20,000 offenders in the federal correctional system and include both those in facilities serving sentences of two years or more and those on conditional release. These offenders are usually individuals who have either committed the most serious of crimes (e.g., murder) or who have been persistent in the commission of crime, such as those who have chosen a "career" in the field of armed robbery. An obvious question then emerges of whether similar patterns would be found among people incarcerated in provincial correctional systems—young offenders or adult offenders serving sentences of up to two years less one day—and especially in those provinces where there was a significant under-representation of visible ethnic minorities and immigrants in the federal correctional system.

A recent study by Gordon and Nelson (1993) of the entire population of provincial youth and adult correctional centres in British Columbia mirrored Thomas's findings in the federal system. Only 8.2% of the prison population were members of non-aboriginal, visible ethnic minorities compared with an estimated 13.5% in the general population of the province. More important, only 11% of inmates—215 of the 1,952 prisoners contained in correctional centres on the day of the census—were not born in Canada compared with 22.3% in the general population of the province, a significant under-representation.

Immigrant inmates came from three main regions: Europe, including Britain (22%), South East Asia (15%), and Central America (12.1%). Other much smaller groups hailed from a variety of regions and countries including India, Fiji, Iran, Hong Kong, and Jamaica, but in each case these individuals accounted for less than 0.5% of the prisoner population. Approximately one-half of the immigrant inmates had been in Canada for a considerable period (ten years or more), and more than two-thirds had been residents for more than five years. Only 59 inmates (3.0% of the inmate population) had been living in Canada for five years or less, and of these only 18 had been resident for one year or less. On the basis of these data, Gordon and Nelson (1993) concluded that less than 1 percent of the total inmate population—18 prisoners out of 1,952—could be described as "newly arrived" immigrants, individuals who had been resident in Canada for one year or less.

Both the study by Thomas (1992) and the census conducted by Gordon and Nelson (1993) examined the kinds of crimes committed by offenders from visible ethnic minorities and those who were immigrants, comparing these with the crimes committed by the rest of the federal and B.C. corrections populations. In the case of immigrants, and regardless of ethnic origin, Gordon and Nelson (1993) analyzed their provincial data by examining, among many other computations, the major offence categories also used by Thomas: break and enter, theft, robbery, murder, assault, sex offences, fraud, conspiracy, extortion, narcotics, prostitution offences, and counselling murder. Separate analyses were conducted for the total provincial inmate population and for all adult inmates not born in Canada.

The data represented below provide a comparison of the numbers of adult inmates in provincial facilities in British Columbia who were, and who were not, born in Canada in each primary offence category. The bar for each offence also shows a line and a number that reflects the expected number of foreign-born offenders in each category, given the proportion of foreign-born individuals in the general population of the province (22.3%). This information is not provided in three categories—conspiracy, extortion, and prostitution—because of the small number of offenders in each category. The figures at the end of each bar are the number of inmates in the offence category who were foreign-born expressed as a fraction of the total number of inmates in that category. So, for example, in the category of break and enter, 14 of the 239 inmates imprisoned for that offence were immigrants. The expected number was 53.

As these data indicate, the actual number of adult inmates who were not born in Canada in each offence category is quite low when compared to the total number of inmates in each category.

The numbers are also much lower than the expected number of foreign-born inmates, and especially with respect to the main types of property crime—break and enter, theft, and fraud. Of all the offence categories, the number of foreign-born inmates convicted of narcotics offences is closest to, and in fact slightly exceeds, the expected number (25), but it should be remembered that the actual number of immigrant offenders in this category (31) is minute when compared to the number of immigrants in the general population of the province (22.3% of the population, or approximately 750,000).

Many of the major offence categories show considerable consistency between the provincial and the federal data. When compared to the percentage of foreign-born people in British Columbia (22.3%), adult foreign-born inmates were underrepresented in the categories of break and enter (5.8%), theft (6.2%), robbery (10.1%), murder (17.6%), assault (10.8%), sex offences (11.8%), and fraud (7.8%). As with Thomas's data, the percentage of foreign-born adult inmates in provincial correctional facilities for conspiracy (20%) was higher than all the offence categories except extortion and narcotics, but unlike the federal data, the percentage did not exceed the percentage of foreign-born people in British Columbia (22.3%). It should be noted that the number of inmates serving time for this offence (five) is very small.

In his study of the federal corrections' population, Thomas (1992) found an overrepresentation for extortion. The percentage of adult provincial inmates who were foreign-born and in this category (42.8%) is nearly twice the expected percentage (22.3%). However, as is the case with the conspiracy category, the number of inmates affected is very small (seven). Offenders not born in Canada were overrepresented in the narcotics category in both Thomas's analysis and the provincial study by Gordon and Nelson (1993). The latter found that 27.2% of inmates in this category were immigrants instead of the expected (and normal) 22.3%.

Gordon and Nelson (1993) gathered considerable information about the kinds of crimes for which individuals from different visible ethnic minorities had been convicted and imprisoned, regardless of their place of birth (i.e., regardless of whether or not they were immigrants). The first, and most important, thing to note about these data is that the number of subjects from non-aboriginal, visible ethnic minorities was quite small (124) when compared with the overall provincial prison population (1,952). It follows that any conclusions drawn from the data must be tentative. There is a danger of unjustly stereotyping and condemning entire ethnic groups because of the concentrated activities of a handful of offenders (e.g., 29 Indo-Canadians, or 29 Blacks). The second point to note is that the majority of the inmates from visible ethnic minorities—98 out of 124, or 79%—were not born in Canada. In the case of those imprisoned for narcotics offences, every inmate from a visible minority was also an immigrant. Again, however, these data should be approached with caution because the actual number of offenders is minute when compared to the numbers of individuals from the different ethnic groups in the general provincial population.

With these important caveats in mind, the data indicate that Indo-Canadian, Black, and Asian inmates were more likely to be in prison for crimes of violence or sex-related crimes. Hispanic inmates were more likely to be serving time for narcotics offences. Overall, inmates belonging to visible ethnic minorities were more likely to be in prison for crimes of violence and sex crimes (47.5%), followed by property crime (23%), and narcotics offences (19.2%).

The study by Gordon and Nelson (1993) included a special examination of all inmates—youth and adult—who were identified by police and corrections personnel as being involved with gangs. Of the 41 subjects in this special study, 22 (53.6%) were from non-aboriginal, visible ethnic minorities, the largest subgroup of these subjects being those of Asian ethnic origin (14 of the 41).

As a point of comparison, an estimated 13.3% of the provincial population are from non-aboriginal visible minorities (Gordon and Nelson, 1993). Clearly, the members of visible ethnic minorities were overrepresented among the gang members in facilities, but no definitive conclusions should be drawn from these data because of the size of the sample. In addition, it is important not to lose sight of the fact that the largest single group of gang-involved inmates were of Caucasian ethnic origin (16/41), the vast majority of whom were born in Canada (Gordon, 1993).

Seventy-four percent (20/27) of those 17 years of age and younger and 50% (7/14) of the adults identified as gang-involved were born in Canada, primarily in British Columbia. Overall, however, 32% of the gang-involved inmates were not born in Canada. As we have seen, 11% of the population of provincial correctional centres were immigrants, compared with approximately 22.3% of the B.C. population (Gordon and Nelson, 1993). The percentage of immigrants among young gang members (17 years of age or younger) was 26%. This is considerably higher than the inmate population as a whole, but only slightly higher than might be expected in a normal and equitable distribution. The *total* percentage of immigrant gang members (32%), however, is higher than both the correctional centres and the provincial populations. Again, these data must be used with caution because of the small number of subjects in the sample. There is also growing concern that the data may be a product of the labelling of individuals from visible ethnic minorities as gang members, and especially those who are of Asian ethnic origin, as a consequence of nearly ten years of negative media attention.

CONCLUSIONS

Recent studies of the correctional populations in Canada indicate that, overall, people from non-aboriginal, visible ethnic minorities and immigrants are significantly underrepresented in the federal corrections system and in British Columbus youth and adult correctional centres. Of particular note is the finding that there are half as many immigrants as one might expect under normal circumstances. Assuming that these findings reflect the situation in the general population of offenders and that there is no massive reverse discrimination in the criminal justice system (a possibility for which there is no supporting evidence), these results invite some interesting new criminological questions. In exploring the relationships among variables such as crime, ethnicity, and immigration, the question "Why criminal activity?" should, perhaps, be rephrased as "Why is there less criminal activity than is found among other groups?"

This requires a significant shift in thinking away from existing bodies of theory, such as strain theories and culture conflict theories, which assume crime is a problem among visible ethnic minorities and immigrants and attempt to explain criminal behaviour, somewhat sympathetically, by reference to the challenges and problems of migration and settlement in a new land. These are theories that have their roots in the work of the Chicago School of sociology as well as famous sociologists such as Robert Merton, and they were constructed in the 1930s and 1940s to account for what were, arguably, quite different immigration practices, policies, and experiences. Since that time, the problems of settlement have been examined and addressed by governments, and an underrepresentation of visible ethnic minorities and immigrants may well be due to effective programming for immigrants, and especially those from ethnic minorities, on their arrival in Canada. It may well be a function of effective screening undertaken by Canadian immigration officials at the place of origin or perhaps simply a product of the type of individuals migrating to Canada.

An examination of the situation in British Columbia helps cast some light on these issues. The province is second only to Ontario in having the highest proportion of its population who are immigrants. Statistics from the 1991 national census indicate that the proportion of immigrants in British Columbia is increasing slightly faster than the increase in the general population. While the province has about 12% of the Canadian population, it attracts approximately 16% of the immigrants who come to Canada. Of these immigrants, the proportion who are European-born has been declining steadily, and the proportion born in Asia has increased. During the period 1988 to 1991, 71.5% of B.C. immigrants were born in Asia, compared with 13.7% born in Europe.

While these data suggest an increasing number of immigrants who are members of visible ethnic minorities in British Columbia, there are also indications of "protective factors" that may assist these people in making successful adjustments and possibly avoiding any contact with the criminal justice system. Many of the immigrants who chose British Columbia were investors (46.1% of all investor immigrants to Canada landed in the province), retired (45.3% of immigrants to Canada), or entrepreneurs (25.1% of immigrants to Canada). The total number of immigrants in these classes totaled 8,941 or approximately one-third of the 27,270 immigrants landing in British Columbia between 1982 and the third quarter of 1992. For Canada as a whole, there were 25,358 of 187,728 or approximately 13.5% of immigrants in these classes. This may suggest that, compared with the Canada-wide proportions, British Columbia has a significantly higher proportion of immigrants who are likely to be financially resourceful. If, as Thomas (1992) suggests, it is important to remove barriers to legitimate opportunities for immigrants and individuals from visible ethnic minorities, then it may be that British Columbia's immigrant population is in a particularly favourable position for doing so. This significant protective factor—the relative abundance of legitimate financial resources—is likely to be important, particularly when coupled with the fact that the majority of people who migrate do not do so in order to find a place where they can commit crime.

Ironically, it is possible that the very factors that buffer or protect many immigrants of visible ethnic minorities from any involvement with crime—their financial resources—may also make them prime targets for a variety of predators, including those who are themselves immigrants and members of visible minorities. In Vancouver, for example, there are occasional spates of "home invasions" usually carried out by small groups consisting primarily of offenders of Asian ethnic origin who target wealthy victims with a similar ethnic background. In a similar vein, Thomas (1992) found an overrepresentation of foreign-born people incarcerated for crimes that are considered characteristic of organized crime (e.g., extortion, narcotics offences, counselling murder, and prostitution), while crime categories such as break and enter, theft, and robbery had the lowest representation of foreign-born prisoners.

Gordon and Nelson (1993) have uncovered a similar situation in the provincial system with the evidence that immigrants and people from visible ethnic minorities are more likely to be imprisoned for particular kinds of offences (notably, narcotics and violence) that are conducted in a particular way—in the company of others in a semi-organized and collective manner (i.e., in "gangs"). But the number of inmates convicted of such offences is small when compared to the overall size of the federal and provincial corrections populations.

Nevertheless, how might we account for the overrepresentation that occurs in specific offence categories? Unlike their more affluent counterparts—the investor and the entrepreneur—many immigrants lack the financial resources necessary for successful settlement and run into significant difficulties making the transition from their former country to their new home (see, for example, Lee, 1992). These individuals encounter a battery of predictable barriers—the lack of language skills, unemployment or employment in low-paying and low-prestige jobs, social isolation, and so forth—that limit a person's choices and may contribute to a decision to engage in certain forms of crime as a way of carving out a living. Faced with indigence and a dependence upon charity, and with little hope of improvement, it is perhaps not surprising that some immigrants, and especially those from visible ethnic minorities, seek employment in company with others in illegitimate business ventures and especially, it would seem, in the sale and distribution of narcotics: a commodity for which there is a large market and a seemingly endless supply of ready and enthusiastic consumers.

Strain theories should not, therefore, be rejected prematurely when attempting to understand the relationships among crime, ethnicity, and immigration. They have their place in the matrix of explanation—but only as possibilities and only as a way of accounting for the activities of what appears to be a relatively small number and proportion of foreign-born individuals who engage in crime. Above all else, strain theories need to be tested in the Canadian context. At this point, the acceptance of such theories is more an act of faith, reinforced by a healthy dose of intuition, than a decision based upon sound research that explores the actual experiences of immigrants (and their families) and especially those from visible ethnic minorities. Hopefully, the discovery that immigrants and members of visible ethnic minorities are underrepresented in corrections systems does not deter researchers from pursuing inquiries in this area. Likewise, it is to be hoped that in this age of problem-focused research the findings of the corrections studies do not contribute to a funding drought as scarce resources are directed to other areas.

Disproportionate Harm:
Hate Crime in Canada

Julian V. Roberts

FINDINGS

Hate Crimes in Other Jurisdictions

As noted in the introduction, the phenomenon of hate crime is truly universal. Although a complete international survey is beyond the scope of this report, some data from the United States and the United Kingdom are presented to give the reader an idea of the extent and nature of the problem in those jurisdictions. These countries have been selected because they most closely resemble the Canadian context (in terms of legal culture and socio-cultural history) as well as because they are the jurisdictions with the most reliable crime statistics relating to hate motivation.

United States

According to the 1990 *Hate Crime Statistics Act* (to be described in greater detail later in this report), the federal Attorney-General is mandated to acquire hate crime statistics. Since that year, these statistics have been available from the United States Federal Department of Justice. Table 1 provides a breakdown of hate crimes recorded by police across the United States in 1992. These data are drawn from law enforcement agencies in over 40 states. These participating agencies covered slightly over half the United States population. As can be

Roberts, J. (1995). Disproportionate harm: Hate crimes in Canada. Ottawa: Department of Justice. Reproduced with permission of the Minister of Public Works and Government Services Canada, 1998.

Table 1:   Hate crimes in America: offence breakdown (1992)

Offence	# of Incidents	% Total Incidents
Threats	3,328	37%
Mischief/Vandalism	2,040	23%
Assault	1,765	20%
Aggravated Assault	1,431	16%
Robbery	172	2%
Break and Enter	69	<1%
Arson	47	<1%
Theft	36	<1%
Murder	17	<1%
Rape	8	<1%
Theft Motor Vehicle	5	<1%
Total	**8,918**	**100%**

Source: Federal Bureau of Investigation, U.S. Department of Justice.

seen, the most frequent offence category of hate crime is threats, accounting for over one-third of all recorded incidents. This is followed by mischief/vandalism (23% of incidents) and simple assault (20%). Personal injury offences account for over one-third of incidents. In total, almost 9,000 incidents were recorded by the Federal Bureau of Investigation in the most recent year for which data are available at the time of writing.

Table 2 presents a classification of the hate crimes in the United States broken down according to the nature of the group targeted, from which it can be seen that the most frequent targets—accounting for almost two-thirds of the incidents—were racial minorities. The three other target categories (ethnic groups, religious groups and certain sexual orientation) each account for approximately the same percentage of incidents (between 10% and 15%). Within these categories, the following trends emerged. The most frequent racial category victimized was Black Americans, accounting for 59% of incidents. White American victims accounted for slightly less than half all the incidents in this category. Hispanic victims accounted for the majority of incidents in the ethnicity category, while anti-semitic incidents accounted for the vast majority (88%) of incidents in the religion category. Almost three-quarters (72%) of the sexual orientation category were crimes against gay persons.

Table 2: Hate crimes in America: target categories (1992)*

Category	# of Incidents	% Total Incidents
Racial	5,050	63%
Religious	1,240	15%
Sexual Orientation	944	12%
Ethnicity/Nationality	841	10%
Total	**8,075**	**100%**

Source: Federal Bureau of Investigation, U.S. Department of Justice.

These data should not be interpreted as firm indicators of the relative incidence of different forms of hate crime. Rather, they presumably reflect both the actual incidence of such crimes as well as the likelihood that victims will report to the police. If some victims such as members of the gay and lesbian community (and as noted earlier, research suggests that this is in fact the case) are less likely to report than other victims, then the pattern of relative frequency revealed by this table is going to be distorted.

Table 3 provides a similar breakdown of hate crimes by target category in a major metropolitan centre which has collected hate crime statistics for some time (New York City). As can be seen in this table, the pattern is fairly similar to that found at the national level.

Table 4 gives a breakdown of hate crime target categories in New York City. This table shows that there is a clear relationship between the nature of

Table 3: Hate crimes in America: target categories in New York City (1987-1988)

Category	# of Incidents	% Total Incidents
Racial	585	59%
Religious	280	28%
Sexual Orientation	66	7%
Ethnicity and Nationality	62	6%
Total	**993**	**100%**

Excludes unclassified cases. Source: Garafolo (1993).

Table 4:   Hate crimes in America: offence categories by target group in
            New York City (1988)

Offence	Racial	Ethnicity/ Nationality	Religious	Sexual Orientation
Assault	42%	42%	6%	41%
Harassment	37%	44%	34%	45%
Mischief	7%	6%	55%	8%
Threats	6%	3%	1%	2%
Burglary/Robbery	5%	2%	3%	2%
Reckless Endanger Life	1%	2%	—	2%
Other	1%	1%	1%	1%
Total	**100%**	**100%**	**100%**	**100%**

Column totals may exceed 100% due to rounding. Source: Garafolo (1993).

the group targeted, and the offence committed. Hate crimes directed against individuals on the basis of their race, ethnicity or sexual orientation are more likely to be crimes against the person (e.g., assault). Thus over 40% of hate crimes against these three target groups were crimes of assault. By contrast, only six percent of hate crimes directed against religious targets were crimes of physical violence. The most likely category of hate crime involving a religious target was mischief, which accounted for over half the incidents recorded.

United Kingdom
    The data from the United Kingdom are of particular interest because they derive from two sources: a victimization survey and criminal incidents recorded by the police. Thus they include reported as well as unreported incidents. It is important to reiterate that the general term "hate crime" is not used in England and Wales; the data pertain only to racially motivated crime.

British Crime Survey (BCS)
    The victimization survey data come from the latest administration of the British Crime Survey. This is a large survey of a nationally representative sample of approximately 10,000 adults in England and Wales which has been carried out repeatedly since 1982. It includes victimizations that occurred in the 12 months preceding the survey, whether they were reported to the police or not (see Mayhew, Maung and Mirrlees-Black, 1993, for further information on

the BCS). Members of ethnic minorities were asked whether or not they thought that an incident had been racially motivated. Table 5 provides estimates of the numbers of incidents that respondents perceived to be racially motivated. Ranges are provided rather than specific numbers. As can be seen, the BCS data suggest that over 100,000 racially motivated crimes occurred in the year covered by the survey. If a broader definition of hate crime had been used, one which included crimes such as anti-semitic incidents, the totals would obviously have been higher still.

Table 6 provides a breakdown of the proportion of incidents reported to the BCS survey for two minority groups: Afro-Caribbean and Asian. As can be seen, high percentages of certain crimes against these groups were perceived

Table 5: Estimates of number of racially motivated crimes in England and Wales (Afro-Caribbeans and Asians)

Assault	23,000-45,000
Threats	29,000-71,000
Vandalism	17,000-41,000
Other Crimes	8,000-26,000
Total	**89,000-171,000**

Source: British Crime Survey, 1992.

Table 6: Racially motivated crimes in England and Wales: proportion of all crimes involving racial motivation

	Afro-Caribbean	Asian
Threats	3.5%	57%
Assault	30%	44%
Robbery	2%	8%
Theft from motor vehicle	2%	2%
Burglary	4%	4%
Motor vehicle theft	2%	2%
All offences reported to British Crime Survey	14%	24%

Source: British Crime Survey (1992); Home Office.

by the survey respondents to have been racially motivated. For example, over half the threats directed at Asian respondents were perceived by the victim to have been racially motivated. Almost half the incidents of assault against Asians, and almost half the incidents of assault against Afro-Caribbeans were racially motivated (see Maung and Mirrlees-Black, 1994, for further information).

By comparing the BCS data to the number of racially motivated crimes reported to the police, we can shed light on the reporting rate of incidents of this crime. Fitzgerald (1995) reports the number of racial incidents reported to the police in England and Wales over the period 1988 to 1992. It is clear that the number of racial incidents reported to the police in 1992 is a small fraction of the number of incidents captured by the British Crime Survey (7,734).

Canada

Hate Crime Statistics Recorded by the Police

The collection of hate crime statistics by different police services across Canada is sufficiently variable to preclude an integrated analysis. Accordingly, statistics from those forces that participated in this survey and who provided data to the Department of Justice Canada will be summarized and discussed on an individual basis. At the conclusion of this section some summary statements will be made. It should be noted that the police forces represented here are those that responded with empirical data, although these data were not always in the form that permitted detailed secondary analysis. Some forces have not yet commenced the collection of hate crime data. The Ontario Provincial Police, for example, do not collect hate crime statistics, and there are no provisions for the collection of such data in the near future. The reason for this appears to be recognition that hate crime is largely an urban problem in Canada. The discussion that follows reflects the information submitted to the Department of Justice Canada. The reader should be aware that other forces may well have similar hate crime units, although this was not made known to the Department at the time that this survey was conducted.

Toronto

The Metropolitan Toronto Police Force began to systematically collect data on hate crimes in January 1993. This activity is part of an extensive hate crime initiative which reaches into the community. In addition to its investigative activities, the Hate Crime Unit also participates in public education in the area. For example, hate crime and hate propaganda posters and pamphlets have been developed and distributed to schools in the Toronto area. Members of the Hate Crime Unit also receive additional training. One benefit of the statistical data collected to date is that the Hate Crime Unit has initiated consultations with educators, community groups as well as other police officers in order to establish additional partnerships aimed at preventing and responding to crimes motivated by hate or bias. Since data for the whole of 1994 were not available at the time this report was written, most of the Toronto data discussed here come from 1993.

Table 7 provides a breakdown of hate crimes as a function of the nature of the group targeted. As can be seen, racial minorities account for the greatest percentage of incidents (50%), followed by religious groups (35%), sexual orientation (10%) and then ethnicity/nationality (5%). It should be noted that this breakdown may well reflect differential willingness to turn to the criminal justice system. If, as the research literature in other countries suggests, gay individuals are less likely to report crimes to the police, these statistics may under-represent the threat to the gay community, relative to other minorities, racial or otherwise.

Table 7:   Hate crimes in Toronto: target categories

Category	# of Incidents	% Total Incidents
Racial	77	50%
Religious	54	35%
Sexual Orientation	16	10%
Ethnicity/Nationality	8	5%
Total	155	100%

Source: Metropolitan Toronto Police.

Additional information was provided by the Toronto Police Service regarding the nature of the targets within specific target groups. Almost half (48%) of the racial incidents were directed against black individuals. The next most frequently targeted groups were East Indians (22% of incidents) and Asians (8%). Thirteen percent of the incidents were classified as multi-bias incidents and 8% were hate crimes directed at white targets. Turning to the classification of crimes in terms of ethnicity rather than race, it is clear that no particular ethnic group was targeted more frequently than any other. Almost all (94%) of the sexual orientation hate crimes were directed at gay males rather than lesbians. Not surprisingly, in light of the data from other sources, the vast majority of religious hate crimes (89%) were anti-semitic in nature.

Table 8 presents a breakdown of the Toronto police data according to offence category. Mischief (over and under combined) accounts for 39% of incidents recorded by the police. Assault is the next most frequent category, accounting for one incident in four.

Table 8:   Hate crimes in Toronto: offence categories

Offence	# of Incidents	% Total Incidents
Mischief Under	38	25%
Assault	37	24%
Threats	27	17%
Mischief Over	21	14%
Bomb Threats	13	8%
Robbery/Break & Enter	7	5%
Other	12	7%
TOTAL	155	100%

Source: Metropolitan Toronto Police.

The data from Toronto also show that personal injury offences are more likely to be directed to racial minorities, as the following statistics for the two most frequent offence categories reveal. Of the assault reports, over three-quarters (77%) were directed at racial groups. Religious groups were more likely to be the victims of property crimes: almost a third of mischief offences were directed at religious groups, but only seven percent of the assaults were directed at this target category (see Table 9).

The Toronto data are also useful because they provide some insight into the typical offender. The majority of the offenders arrested for a hate crime were young males under 20 years of age. Most were first offenders. These findings are consistent with research conducted in other jurisdictions. Thus Levin and McDevitt (1993) report that in New York City, the median age of hate crime offenders was 18, almost 10 years younger than the median for offenders in general. In Sweden, most hate crime offenders were under twenty at the time of the commission of the offence (see Loow, 1995).

Data from the first six months of 1994 show a modest increase in the proportion of all hate crimes directed at racial groups (50 to 58%) with a

Table 9:   Hate crimes in Toronto: offence category by target category

Target Category	Crime	
	Assault	**Mischief**
Racial	77%	58%
Religious	7%	31%
Ethnicity/Nationality	9%	8%
Other	19%	3%
Total	**100%**	**100%**

Source: Metropolitan Toronto Police.

corresponding decline in the amount of hate crime involving religious groups. This is worth noting because it means there has been an increase in the proportion of hate crimes involving offences against the person, since racial hate crimes are far more likely to involve violence (than are hate crimes directed at religious targets—see below).

The data from the first half of 1994 are also noteworthy because they suggest an increase in the *absolute* level of hate crime activity in the city of Toronto. A total of 112 occurrences were recorded in this period. This is a 55% increase in reported hate crime incidents over the preceding year. However, it is important to point out that as with changes in other crime trends, this increase could also reflect an increased willingness to report such incidents to the criminal justice system. The police appear to attribute the increase to greater public confidence in the Metropolitan Toronto Force.

It seems more likely that the increase reflects a genuine increase in the number of hate crimes as well as a shift in the mix of offences. The trend observed in the police statistics confirms what was noted in the B'nai Brith data from the same year (see later section of this report). Since the B'nai Brith data are independent of the police and are unaffected by public expectations of the criminal justice response, this suggests a genuine increase in offending. As for the offence mix, it is clear that there has been an increase in the proportion of hate crimes that involve violence, and personal injury offences are more likely to be reported to the police than crimes involving property. This would have the effect of inflating the statistics.

Police de la Communauté Urbaine de Montréal

This police service began collecting data on anti-semitic incidents in 1988. In 1990, racially motivated crimes were added and this was followed in 1992 by the creation of a computerized database, to which officers were required to submit reports. The hate crime initiative was formally created in 1994, and comprehensive reports on hate crime activity are now released on a regular basis (three times a year). As well, an annual report is published. In addition to the collection of systematic statistics and the prosecution of hate crimes, individuals from the Montréal force also participate in conferences and workshops on the subject of responding to hate crimes. For the purposes of the present report, findings derive from the period January 1, 1994 to December 31, 1994. In this period there were 199 incidents of hate-motivated crimes in the Montréal community that were recorded by the police. Of these, the vast majority (79%) were directed at racial minorities: no other target category accounted for more than nine percent of the incidents recorded (see Table 10).

Table 10:   Hate crimes in Montréal: target categories

Category	# of Incidents	% Total Incidents
Racial	157	79%
Religious	8	4%
Sexual Orientation	17	9%
Ethnicity/Nationality	7	4%
Other	10	5%
Total	**199**	**100%**

Source: Montréal Police.
The total of 199 reflects the fact that one incident was directed at two distinct categories of victims (Jewish people and homosexuals), accordingly it was counted twice.

Overall, two-thirds of the hate crime incidents recorded in Montréal in 1994 involved crimes against the person, with the remaining one-third classified as property crimes. A more detailed offence breakdown is provided in Table 11. As can be seen, assault was the offence which accounted for the greatest percentage of reports (34%).

An interesting interaction exists between the nature of the crime and the particular group targeted. Hate crimes directed against gays are significantly more likely to involve violence. Thus almost nine out of ten hate crimes against

Table 11:   Hate crimes in Montréal: offence categories

Offence	# of Incidents	% Total Incidents
Assault	68	34%
Mischief	57	29%
Threats	47	24%
Hate Literature	9	5%
Robbery	8	4%
Break and Enter	5	3%
Theft	4	2%
Total	**198**	**100%**

Source: Montréal Police.

gay targets involve violence, while only 30% of anti-semitic hate crimes involved a crime against the person. Anti-black hate crimes fell between these two extremes: 69% of hate crime incidents were crimes against the person. The 1994 annual report concludes from this that the anti-semitic incidents are the work of racist organizations, while the other two categories are more likely to be accounted for by individual acts of racial intolerance.

Since 1994 was the first year of full collection of comprehensive data, historical comparisons are problematic. However, examination of the anti-semitic statistics show a relatively stable pattern over the period 1988 to 1992, with a significant increase over the last two years for which such statistics are available (1992-1994). It is not clear what is responsible for this recent increase, although it seems consistent with increases elsewhere. The final observation about the Montréal data is that several districts have particularly high rates of hate crime incidents. Thus while two-thirds of the districts have relatively uniform rates, five districts report numbers of incidents up to five times in excess of the area average.

Data from the Montréal police also provide information on the criminal justice outcome in hate crime incidents. A criminal charge was laid in 17% of the 198 incidents reported. While this may seem like a small percentage, two considerations should be borne in mind. First, a significant number of hate crimes are directed against property, and a criminal charge is laid in only a small percentage of property crimes recorded by the police. For example, in 1993 (the most recent year for which data are available), the "cleared by charge" statistic for Canada (aggregated across offences) was 16% (Canadian Centre for Justice

Statistics, 1994). Second, it is clear from research in other jurisdictions that hate crimes are notoriously hard to clear by the laying of a charge. A charge rate for hate crimes that is slightly higher than the average rate of charging shows the additional effort that police agencies have directed to this form of criminality.

Ottawa

The Ottawa Police Service has perhaps the most organized bias crime unit in the country. The unit evolved out of sustained liaison with the community of Ottawa. The experience in Ottawa shows that the police-community partnership is a critical way of responding to the special problems created by hate crimes. The Ottawa Unit is unique in other respects too. As a recent publication notes:

> What makes the [Ottawa Carleton Regional Police Bias Crime] Unit different is that there is a legitimate investigative function. In addition, the Unit has an intelligence and educational component. We believe that all three are necessary in order to properly address the concern of bias motivated crimes. (Ottawa Police Service, 1994: 1)

The Ottawa Carleton Regional Police Bias Crime Unit was established in January 1993. Modeled on the Boston Police Department's Community Disorders Unit, it reflects a grass-roots approach to the problem of hate crimes which stresses the importance of consultation with community groups. The unit is comprised of two investigators and a sergeant. In addition to its investigative function, the unit is also very active in community education. Members of the unit deliver lectures to community groups, minority groups as well as the news media.

The Ottawa Police Service submission to the Department of Justice Canada request contains hate crime statistics for a two-year period from January 1993 to December 1994. In 1993, there were 176 hate crime incidents recorded by the Ottawa Police Bias Crime Unit. This rose to 211 in 1994. Over the two-year period covered by the data, there were 387 cases. Consistent with the trends in Toronto and Montréal, Table 12 shows that the most frequent targets of hate crimes in Ottawa were racial minorities, followed by religious groups. Table 13 shows that Blacks are the most frequently targeted racial group. Anti-semitic incidents accounted for almost all (87%) of the religious category. Of the 45 incidents directed at individuals on account of their sexual orientation, 93% were directed at males, 7% at females.

It is clear that the interaction between the nature of the crime and the nature of the target group is replicated in the Ottawa statistics. That is, the vast

Table 12: Hate crimes in Ottawa: target categories

Category	# of Incidents	% Total Incidents
Racial	215	54%
Religious	110	29%
Sexual Orientation	45	11%
Ethnicity/ Nationality	25	6%
Total	**395**	**100%**

Source: Ottawa Police Service.

Table 13: Hate crimes in Ottawa: detailed breakdown of racial categories

	# of Incidents	% Total Incidents
Anti-Black	161	75%
Anti-White	27	13%
Anti-Asian	12	6%
Anti-Multi-Racial	9	4%
Anti-Aboriginal	6	3%
Total	**215**	**100%**

Source: Ottawa Police Service.

Table 14: Hate crimes in Ottawa: breakdown of religious target category

Religious Offence	# of Incidents	% Total Incidents
Anti-Semitic	96	87%
Anti-Islamic	8	7%
Anti-Catholic	3	3%
Anti-Protestant	1	<1%
Other	2	2%
Total	110	100%

Source: Ottawa Police Service.

majority of hate crimes directed against racial minorities involved violence or the threat of violence. Cases of vandalism against this target group accounted for a small percentage of incidents. Anti-semitic hate crimes on the other hand were far more likely to involve mischief or vandalism.

Ontario Provincial Police

While it is anticipated that such information may be required in the future, at the present time the O.P.P. have not yet begun to collect hate crime statistics. It is worth noting however that guidelines exist for the investigation of hate-motivated crime. These guidelines include an explanatory description of hate crimes, along with explicit criteria for identifying hate-motivated incidents.

Sûreté du Québec

Since hate crimes are concentrated in urban centres (in Canada at least), this organization has no statistical data relating to such offences.

City of Halifax Police Department

Collection of statistics relating to hate crimes began in January 1994. The Halifax Police Department has taken steps to ensure that all members of the force are aware of the existence of hate crimes. The Halifax Police Department has appointed a Race Relations Coordinator, with a mandate to raise and promote awareness both in the community and the force itself, of the problem of hate crimes. This police department recorded only three hate crime incidents over the most recent period for which data are available (January to October, 1994).

Edmonton Police Service

The Edmonton Police Service has been involved in identifying and collecting statistics on bias-motivated crimes since September 1994. Since that time, all members of the force have been trained in responding to incidents of hate-motivated crime. This police service recorded three incidents of hate crimes for the period September to November 1994. Two of these were directed against racial minorities, the third was an incident of anti-semitism.

Other Police Agencies

Finally, it is worth noting that some police agencies (such as the Vancouver Police) have a hate crime policy in practice, and also record hate crimes, although they did not participate in the survey which gave rise to this report.

Aggregate Trends

Since there is considerable variability in terms of the targets selected in different parts of the country, Table 15 provides a breakdown of target categories

Table 15:   Hate crime targets: Canada v. U.S. (police statistics)

Target Category	% Hate Crimes in Canada (1993-1994)	% Hate Crimes in U.S. (1992)
Racial Minorities	61%	62.5%
Religious Minorities	23%	15.4%
Sexual Orientation	11%	11.7%
Ethnic Minorities	5%	10.4%
Total	**100%**	**100%**

Sources: Canada: Department of Justice Canada; U.S.: Department of Justice, Federal Bureau of Investigation.

for all reported incidents combined. These percentages are weighted to reflect the different rates of reporting, and do not include the B'nai Brith data or incidents of crimes against gays or lesbians (which will be discussed later in this report). As can be seen, 61% of the almost 1,000 hate crime incidents recorded by the police were directed at racial minorities. The next most frequent category was religious groups, (almost all anti-semitic incidents), followed by sexual orientation and ethnic origin. This table also presents a breakdown of hate crime targets from the United States. It is interesting to note that the pattern of victimization is very similar in the two countries: racial minorities account for almost two-thirds of all incidents recorded by the police.

Following analyses used in other countries, it is possible to generate an estimate of the number of hate crimes that occur in Canada on an annual basis. Such an estimate will of course be highly speculative. Nevertheless, using the Ottawa police statistics as a basis, we can perform some extrapolations. There is no reason to suppose that Ottawa has a higher than average incidence of hate crimes. Indeed, the relatively small percentage of non-white residents (compared to Toronto for example) suggests that a broader estimate of the number of hate crimes based on the Ottawa statistics is likely to underestimate the magnitude of the problem.

Since hate crime is largely (although not necessarily exclusively) an urban phenomenon, we shall restrict the analysis to the following major urban centres: Halifax, Montréal, Ottawa, Toronto, Winnipeg, Regina, Calgary, Edmonton, and Vancouver. The analysis that follows draws upon recently published crime statistics for these cities (see Hendrick, 1995). The data are drawn from 1994. In that year, the police in Ottawa recorded 211 hate crimes. If we assume a reporting rate of one third, this means that 633 verified (i.e., founded) incidents occurred in that year. Since Ottawa accounts for 7% of the total Criminal Code infractions for this group of urban centres, an estimate of the total number of hate crimes committed in these cities would be slightly under 60,000 (59,502). Such an estimate is not out of line with other countries. It will be recalled that it was estimated that there were over 100,000 racially motivated crimes in the United Kingdom, and this estimate was based on a single form of hate crime. If a lower reporting rate was used in the calculation, the total number of estimated incidents would obviously be higher. The accuracy of an estimate of this kind remains to be verified by future research drawing upon victimization surveys. However accurate it turns out to be, one trend is clear: using police statistics as the sole index of hate crime activity is going to seriously underestimate the magnitude of the problem across the country.

As noted in the introduction, hate crimes are among the most under-reported offences. This means that an examination of hate crimes derived from the criminal justice system (i.e., incidents recorded by the police) would seriously underestimate the prevalence of these incidents, as well as distort the nature of the problem. For this reason, at this point we turn to hate crime statistics derived from two sources outside the criminal justice system. These two sources were selected because they represent the groups most often affected by hate.

B'nai Brith Data

The best data available on the incidence of hate crimes of a particular category in Canada come from the League for Human Rights of B'nai Brith Canada. These statistics have been compiled for over a decade now, and are publicly available in the annual "Audit of Anti-Semitic Incidents". Since the same definitions (and criteria for inclusion) have been used over this period, and the same mechanisms employed to record incidents, this database provides a unique historical record of hate crimes in Canada over the past 13 years. The B'nai Brith database is therefore a vital resource for anyone wishing to know more about the incidence of hate crimes. These data are restricted to incidents of anti-semitism. However, anti-semitic hate crimes constitute one of the principal hate crime targets in Canada, and the principal hate crime target in other jurisdictions as well. The B'nai Brith data are presented separately in this report because they are qualitatively different from the statistics recorded by the police (although some of the incidents recorded by the B'nai Brith will presumably have also been reported to the police).

Incidents included in the database are classified either as episodes of vandalism or harassment. The annual document describes the former as:

> an act involving physical damage to property. It includes graffiti, swastikas, desecrations of cemeteries and synagogues, other property damage, arson and other criminal acts such as thefts and break-ins where an anti-semitic motive can be determined. (League for Human Rights, 1995: 3)

> "Harassment" includes "anti-semitic hate propaganda distribution, hate mail and verbal slurs or acts of discrimination against individuals. Death threats and bomb threats against individuals and property, as well as any kind of physical assault." (League for Human Rights, 1995: 3)

It is clear then, that the B'nai Brith data are more inclusive than hate crime statistics gathered by the police. Some of the incidents that are included in the B'nai Brith database would not be considered crimes, even though the social harm may be as great or greater than a crime and the acts may be even more morally reprehensible. The B'nai Brith data provide a broader insight into hate-motivated behaviour than can be obtained from police reports. For this reason, the B'nai Brith data will be referred to as hate activity incidents, rather than crimes, *per se*.

Before describing recent trends in anti-semitic incidents, it is worth making a few observations about the B'nai Brith statistics. First, these incidents are primarily the result of reports by victims themselves. This differs from police statistics, where a higher proportion are likely to arise from witnesses. Second, not all reports result in an entry in the annual audit. The League for Human Rights conducts a thorough investigation of each incident in order to establish that anti-semitism was indeed the underlying motivation. Third, an attempt is made to ensure comparability from year to year, so that the database is unaffected by changing thresholds of proof. The criteria for inclusion have been constant since the audit was established in 1982. In this sense, on a national level the B'nai Brith statistics are purer than criminal justice statistics which, as noted earlier, use variable definitions of what constitutes a hate crime. Finally, it is important to point out that, as with police statistics, the B'nai Brith data represent but a fraction of incidents of anti-semitism in this country. For a number of reasons, a great deal of anti-semitism passes unrecorded by either the police or B'nai Brith. *When the 1994 audit reports 290 incidents, it should not be taken that this represents anything other than a fraction of the true total of anti-semitic incidents across Canada.*

Table 16 provides a breakdown of anti-semitic incidents recorded by the League for Human Rights since 1982. Several trends are apparent from this table. First, there has been a steady increase in the recorded number of anti-semitic incidents over the decade, rising from 63 in 1982 to almost 300 in 1994, the most recent year for which data are currently available. Second, harassment incidents have accounted for approximately two-thirds of all incidents over the entire period. Third, there has been a dramatic increase in the number of incidents recorded in recent years. Thus there were 196 incidents recorded in 1992. The total for 1994 was 290, which represents an almost 50% increase in two years. These data underline the fact that anti-semitism is clearly a social problem in Canada.

Table 17 makes it clear that incidents of anti-semitism reported to and recorded by the League for Human Rights are concentrated in three principal

Table 16: Anti-semitic incidents, Canada 1982-1994

Year	Offence Category				Total # of incidents	Total %
	Vandalism		Harassment			
	# of incidents	% Total	# of incidents	% Total		
1982	19	(30%)	44	(70%)	63	(100%)
1983	25	(52%)	23	(48%)	48	(100%)
1984	60	(48%)	66	(52%)	126	(100%)
1985	52	(55%)	43	(45%)	95	(100%)
1986	23	(42%)	32	(58%)	55	(100%)
1987	18	(33%)	37	(67%)	55	(100%)
1988	52	(46%)	60	(54%)	112	(100%)
1989	63	(36%)	113	(64%)	176	(100%)
1990	60	(29%)	150	(71%)	210	(100%)
1991	50	(20%)	201	(80%)	251	(100%)
1992	46	(23%)	150	(77%)	196	(100%)
1993	105	(41%)	151	(59%)	256	(100%)
1994	92	(32%)	198	(68%)	290	(100%)

Source: League for Human Rights (1994).

Table 17: Anti-semitic incidents in Canada: principal cities affected, 1994

Offence	# of Incidents	% Total Incidents in Canada
Toronto	146	50%
Montréal	55	19%
Ottawa	36	12%

Source: League for Human Rights (1994).

cities: Montréal, Toronto and Ottawa. Together these cities account for over 80% of the incidents of anti-semitism in Canada that are captured by this database. There are several possible explanations for this finding. These three cities have large Jewish communities. This increases the number of potential targets. As well, awareness of the League for Human Rights audit may be greater in these cities, thereby increasing the likelihood that a victim will contact the B'nai Brith.

Hate Crimes Directed at Gays and Lesbians

The second non-criminal justice source of data drawn upon in this report concerns hate-motivated crimes directed against gays and lesbians. The research literature in other jurisdictions makes it clear that gays and lesbians are a prime target for hate-motivated crimes, and have been for many years. In addition, gay and lesbian victims are probably less likely to report to the police than any other group. *For this reason, a portrait of hate crime incidents in Canada would be inadequate without some information about crimes directed against gays and lesbians.* The data provided in this report are far from exhaustive; they derive from organizations in two major cities: Toronto and Montréal. They are provided to give an indication of the scope of the problem within the gay community.

Toronto

The principal source of information about hate crimes in Toronto is the 519 Church St. Community Centre. One of the activities of this community centre was the creation, in 1990, of a "Gay and Lesbian Bashing Hotline". A confidential report is completed about all calls to this line. This information is then communicated to the police for further investigation. The line is available during the centre's opening hours. In mid-November 1994, the centre hired a full-time trainer and educator for the Victim Assistance Program. This individual currently processes all the reports made to the line. As well, she trains volunteers to handle incoming reports. The line is now known as the Lesbian and Gay Bashing Reporting and Information Line.

Two caveats are worth making regarding these data. First, it is important to note that, as with police statistics, these data do not capture the all the incidents of anti-gay activity taking place in Toronto. The majority of incidents are, for a variety of reasons, reported neither to the hotline nor the police. Second, these data—like the British Crime Survey data (but unlike the police statistics)— consist of reports of incidents in which the victim reports the hate motivation. It is possible that some of these incidents involve crimes that were not motivated by hatred of gays or lesbians, but were seen that way by the victim.

Over 90% of the calls to the Toronto hotline were made by gay men. However, this statistic should not be taken to suggest that lesbians are significantly less likely to be the target of harassment or assault on the grounds of their sexual orientation. Although no direct evidence is available in Canada, research in other countries suggests that the nine to one ratio represents a differential willingness to report incidents to either a hotline or the police and that, in fact, lesbians are almost as likely to be the target of hate-motivated crimes as gay men.

Table 18 presents a breakdown of incidents reported to the hotline over the period January 1, 1990 to April 1, 1995. As can be seen, there is a high incidence of physical assault: almost half (46%) of the incidents involved some form of physical assault. Almost a third of incidents involved some form of verbal harassment, while 15% of reports involved a threat of some form. Less than 10% were hate-motivated cases of vandalism or theft. A further 12 reports

---

Table 18: Statistics from lesbian/gay hotline in Toronto 1990-1995

Assault Reported	# of Incidents	% Total Incidents
Physical & Verbal	175	36%
Verbal harassment	136	30%
Threatening	72	15%
Physical Assault	51	10%
Vandalism/Theft	43	9%
Sexual Assault	10	<1%
Total	**487**	**100%**

Source: 519 Church Street Community Centre.

---

were made concerning reports of assaults against gays by police officers (these are not included in Table 18). Some indication of the gravity of the incidents reported to the hotline can be found in Table 19, which provides a breakdown of the 50% of respondents who reported some form of injury. All respondents reported bruising of some kind, with almost one in five reporting a fracture (percentages exceed 100% due to multiple responses). Of the 22 cases of head injuries, one-third resulted in concussion. These data suggest that crimes of violence directed against gays and lesbians involve a greater degree of injury than the average assault. The revised U.C.R. survey contains information on the severity of assaults reported to the police across Canada. Recent statistics show that of all assaults reported involving a male victim, major injuries were involved in fewer than one case in ten reported to the police (see Roberts, 1994c: 83). This is also consistent with research in the United States.

Table 19: Injuries reported to gay/lesbian hotline

Injury Reported	Percentage Reporting
Head injuries	16%
Bruises	100%
Lacerations	29%
Scratches	6%
Sprains	6%
Rapes	1%
Groin injuries	2%
Fractures	17%
Emotional trauma requiring time off	1%

Note: Percentages exceed 100% due to multiple responding Source: 519 Church Street Community Centre.

The majority of these incidents (53%) had not been reported to the police. Approximately 40% had been reported to the police, while a further three individuals planned to report the incident. This information was unavailable for 14 cases (no information is directly available on why individual victims did not report the incident). The fact that most incidents had not been reported to the police explains, in part, why such a small number result in official action by the criminal justice system. Of the 239 reports recorded by the hotline, only 104 were reported to the police. Of these, charges were laid in 8 cases, and convictions recorded in only 2 cases. Convictions are recorded in a very small percentage of crimes committed.

However, the data from the 519 Church Street Toronto hotline suggest that a much smaller percentage of hate crimes result in a conviction. Recent data from Statistics Canada show that on average, a conviction is recorded in approximately one crime in twenty. *The percentage of hate crimes resulting in a conviction is clearly much smaller.*

An analysis of calls to a hotline is no substitute for systematic research. For obvious reasons, such calls are likely to represent a somewhat distorted image of violence against the gay community. Nevertheless, in the absence of more rigorous research, this source of information is the best available. However, superior data relating to anti-gay incidents in Toronto will soon be available. In 1995, the 519 Church Street Community Centre conducted a survey of the gay and lesbian community in Toronto. The questionnaire contained a number of in-depth questions relating to harassment and physical and verbal abuse. Since it was a survey, and not an analysis of calls to a hotline, the responses are likely to give a far more accurate image of anti-gay violence in the Toronto community.

Montréal

Unfortunately, statistics on hate crimes in Montréal are restricted to the police data. The only non-criminal justice data come from a study conducted by the Table de concertation des lesbiennes et des gais du Grand Montréal. This study was conducted over a three-month period in 1993. It was discontinued only as a result of a lack of resources. Over the period covered there were 54 reported incidents. However, some of these reports (as with other victimization surveys) concerned incidents that took place prior to the period covered by the survey. Accordingly, it is impossible to draw conclusions about the numbers of incidents, and whether the rate of anti-gay crime is higher in Montréal than Toronto. However, the data are useful for providing information on the nature of the crimes. The Montréal statistics confirm the picture emerging from Toronto. Thus, over half the incidents involved violence. In fact, acts of aggression were the most frequent category of incident reported. Almost all (83%) of the victims were gay men. Almost half the incidents resulted in physical trauma, and one-quarter resulted in material loss of some kind.

These data support the findings from other jurisdictions which show that crimes of hate directed against the gay community are more likely to involve violence, or the threat of violence, than hate crimes directed at other groups.

Before leaving the Montréal data it is worth noting that evidence exists in that city of the most extreme form of hate crime. In December 1992, two gay men were murdered by groups of teenagers, and since then there have been several more such incidents. Over the period 1988 to 1995, thirty gay individuals have been murdered under conditions that strongly suggest a homophobic motivation. In March, 1995, *The Globe and Mail* reported the murder of Quebec actor Richard Niquette, who was stabbed to death by men who preyed on homosexuals. *The Globe* noted that he was the "19th gay man to be killed under similar circumstances in the past four years" (*Globe and Mail*, March 3, 1995). This most extreme form of hate crime, which can provoke widespread alarm among members of the community, clearly requires a vigorous response from the criminal justice system, beginning with the police.

Finally, it should be noted that some respondents in both cities reported acts of aggression by police officers. These remain unsubstantiated at present, and until evidence is adduced to substantiate them it would be unwise to judge the officers concerned. However, acts of aggression by police officers are obviously far more serious than similar crimes by civilians as they undermine public confidence and reduce still further the likelihood that these crimes will be reported to the criminal justice system.

Unit IV
Women

In the 1990s, a number of articles appeared about the abuse of women in the Canadian Forces. One such case involved former Tracey Constable who while serving as a medical assistant was raped by a military doctor. Knowing how the military operated she was unable to have any actions taken against the doctor. She left the forces. In 1998, Maclean's *gave women who have served in the Forces a platform to express their pain and frustration. However, other than to tell their stories, justice has been slow in unfolding. (O'Hara, 1998)*

Until 1995, all federally-sentenced women, regardless of their security classification had to serve their time at the only federal penitentiary for women in Canada, the Prison for Women (P4W) in Kingston, Ontario. (50 years of human rights developments in federal corrections, 1998)

W omen have been struggling for identity and equal representation in society for decades. This general fact has also been observed within the criminal justice system. We only need to reflect on scathing observations in the Arbour Commission Report on the "P4W incident" in Kingston back in early 1990s when several women inmates were violently handled by several male guards. The incident is not an isolated or recent phenomena. Shortly after opening in 1934, the Archambault Commission commented on the appalling conditions of "P4W" and recommended its closing. Similar recommendations followed in 1956, 1977 and 1981 by the Canadian Human Rights Commission. In fact, since its opening, P4W has been the subject of fourteen inquiries and commissions that all called for its closure. Perhaps because women continue to be under-represented within our criminal justice system and the general gender insensitivity, they continue to experience varying degrees of systematic discrimination and violence at all levels of the system. Yet, as University of British Columbia psychologist Don Dutton observed in a 1998 study, workplace harassment has become the crime of the 90s (Jimenez, 1998).

More recently, a study revealed that women on the Supreme Court of Canada (only two in 1999) were generally treated as "outsiders." Not only are they under-represented but Peter McCormick, author of the study, suggests that in order for women to be appointed to the Supreme Court they appear to be the "ones who have learned to dig into their own foxhole and stand everybody off." The study found that the two female justices, for example, have been prone to ruling against the majority and show no allegiance to the plight of women's rights (Tibbetts, 1999).

It was not until 1978 that the first female correctional officers were hired in male institutions. By 1984, women constituted approximately 10% of correctional officers and 22% in 1998. In 1998, there were just over a dozen women institutional heads in federal penitentiaries.

The 1998 United Nations meeting on women rights observed that judicial bodies around the world (Canada included) continually neglect to properly investigate and prosecute suspected offenders of women. In one recent survey of federally sentenced women, Pate (1998) found that in spite of the Declaration of Human Rights and the charter, most women do not know their rights, let alone choose to exercise them. Pate found that women with mental health problems and women in maximum security institutions are still imprisoned in all-male prisons. These general views were also expressed recently by the Pope when he condemned the "social sins which cry out to heaven" among which he mentioned the exploitation of women (Pope calls..., 1999).

Fortunately, a number of scholars have championed their plight. Following in the footsteps of the women's movement of the early 1970s, a number of scholars began to write about the plight of women in the criminal justice system. In 1974, Carol Smart's book, *Women, Crime and Criminality: A Feminist Critique*, and in 1975, Freda Adler's book, *Sisters in Crime*, helped to forge the emergence of feminist theories in criminology. More recently, Karleen Faith (1993) observed that not only does the system discriminate against women but that the images are also distorted by the media and the movies. In response to the growing body of research being conducted in the field of gender-based violence, the journal *Violence Against Women* in 1999 doubled its publications to one issue per month. In 1994, British Columbia became one of the first provinces to provide an annual report to the Ministry of Attorney-General's Department of Equality Initiative on the steps towards justice for women. Finally, the Canadian Association of Elizabeth Fry Societies continues to maintain a vigil to ensure that women are not discriminated against in the criminal justice system.

Today, there are at least five differing expressions of feminist theories. But, they all share a common theme—that is, recognizing the injustices women have had to endure at all levels of the criminal justice system. However, as noted in the introduction to Unit III, the road has been long and the end does not appear in sight. In fact, in late 1998, the National Action Committee on the Status of Women (an Ottawa-based political lobby group) announced that they were closing. The reason being a lack of funding. Regionally, cities like Calgary have also experienced hardship. The Women's Centre had to close down for eighteen months and as of late 1998 were uncertain whether their current funding from the community and the United Way would allow they to stay open after 1999.

In this unit, we offer two articles that serve to highlight the nature and extent of female crime and the general attitude towards female offenders. The first article is a portion of a recent Statistics Canada report entitled *Women in Canada: A Statistical Report*. The section we have included relates to women in the Canadian criminal justice system. Information is provided on the extent of reported criminality by, and against, women. The second article is by M. Chesney-Lind, a recognized expert in the area of female offenders and women in the justice system, who offers an overview of the nature of female criminality as well as presents reasons for their increasing involvement in the system. Chesney-Lind also draws attention to some of the inequalities women experience when they come into contact with the justice system.

DISCUSSION QUESTIONS:

1. Why do women continue to experience discriminatory attention?
2. To what extent might social, cultural and/or patriarchal factors hinder the plight of women?
3. How can the criminal justice system begin to rectify the injustices directed towards women?
4. Examine current data on such topics as wife rape, battered women, sexual harassment, violence against women. What are the trends and how might we explain them? How do they reflect discrimination of women?
5. To what extent might our moral and ethical sensitivity to women's issue been compromised by not always relying on careful scientific analysis?

REFERENCES

Faith, K. (1993). *Unruly women: The politics of confinement and resistance*. Vancouver, BC: Press Gang.

50 Years of Human Rights Developments in Federal Corrections. (1998, August). Ottawa: Human Rights Division—Correctional Service of Canada.

O'Hara, J. (1998, December 11). Of rape and justice. *Maclean's*. On-line service.

Jimenez, M. (1998, November 7). Sexual harassment an epidemic in B.C. *National Post*, A8.

Pate, K. (1998, November). Correcting corrections for federally sentenced women. *Let's Talk*, 23(4):16-17.

Pope calls on Americas to rid continents of racism, drug-trafficking and abortion. (1999, January, 24). *Calgary Herald*, A3.

Tibbetts, J. (1999, January 21). Women on Supreme Court 'outsiders', study concludes. *Calgary Herald*, A8.

Web watch: http://www.uottawa/~hrrec/projects/internat/women.html. Again, the list of possible web sites is virtually endless. Two interesting starting points might be the Human Rights and Education Centre located at the University of Ottawa—http://www.ichrdd.ca/. The other site is the International Centre for Human Rights and Democratic Development—http://www.ichrdd.ca/.

Women and the Criminal Justice System

Catherine Trainor, Josee Narmond, and Lisa Verson

INVOLVEMENT IN CRIMINAL ACTIVITY

Women make up a relatively small percentage of adult offenders in the criminal justice system. In fact, only 17% of all persons aged 18 and over charged with criminal offences in 1993 were women. The share of all criminal offenders accounted for by women, however, has increased somewhat from 14% in 1987 (see Figure 1).

Women make up a particularly small share of adults charged with violent crimes. In 1993, only 11% of persons aged 18 and over charged with violent crimes were women. That year, women made up 14% of those charged with homicide, 14% of those charged with attempted murder, 13% of those charged with non-sexual assaults, 8% of those charged with robbery and only 2% of those charged with sexual assault.

Women account for a somewhat greater share of those charged with property offences than those charged with violent crimes. In 1993, 24% of all adults charged with crimes against property were women, compared with 11% of those charged with violent crimes.

Trainor, C., Normand, J., and Verdon, L. (1995). Women and the criminal justice system. In Statistics Canada, *Women in Canada: A statistical report* (3rd ed.). Catalogue No. 85-503E (101-109).

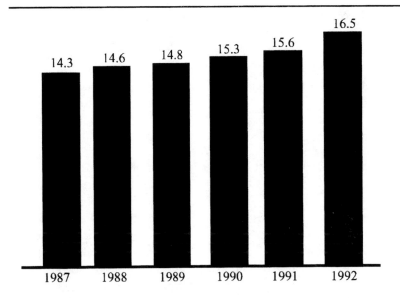

Figure 1: Women as a percentage of all adults charged with criminal offences, 1987-1993

| 14.3 | 14.6 | 14.8 | 15.3 | 15.6 | 16.5 |
| 1987 | 1988 | 1989 | 1990 | 1991 | 1992 |

Source: Statistics Canada, Catalogue 85-205.

There is considerable variation, though, in women's involvement in different types of property crime. In 1993, for example, women made up 35% of those charged with theft under $1,000 and 30% of those charged with fraud.

In contrast, only 5% of adults charged with either breaking and entering or theft of a motor vehicle were women.

About half of all adults charged with prostitution-related offences, including communicating for the purpose of prostitution, operating a bawdy house, and procuring, that is, recruiting new prostitutes, are women. In 1993, 4,200 women were charged with prostitution-related offences; these women represented 48% of all adults charged with this type of offence that year.

These data include both prostitutes and customers charged with prostitution-related offences, since police and court information do not distinguish between prostitutes and customers. It is generally acknowledged, however, that most prostitutes who are charged are female, while most customers who are charged are male.

Overall, relatively few women are charged with drug offences. In 1993, women represented 14% of persons aged 18 and over charged under the Narcotic Control Act and the Food and Drug Act. That year, women accounted for 17% of adults charged with cocaine offences, 15% of those involved with heroin, and 13% of those involved with cannabis.

As with men, however, the majority of drug-related charges brought against women are for cannabis-related offences. In 1993, 54% of all drug charges against women were for cannabis-related offences, while the figure for men was 61%.

YOUNG FEMALE OFFENDERS

Female youths also account for a relatively small proportion of all reported youth crime. In 1993, just 21% of 12- to 17-year-olds charged in criminal incidents were female.

Unlike adult women, female young offenders account for a greater share of those charged with violent offences than those charged with property crimes. In 1993, females aged 12-17 made up 24% of all young offenders charged with violent offences, compared with 21% of those charged with property crimes.

As well, the percentage of all youths charged with crimes against property accounted for by female youths declines the more serious the offence. For example, female youths made up 33% of young offenders charged with theft under $1,000 and 30% of those charged with fraud in 1993, versus13% of those charged with theft over $1,000, 10% of those charged with motor vehicle theft, and 7% of those charged with breaking and entering.

WOMEN IN CORRECTIONAL FACILITIES

Women make up a relatively small proportion of the population sentenced to correctional facilities. In 1994, a total of 312 women were sentenced to federal penitentiaries. These women represented only 3% of all persons sentenced to federal institutions that year.

Women make up a slightly larger share of those admitted to provincial facilities. In 1993-94, a total of 10,696 women were admitted to provincial facilities, representing 9% of all adult admissions to these institutions that year.

VICTIMS OF CRIMES

Overall, women and men are about equally likely to be victims of crime. In 1993, 23% of women and 24% of men aged 15 and over reported that they had been the victim of at least one personal or household crime (Table 1). As well, the likelihood of being victimized has not changed substantially for either women or men over the past five years.

Table 1: Personal victimizations per 1,000 population aged 15 and over, by type of incident, 1993

	Women	Men
Theft of personal property	51	51
Sexual assault	29	---
Robbery	6	17
Assault	66	68

Source: Statistics Canada, General Social Survey.

However, women are more likely than men to be the victims of a personal crime, such as sexual assault, robbery attempted robbery and assault. In 1993, there were 151 incidents of these crimes for every 1,000 women aged 15 and over, compared with 136 for men.

The likelihood of women and men being victims of a personal crime also varies by the type of crime. Women, for example, are considerably more likely than men to be victims of sexual assault. In 1993, there were 29 such incidents for every 1,000 women aged 15 and over, whereas there were too few of these crimes committed against men to produce a statistically reliable estimate.

At the same time, women were only about half as likely as men to be the victims of a robbery while about the same percentage of women and men were victims of either personal thefts or non-sexual assaults.

Young women are particularly likely to be the victims of a personal crime. In 1993, there were 333 personal crimes committed for every 1,000 women aged 15-24, compared with 178 among 25- to 44-year-old women and 74 among those aged 45-64. The number of personal crimes committed against women aged 65 and over was too small to be expressed reliably.

WOMEN VICTIMIZED BY MEN THEY KNOW

Women who are victims of violent attacks are more likely than male victims to know their assailants. In fact, acquaintances or relatives were responsible for 72% of the violent incidents committed against women in 1993, compared with 37% of those committed against men. In comparison, strangers perpetrated 24% of violent attacks against women, versus 56% of attacks against men.

MOST PERSONAL VICTIMIZATIONS GO UNREPORTED

The majority of personal crimes committed against women are not reported to the police. In 1993, 69% of all personal victimizations experienced by women were not reported to police, slightly higher than the corresponding figure for male victims (62%).

Violent personal crimes committed against women are even less likely to be reported to police. In 1993, 75% of all violent attacks against women were not reported to the police, compared with 65% of those committed against men. In fact, 90% of sexual assaults committed against women went unreported that year.

The most common reason cited by women for not reporting personal victimizations to the police in 1993 was that the incidents were dealt with in another manner (58%). As well, in many cases the incident was not reported because the woman considered it to be a personal matter (49%), she did not want to get involved with the police (45%), or she considered the incident to be minor (38%). At the same time, though, 33% of these incidents were not reported because the victim felt the police could do nothing about it, while in 24% of cases, the woman feared revenge from the offender.

Women and men tend to have different reasons for not reporting personal victimizations to the police. While one in five personal victimizations against women were not reported because the woman feared revenge from the attacker, so few male victims cited this reason that the figure could not be expressed reliably. In contrast, women were less likely than men to keep incidents from the police because they were too minor, or because the victim felt that the police could not do anything or would not help.

EFFECTS OF PERSONAL VICTIMIZATION

Incidents of personal victimization are more likely to disrupt the daily activities of female than male victims. In 1993, 27% of female personal victimizations resulted in the woman finding it difficult or impossible to carry out her main activity for at least one day, more than twice the figure reported by male victims (12%) (see Figure 2).

Percent of personal victimizations resulting in difficulty carrying out main activity, 1993

Source: Statistics Canada, General Social Survey.

FEMALE VICTIMS OF HOMICIDE

Fewer women than men are victims of homicide. In 1993, there were 208 female homicide victims, representing about one out of three of all homicides that year. The number of female homicide victims, however, has fallen in recent years, from 271 in 1991 to 208 in 1993. Female victims as a percentage of all homicide victims, though, has not changed.

MORE DOMESTIC HOMICIDES

Although women account for only a third of all homicide victims, they make up the majority of those killed by a family member. In 1993, women made up 59% of all homicide victims killed in a domestic relationship, while they represented only 22% of those killed by an acquaintance and just 12% of those killed by a stranger.

Women killed by their husbands or common-law partners account for the single largest group of victims in family-related homicides. In 1993, 38% of all domestic homicides involved women killed by their husbands, common-law partners or former partners, while only 15% involved men murdered by their current or former partners.

WIFE ASSAULT

During the 12 months prior to the 1993 Violence Against Women Survey, 3% of all women who were married or living common law at the time reported that they had experienced violence at the hands of their current husband or common-law partner at least once.

Overall, 29% of all women who had ever been married or lived in a common-law relationship, had been physically or sexually assaulted by their partner on at least one occasion since the age of 16.

In general, women were more likely to report experiences of wife assault by previous partners than by current partners. As of 1993, 48% of all women who had ever been married or lived common law reported that their ex-partners had assaulted them. In comparison, 15% of those who were presently married or living common law had been assaulted by their current partner.

TYPES OF WIFE ASSAULT

As of 1993, 16% of all ever-married women reported that the most serious types of wife assault they had ever experienced involved being kicked, hit, beaten up or choked, having a gun or knife used against them, or being sexually assaulted. At the same time, 11% reported that being pushed, grabbed, shoved or slapped was the most serious form of violence ever experienced, while 2% had only experienced non-physical assaults, such as being threatened or having something thrown at them.

LIFE-THREATENING WIFE ASSAULT

One in three ever-married women (34%) in violent partnerships had feared at some point that their lives were in danger. Once again, wife assault victims were more likely to have experienced life-threatening violence in previous relationships. In 1993, 45% of women in previous violent marital relationships or common-law unions had feared for their lives, compared with 13% of women in current violent partnerships.

MOST VICTIMS ASSAULTED MORE THAN ONCE

Almost two out of three women who have ever experienced wife assault had been victimized on more than one occasion. As of 1993, 63% of women who had ever experienced spousal abuse had been victimized more than once.

This included 32% who were victimized on at least 11 occasions, while 9% were assaulted between 6 and 10 times, and 22% were victimized between 2 and 5 times.

As well, the incidence of repeated abuse was higher for previous partnerships than for current unions, perhaps indicating that women tend to leave violent partnerships. For example, 41% of women who had been assaulted by a previous partner experienced more than 10 separate assaults, compared with 10% of those currently living with a violent partner.

RISK OF ASSAULT AT SEPARATION

For most women who experienced wife assault in a former relationship, the violence ended at the time of separation. In fact, 81% of ever-married women who experienced wife assault in a past relationship reported no further violence after they separated from their partner. However, for 19% of these women, the violence continued even after separation.

Indeed, for some women, the assaults only began at the time of separation, while for others, the violence escalated. For example, 8% of ever-married women who experienced violence after separation reported that the assaults first began when they left the relationship. As well, the violence increased in severity and/ or frequency after separation for 35% of women whose partner had assaulted them after separation.

NON-SPOUSAL MALE VIOLENCE

Many women experience violence at the hands of men other than their husbands or common-law partners, including dates or boyfriends, other known men or strangers. In the 12 months prior to the Violence Against Women Survey, 8% of women in Canada were sexually or physically assaulted by a man other than a spouse. That year, 6% of women were sexually assaulted and 3% were physically assaulted.

Young women are more likely than older women to be victims of non-spousal violence. In the 12 months prior to the survey, 23% of women aged 18-24 were assaulted by a date, boyfriend, acquaintance or stranger, compared with 11% of women aged 25-34 and 6% or less of those in groups aged 35 and over (see Figure 3).

As of 1993, a total of 4.4 million women aged 18 and over, 42% of all adult women in Canada, had experienced at least one incident of either non-spousal sexual or physical assault since the age of 16. In fact, over one in three women

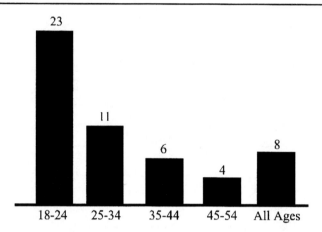

Figure 3:   Percent of women aged 18 and over who experienced
non-spousal violence, by age, 1993

*During the 12 months prior to the survey

Source: Statistics Canada, Violence Against Women Survey.

(37%) had been victims of sexual assault, while 17% had been physically assaulted.

As well, over half of women who had ever experienced sexual assault since the age of 16 had been assaulted on more than one occasion. As of 1993, 26% of female victims of sexual assault had experienced this type of violent incident on four or more occasions, while 11% had experienced three sexual assaults and 20% reported two such incidents.

As of 1993, over half (54%) of all incidents of non-spousal violence against women were perpetrated by men known to the victims. More specifically, 20% of non-spousal violent incidents against women were perpetrated by a date or boyfriend, while 34% were committed by other known men. Strangers were responsible for the remaining 45% of violent incidents (see Figure 4).

SOURCES OF ASSISTANCE FOR ABUSED WOMEN

In most instances, women who experience violence do not contact formal organizations such as the police or social service agencies for help. Indeed, only 14% of incidents of wife assault or non-spousal physical or sexual assault were reported to the police, while in just 9% of cases the victim contacted a

Figure 4: Percent of non-spousal violent incidents ever experienced by women aged 18 and over, by relationship to assailant

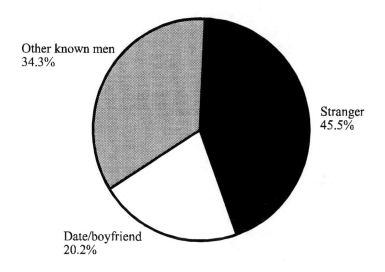

Other known men
34.3%

Stranger
45.5%

Date/boyfriend
20.2%

Source: Statistics Canada, Violence Against Women Survey.

social service agency. Rather, women most often sought the help of friends and neighbours (51%) or family members (42%) after these incidents.

However, many female victims of violence at the hands of men tell no one about their experience. As of 1993, victims of 22% of wife assault or other physical or sexual assault incidents had not told anyone about the experience prior to the Violence Against Women Survey.

WORK-RELATED SEXUAL HARASSMENT

During the 12 months prior to the 1993 Violence Against Women Survey 389,000 women, 6% of all employed women aged 18 and over, reported they had been subjected to sexual harassment in the workplace on at least one occasion.

Young women were at the greatest risk of workplace sexual harassment (see Table 2). In 1993, 10% of employed women aged 18-24 reported that they had experienced work-related sexual harassment in the past 12 months, compared with 8% of those aged 25-34 and 6% of those in the 35-44 age range.

Table 2:   Percentage of women aged 18 and over who ever experienced
            workplace sexual harassment, by type of harassment

Inappropriate comments about body or sex life	77%
Leaning over unnecessarily, getting too close, or cornering victim	73%
Repeatedly asking for a date and not taking "no" for an answer	50%
Saying job situation might suffer if victim did not have a sexual relationship with harasser	18%

Source: Statistics Canada, Violence Against Women Survey.

There are also differences in the incidence of sexual harassment depending on marital status. In 1993, 9% of employed women who were single and 8% of those who were divorced or separated reported they had experienced sexual harassment at work, versus 5% of married women.

The most common form of workplace sexual harassment experienced by women involves inappropriate comments about their bodies and sex life. As of 1993, 77% of employed women who had ever been harassed at work reported that they had been subjected to this type of harassment at least once, while 73% had been made uncomfortable by a man either leaning over them unnecessarily, getting too close or cornering them. At the same time, 50% had been harassed by a man who repeatedly asked for a date, and 18% had been told that they could lose their jobs or their employment situations could be affected if they did not have a sexual relationship with him.

FEAR OF CRIME

Women are much more likely than men to feel worried or unsafe about their personal security. For instance, 42% of women aged 15 and over reported they felt unsafe walking alone in their neighbourhood after dark, over four times the figure for men (10%).

Many women also feel worried when they are alone at home at night. In 1993, 37% of women aged 15 and over reported feeling very or somewhat worried when they were alone in their homes in the evening or at night, three times the figure for men (12%).

Young women are the most likely to be worried when home alone in the evening or at night. In 1993, 42% of women aged 15-24, compared with 39% of those aged 25-44, 37% of those aged 45-64, and 27% of senior women reported that they worried when they were alone in their homes in the evening or at night.

CRIME PREVENTION MEASURES

Many women have begun to take special measures to protect themselves from crime. In 1993, 36% of women aged 15 and over reported that they either modified their activities or routines or began to avoid certain places specifically to protect themselves from crime. At the same time, 22% installed security devices such as new locks or burglar alarms, 5% changed their telephone number, 4% obtained a dog, and 4% took a self-defence course. As well, women were generally more likely than men to have adopted these behaviours to protect themselves from crime.

In addition, many women routinely take measures to protect themselves from crime. For instance, in 1993, 68% of women reported that they routinely locked their car doors when alone, 58% planned their route for reasons of safety, 58% checked the back seat of their parked car before getting in, 24% stayed at home at night, and 17% carried some kind of weapon. Again, these figures were all considerably higher than those for men.

WOMEN IN THE POLICE FORCE

Women make up a relatively small share of all people employed in police forces across Canada, including police officers, civilians and other personnel. In 1993, women represented only 23% of total police personnel, although this figure has increased from 21% in 1990 and 15% in the early 1980s.

However, women make up an even smaller percentage of police officers. In 1993, women represented only 8% of all police officers, while they accounted for 66% of all civilian police personnel working in administrative support positions.

Nevertheless, the number of women police officers has grown considerably in the last decade. Between 1980 and 1993, the number of female police officers more than quadrupled, while there was little change in the number of male officers. As a result, the representation of women among police officers rose from 2% to 8% over this period.

WOMEN IN LAW AND JURISPRUDENCE OCCUPATIONS

There are also relatively few women employed in law and jurisprudence occupations. In 1991, just 37% of all judges and magistrates, lawyers and notaries, and people in related occupations, such as paralegals and law clerks, were women.

The representation of women in each of these three occupational groups also varies considerably. In 1991, women represented only 29% of lawyers, whereas they accounted for 70% of all persons employed in other related law and jurisprudence occupations.

As well, women made up only 20% of all judges and magistrates in Canada in 1991, although this was up from 13% in 1986. In addition, Madame Justice Bertha Wilson became the first women appointed to the Supreme Court of Canada in 1982. She was followed by Madame Justice Claire L'Heureux-Dube in 1987 and Madame Justice Beverly McLachlin in 1989. By 1994, two out of nine judges on the Supreme Court of Canada were women.

Trends in Women's Crime

M. Chesney-Lind

Women's crime, like girls' crime, is deeply affected by women's place. As a result, women's contribution to serious crime, like that of girls', is minor. Of those adults arrested for serious crimes of violence in 1994 (murder, forcible rape, robbery, and aggravated assault), only 14% were female. Indeed, women constituted only 18.8% of all arrests during that year (Federal Bureau of Investigation, 1995, p. 222). This also means that adult women are an even smaller percentage of those arrested than their girl counterparts (who now comprise about one out of four juvenile arrests).

Moreover, the majority of adult women offenders, like girls, are arrested and tried for relatively minor offences. In 1994, women were most likely to be arrested for larceny theft (which alone accounted for 15.5% of all adult women's arrests), followed by drug abuse violations (9.3%). This means that over a quarter of all the women arrested in the United States that year were arrested for one of these two offences. Women's offences, then, are concentrated in just a few criminal categories, just as women's employment in the mainstream economy is concentrated in a few job categories. Furthermore, these offences, as we shall see, are closely tied to women's economic marginality and the ways women attempt to cope with poverty.

Chesney-Lind, M. (1997). Trends in women's crime. In M. Chesney-Lind (Ed.), *The female offender*. Thousand Oaks, CA: Sage. (pp. 95-119). Canadian spellings have been used throughout for consistency. Copyright ©1997 by Sage. Reprinted with permission of Sage Publications Inc.

Unruly Women: A Brief History of Women's Offences

Women's concentration in petty offences is not restricted to the present. A study of women's crime in fourteenth-century England (Hanawalt, 1982) and descriptions of the backgrounds of the women who were forcibly transported to Australia several centuries later (Beddoe, 1979) document the astonishing stability in patterns of women's lawbreaking.

The women who were transported to Australia, for example, were servants, maids, or laundresses convicted of petty theft (stealing, shoplifting, and picking pockets) or prostitution. The number of women transported for these trivial offences is sobering. Between 1787 and 1852, no less than 24,960 women, fully a third of whom were first offenders, were sent to relieve the "shortage" of women in the colonies. Shipped in rat-infested holds, the women were systematically raped and sexually abused by the ships' officers and sailors, and the death rate in the early years was as high as one in three. Their arrival in Australia was also a nightmare, no provision was made for the women and many were forced to turn to prostitution to survive (Beddoe, 1979, pp. 11-21).

Other studies add different but important dimensions to the picture. For example, Bynum's (1992) research on "unruly" women in antebellum North Carolina adds the vital dimension of race to the picture. She notes that the marginalized members of society, particularly "free black and unmarried poor white women" were most often likely both to break social and sexual taboos and to face punishment by the courts. Indeed, she observes that "if North Carolina lawmakers could have done so legally, they would have rid society altogether" of these women (Bynum, 1992, p. 10). As it was, they harshly enforced laws against fornication, bastardy, and prostitution in an attempt to affect these women and their progeny.

The role of urbanization and class is further explored in Feeley and Little's (1991) research on criminal cases appearing in London courts between 1687 and 1912, and Boritch and Hagan's (1990) research on arrests in Toronto between 1859 and 1955. Both of these studies examine the effect of industrialization and women's economic roles (or economic marginalization) on women's offences. Both works present evidence that women were drawn to urban areas, where they were employed in extremely low-paid work. As a result, this forced many into forms of offending, including disorderly conduct, drunkenness, and petty thievery. Boritch and Hagan make special note of the large numbers of women arrested for property offences, "drunkenness" and "vagrancy," which can be seen as historical counterparts to modern drug offences (Boritch & Hagan, 1990). But what of women who committed "serious" offences such as murder? Jones's (1980) study of early women murderers in the United States reveals that many of America's early women murderers were indentured servants. Raped by calculating masters who understood that giving birth to a "bastard" would add 1 to 2 years to a woman's term of service, these desperate women hid their pregnancies and then committed infanticide. Jones also provides numerous historical and contemporary examples of desperate women murdering their brutal "lovers" or husbands. The less dramatic links between forced marriage, women's circumscribed options, and women's decisions to kill, often by poison, characterized the Victorian murderesses. These women, though rare, haunted the turn of the century, in part because women's participation in the methodical violence involved in arsenic poisoning was considered unthinkable (Hartman, 1977).

In short, research on the history of women's offences, and particularly women's violence, is a valuable resource for its information on the level and character of women's crime and as a way to understand the relationship between women's crime and women's lives. Whenever a woman commits murder, particularly if she is accused of murdering a family member, people immediately ask, "How could she do that?" Given the enormous costs of being born female, that may well be the wrong question. The real question, as a review of the history of women's crime illustrates, is not why women murder but rather why so few murder

Take a look at some facts. Every 15 seconds a woman is beaten in her own home (Bureau of Justice Statistics, 1989a). A National Institute of Mental Health study (based on urban area hospitals) estimated that 21% of all women using emergency surgical services had been injured in a domestic violence incident; that half of all injuries presented by women to emergency surgical services occurred in the context of partner abuse; and that over half of all rapes of women over the age of 30 had been perpetrated by an intimate partner (Stark et al., 1981). In the United States, for example, former Surgeon General C. Everett Koop estimated that 3 to 4 million women are battered each year; roughly half of them are single, separated, or divorced (Koop, 1989). Battering also tends to escalate and become more severe over time. Almost half of all batterers beat their partners at least three times a year (Straus, Gelles, & Steinmetz, 1980). This description of victimization doesn't address other forms of women's abuse, such as incest and sexual assault, which have rates as alarmingly high (see Center for Policy Studies, 1991).

The real question is why so few women resort to violence in the face of such horrendous victimization—even to save their lives. In 1994, in the United States, only 10.8% of those arrested for murder were women—meaning that murder, like other forms of violent crime, is almost exclusively a male activity. In fact, women murderers, as both Jones and Hartman document, are interesting precisely because of their rarity. The large number of women arrested for trivial property and morals offences, coupled with the virtual absence of women from those arrested for serious property crimes and violent crimes, provides clear evidence that women's crime parallels their assigned role in the rest of society (Klein & Kress, 1976). In essence, women's place in the legitimate economy largely relegates them to jobs that pay poorly and are highly sex segregated (like secretarial and sales jobs); likewise, in the illicit or criminal world, they occupy fewer roles and roles that do not "pay" as well as men's crime. There is, however, little understanding of why this is the case, and, until recently, little scholarship devoted to explaining this pattern. In this article we will attempt to address both the reality of women's crime and the fascination with the atypical woman offender who is violent and defies her "conventional role" in both the mainstream and the criminal world.

TRENDS IN WOMEN'S ARRESTS

Over the years, women have typically been arrested for larceny theft, drunk driving, fraud (the bulk of which is welfare fraud and naive check forgery), drug abuse violations, and buffer charges for prostitution (such as disorderly conduct and a variety of petty offences that fall under the broad category of "other offences") (Steffensmeier, 1980; Steffensmeier & Allan, 1990).

Arrest data certainly suggest that the "war on drugs" has translated into a war on women. Between 1985 and 1994, arrests of adult women for drug abuse violations increased by 100.1%, compared to 53.7% for men (Federal Bureau of Investigation, 1992, p. 222). The past decade (1985-1994) has also seen increases in arrests of women for "other assaults" (up 126%) (not unlike the pattern seen in girls' arrests). Arrest rates show much the same pattern. In the past decade, arrests of women for drug offences and other assaults have replaced fraud and disorderly conduct as the most common offences for which adult women are arrested.

These figures however should not be used to support notions of dramatic increases in women's crime. As an example, although the number of adult women arrested between 1993 and 1994 did increase by 5.8%, that increase followed a slight decline in women's arrests between 1992 and 1993 (Federal Bureau of Investigation, 1994, p. 226; Federal Bureau of Investigation, 1995, p. 226).

The arrests of women for Part One or "index" offences (murder, rape, aggravated assault, robbery, break-and-enter, larceny theft, motor vehicle theft, and arson) increased by 25.2% (compared to an increase in male arrests of 14.3%) between 1985 and 1994 (Federal Bureau of Investigation, 1993, p. 222).

Trends in adult arrest by gender, 1985-1994

Offence	Percentage Change (1985—1994)	
	Male	**Female**
Total	15.4	36.4
Murder and non-negligent manslaughter	13.4	-4.2
Forcible rape	-5.1	-4.4
Robbery	10.1	32.5
Aggravated assault	65.1	110.5
Break-and-enter	-14.4	25.0
Theft	7.5	14.1
Motor vehicle theft	29.1	77.1
Arson	-23.6	-12.4
Violent crime	42.5	89.9
Property crime	3.1	16.1
Crime index total	14.3	25.2
Other assaults	80.7	126.2
Forgery and counterfeiting	29.0	41.6
Fraud	32.0	11.4
Embezzlement	16.2	40.8
Stolen property; buy, receive, possess	18.2	37.3
Vandalism	14.9	60.7
Weapons: carrying, possessing etc.	26.1	29.2
Prostitution and commercialized vice	8.4	-24.9
Sex offences (except forcible rape and prostitution)	-4.5	15.5
Drug abuse violations	53.7	100.1
Gambling	-44.8	-40.5
Offences against family and children	80.0	264.6
Driving under the influence	-24.2	-4.7
Liquor Laws	-0.7	38.1
Drunkenness	-32.1	-8.0
Disorderly conduct	-5.2	1.7
Vagrancy	-43.0	29.7
All other offences (except traffic)	45.7	78.5
Suspicion (not included in totals)	1.0	19.9
Curfew and loitering law violations	0.0	0.0
Runaway	0.0	0.0

Source: Federal Bureau of Investigation. (1994). *Crime in the States—1993*. Washington, D.C: Department of Justice, p. 222.

Much of this increase, however, can be explained by increases in larceny theft, which some contend often involves such minor offences that it should not be confused with "serious" crime (see Steffensmeier & Allan, 1990).

Moreover, looking at these offences differently reveals a picture of stability rather than change over the past decade. Women's share of these arrests (as a proportion of all those arrested for this offence) rose from 21.8% to 23.4% between 1985 and 1994. Women's share of arrests for serious violent offences rose from 10.9% to 14% during the same period (Federal Bureau of Investigation, 1994, p. 222)— hardly anything to get excited about. At the other extreme is the pattern found in arrests for prostitution—the only crime among the 29 offence categories tracked by the FBI for which arrests of women account for the majority (6 1.3%) of all arrests.

Overall, the increase in women's arrests is largely accounted for by more arrests of women for nonviolent property offences, such as shoplifting (theft, which was up 14.1%), check forgery (forgery/counterfeiting, which was up 41.6%), welfare fraud ("fraud", which was up 11.4%), and, most important, drug offences (up 100.1%) (Federal Bureau of Investigation, 1993, p. 222). Here, the increases in arrests are real, because the base numbers are large and, as a result, these offences make up a large portion of women's official deviance. Whether they are the product of actual changes in women's behaviour over the past decade or changes in law enforcement practices is an important question, and one to which we now turn.

How Could She? The Nature and Causes of Women's Crime

The pattern of women's crime, as represented in official arrest statistics, is remarkably similar to the pattern seen earlier for girls. Adult women have been, and continue to be, arrested for minor crimes (generally shoplifting and welfare fraud) and what might be called "deportment" offences (prostitution, disorderly conduct, and, arguably, "driving under the influence"). Their younger counterparts are arrested for essentially the same crimes, in addition to status offences (running away from home, incorrigibility, truancy, and other noncriminal offences for which only minors can be taken into custody). Arrests of adult women, like arrests of girls, have increased for both aggravated and other assaults. Finally, and most important, adult women's arrests for drug offences have soared.

Where there have been increases in women's arrests for offences that sound nontraditional, such as embezzlement (or, as we shall see later in this chapter, robbery), careful examination reveals the connections between these offences and women's place.

EMBEZZLEMENT

In the case of embezzlement, for which women's arrests increased by 40.8% in the past decade, careful research disputes the notion of women moving firmly into the ranks of big-time, white-collar offenders. Because women are concentrated in low-paying clerical, sales, and service occupations (Renzetti & Curran, 1995), they are "not in a position to steal hundreds of thousands of dollars but they [are] in a position to pocket smaller amounts" (Simon & Landis, 1991, p. 56). Moreover, their motives for such theft often involve family responsibilities rather than a desire for personal gain (Daly, 1989; Zietz, 1981).

Daly's analysis of gender differences in white-collar crime is particularly useful. In a review of federal "white-collar" crime cases in seven federal districts (which included people convicted of bank embezzlement, income tax fraud, postal fraud, etc.), she found that gender played a substantial role in the differences between men's and women's offences. For example, of those arrested for bank embezzlement, 60% of the women were tellers and 90% were in some sort of clerical position. By contrast, about half of the men charged with embezzlement held professional and managerial positions (bank officers and financial managers). Therefore it is no surprise that for each embezzlement offence, men's attempted economic gain was 10 times higher than women's (Daly, 1989). In commenting on this pattern, Daly notes, "the women's socio-economic profile, coupled with the nature of their crimes, makes one wonder if 'white collar' aptly described them or their illegalities" (Daly, 1989, p. 790).

Embezzlement is a particularly interesting offence to "unpack" because it is one of the offences for which, if present trends continue, women may comprise about half of those charged with this offence (Renzetti & Curran, 1995, p. 310). In fact, women composed 41.8% of those charged with embezzlement in 1994 (Federal Bureau of Investigation, 1995, p. 222). Yet these increases cannot be laid at the door of women breaking into traditionally "male" offence patterns. Women's increased share of arrests for embezzlement is probably an artifact of their presence in low-level positions that make them more vulnerable to frequent checking and hence more vulnerable to detection (Steffensmeier & Allan, 1990). Combining this with these women's lack of access to resources to "cover" their thefts prompts Steffensmeier and Allan to draw a parallel between modern women's involvement in embezzlement and increases in thefts by women in domestic service a century ago.

Driving Under the Influence

Arrests of women driving under the influence (DUI) account for almost 1 arrest in 10 women. One study (Wells-Parker, Pang, Anderson, McMillen, & Miller, 1991) found that women arrested for DUI tended to be older than men (with nearly half of the men but less than a third of the women under 30), more likely to be "alone, divorced or separated" and to have fewer serious drinking problems and fewer extensive prior arrests for DUI or "public drunkenness" (Wells-Parker et al., 1991, p. 144). Historically, women were arrested for DUI only if "the DUI involved a traffic accident or physical/verbal abuse of a police officer" (Coles, 1991, p. 5). These patterns have probably eroded in recent years because of public outrage over drinking and driving and an increased use of roadblocks. Changes in police practices, rather than changes in women's drinking, could easily explain the prominence of this offence in women's official crime patterns.

Women tend to drink alone and deny treatment (Coles, 1991). Also, in contrast to men, they tend to drink for "escapism and psychological comfort" (Wells-Parker et al., 1991, p. 146). For these reasons, intervention programs that attempt to force women to examine their lives and the quality of relationships, which tend to work for male DUI offenders, are not successful with women. Indeed, these interventions could "exacerbate a sense of distress, helplessness and hopelessness" that could, in turn, trigger more drinking (Wells-Parker et al., 1991, p. 146).

Larceny Theft/Shoplifting

Women's arrests for theft are composed largely of arrests for shoplifting. Steffensmeier (1980) estimates that perhaps as many as four fifths of all arrests on larceny charges are for shoplifting. Cameron's (1953) early study of shoplifting in Chicago explains that women's prominence among those arrested for shoplifting may not reflect greater female involvement in the offence but rather differences in the ways men and women shoplift. Her research revealed that women tend to steal more items than men, to steal items from several stores, and to steal items of lesser value. Store detectives explained this pattern by saying that people tended to "steal the same way they buy" (Cameron, 1953, p. 159). Men came to the store with one item in mind. They saw it, took it, and left the store. Women, on the other hand, shopped around. Because the chance of being arrested increases with each item stolen, Cameron felt that the stores probably underestimated the level of men's shoplifting.

Although women stole more items than men, the median value of adult male theft was significantly higher than that of women's (Cameron, 1953, p. 62). In addition, more men than women were defined as "commercial shoplifters" (people who stole merchandise for possible resale).

Perhaps as a result of women's shopping and shoplifting patterns, studies done later (Lindquist, 1988) have found that women constitute 58% of those caught shoplifting. Steffensmeier and Allan (1990) go so far as to suggest that shoplifting may be regarded as a prototypically female offence. Shopping is, after all, part of women's "second shift" of household management, housework, and childcare responsibilities (Hochschild, 1989). Shoplifting can be seen as a criminal extension of expected and familiar women's work.

Even the reasons for shoplifting are gendered. Men, particularly young men, tend to view stealing as part of a broader pattern of masculine display of "badness" and steal items that are of no particular use to them (Steffensmeier & Allan, 1990). At the other extreme, they may be professional thieves and thus more likely to escape detection (Cameron, 1953).

Girls and women, on the other hand, tend to steal items that they either need or feel they need but cannot afford. As a result, they tend to steal from stores and to take things such as clothing, cosmetics, and jewelry. Campbell (1981) notes that women—young and old—are the targets of enormously expensive advertising campaigns for a vast array of personal products. These messages, coupled with the temptations implicit in long hours spent "shopping," lead to many arrests of women for these offences.

Despite some contentions that women actually shoplift more than men, self-report data in fact show few gender differences in the prevalence of the behaviour (see Chesney-Lind & Shelden, 1992, for a review of these studies). What appears to be happening is that girls and women shoplift in different ways than men. In addition, they are more often apprehended because store detectives expect women to shoplift more than men and thus watch women more closely (Morris, 1987).

BIG TIME/SMALL TIME

English (1993) approached the issue of women's crime by analyzing detailed self-report surveys she administered to a sample of 128 female and 872 male inmates in Colorado. She examined both "participation rates" and "crime frequency" figures for a wide array of different offences. She found few differences in the participation rates of men and women, with the exception of three property crimes. Men were more likely than women to report participation in break-and-enter, whereas women were more likely than men to have participated in theft and forgery. Exploring these differences further, she found that women "lack the specific knowledge needed to carry out a burglary" (English, 1993, p. 366).

Women were far more likely than men to be involved in "forgery" (it was the most common crime for women and fifth out of eight for men). Follow-up research on a subsample of "high crime"-rate female respondents revealed that many had worked in retail establishments and therefore "knew how much time they had" between stealing the checks or credit cards and having them reported (English, 1993, p. 370). The women said that they would target "strip malls" where credit cards and bank checks could be stolen easily and used in nearby retail establishments. The women reported that their high-frequency theft was motivated by a "big haul," which meant a purse with several hundred dollars in it, in addition to cards and checks. English concludes that "women's over representation in low-paying, low status jobs" increases their involvement in these property crimes (English, 1993, p. 171).

English's findings with regard to two other offences, for which gender differences did not appear in participation rates, are worth exploring here. She found no difference in the "participation rates" of women and men in drug sales and assault. However, when examining the frequency data, English found that women in prison reported making significantly more drug sales than men but not because they were engaged in big-time drug selling. Instead, their high number of drug sales occurred because women's drug sales were "concentrated in the small trades (i.e., transactions of less than $10)" (English, 1993, p. 372). Because they made so little money, English found that 20% of the active women dealers reported making 20 or more drug deals per day (English, 1993, p. 372).

A reverse of the same pattern was found when she examined women's participation in assault. Here, slightly more (27.8%) of women than men (23.4%) reported assaulting someone in the past year. However, most of these women reported making only one assault during the study period (65.4%), compared to only about a third of the men (37.5%).

English found that "economic disadvantage" played a role in both women's and men's criminal careers. Beyond this, however, gender played an important role in shaping women's and men's response to poverty. Specifically, women's criminal careers reflect "gender differences in legitimate and illegitimate opportunity structures, personal networks, and in family obligations" (English, 1993, p. 374).

Pathways to Women's Crime

As with girls, the links between adult women's victimization and crimes are increasingly clear. As was noted in earlier chapters, the backgrounds of adult women offenders hint at links between childhood victimization and adult offending. In an important study of such links, Gilfus (1992) interviewed 20 incarcerated women and documented how such childhood injuries were linked to adult crimes in women.

Gilfus extends the work of Miller (1986) and Chesney-Lind and Rodriguez (1983) on the ways in which women's backgrounds color their childhoods and ultimately their adulthoods. She conducted in-depth interviews in 1985 and 1986 with the women in a northeastern women's facility that, at the time, served as both a jail and a prison. From these lengthy interviews, she reconstructed "life event histories" for each of the women. The group had a mean age of 30 (ranging from 20 to 41 years of age), and included 8 African American and 12 white women. All of the women had life histories of what Gilfus characterized as "street crimes"—by which she meant prostitution, shoplifting, check or credit card fraud, and drug law violations. Their current offences included assault and battery, accessory to rape; breaking and entering; and multiple charges of drug possession, larceny, and prostitution (Gilfus, 1992). Sentence lengths ranged, for this group, from 3 months to 20 years. Most of the women were single mothers, three-quarters were intravenous drug users, and almost all (17) had histories of prostitution (seven of the women had begun as teenage prostitutes). Most of these women had grown up with violence; 13 of the 20 reported childhood sexual abuse and 15 had experienced "severe child abuse" (Gilfus, 1992, p. 70). There were no differences in the levels of abuse reported by black and white respondents, although African American women grew up in families that were more economically marginalized than their white counterparts. Although some women's childhood memories were totally colored by their sexual abuse, for most of the women in Gilfus's sample, coping with and surviving multiple victimization was the more normal pattern. In the words of one of these women, "I just got hit a lot.... 'Cause they would both drink and they wouldn't know the difference. I was picked up, thrown against walls, everything, you name it" (Gilfus, 1992, p. 72).

Despite the abuse and violence, these women recall spending time trying to care for and protect others, especially younger siblings, and attempting to do housework and even care for their abusive and drug or alcohol dependent parents. They also recall teachers who ignored signs of abuse and who, in the case of African American girls, were hostile and racist. Ultimately, 16 out of the 20 dropped out of high school (Gilfus, 1992, p. 69). The failure of the schools to be responsive to these young women's problems meant that the girls could perceive no particular future for themselves. Given the violence in their lives, drugs provided these girls with a solace found nowhere else.

Many (13) ran away from home as girls. "Rape, assault, and even attempted murder" were reported by 16 of the 20, with an average of three "rape or violent rape attempts" per woman; many of these occurred in the context of prostitution, but when the women attempted to report the assault, the police simply "ridiculed" the women or threatened to arrest them. In some cases, the police would demand sexual services for not arresting the woman (Gilfus, 1992, p. 79).

Violence also characterized these women's relationships with adult men; 15 of the 20 had lived with violent men. The women were expected to bring in money, generally through prostitution and shoplifting. These men functioned as the women's pimps but also sold drugs, committed robberies, or fenced the goods shoplifted by the women. Thirteen of the women had become pregnant as girls, but only four kept their first baby. Most of the women had subsequent children whom they attempted to mother despite their worsening addictions, and they tended to rely on their mothers (not their boyfriends) to take care of their children while in prison. The women continued to see their criminal roles as forms of caretaking; taking care of their children and of their abusive boyfriends. As Gilfus puts it, "the women in this study consider their illegal activities to be a form of work which is undertaken primarily from economic necessity to support partners, children, and addictions" (1992, p. 86). Gilfus further speculates that violence "may socialize women to adopt a tenacious commitment to caring for anyone who promises love, material success, and acceptance" (p. 86), which, in turn, places them at risk for further exploitation and abuse.

The interviews Arnold (1995) conducted, based on this same hypothesis, with 50 African American women serving sentences in a city jail and 10 additional interviews with African American women in prison are an important addition to the work of Gilfus. Arnold notes that African American girls are not only sexually victimized but are also the victims of "class oppression." Specifically, she notes that "to be young, Black, poor and female is to be in a high-risk category for victimization and stigmatization on many levels" (Arnold, 1995, p. 139). Growing up in extreme poverty means that African American girls may turn earlier to deviant behaviour, particularly stealing, to help themselves and their families. One young woman told Arnold that "my father beat my mother and neglected his children.... I began stealing when I was 12. I hustled to help feed and clothe the other [12] kids and help pay the rent" (Arnold, 1995, p. 139).

Thus, the caretaking role noted in women's pathways to crime is accentuated in African American families because of extreme poverty. Arnold also noted that economic need interfered with young black girls' ability to concentrate on schoolwork and attend school. Finally, Arnold noted, as had Gilfus, that African American girls were "victimized" by the school system (1995, p. 140); one of her respondents said that "some [of the teachers] were prejudiced, and one had the nerve to tell the whole class he didn't like black people" (p. 140). Most of her respondents said that even if they went to school every day, they did not learn anything. Finally, despite their desperate desire to "hold on. . . to conventional roles in society," the girls were ultimately pushed out of these, onto the streets, and into petty crime (p. 141).

The mechanics of surviving parental abuse and educational neglect were particularly hard on young African American girls, forcing them to drop out of school, on to the streets, and into permanent "structural dislocation" (Arnold, 1995, p. 143). Having no marketable skills and little education, many resorted to "prostitution and stealing" while further immersing themselves in drug addiction.

BEYOND THE STREET WOMAN: RESURRECTING THE LIBERATED FEMALE CROOK?

Issues of women's violence and the relationship between that violence and other changes in women's environment are recurring themes in discussions of women's crime. As others have noted, a persistent theme in women's criminality is the presumed link between efforts to improve women's economic and political position and levels of girls' and women's crime—particularly violent crime. We also saw that there is nothing particularly "new" about the concern. During the early 1970s, newspapers and periodicals were full of stories about the "new female criminal" (Foley, 1974; Klemesrud, 1978; *Los Angeles Times Service*, 1975; Nelson, 1977; Roberts, 1971). Presumably inspired by the women's movement, the female criminal supposedly sought equality in the underworld just as her more conventional counterparts pursued their rights in more acceptable arenas.

Such media accounts, like contemporary "girls in the hood" stories, generally relied on two types of evidence to support the alleged relationship between the women's rights movement and increasing female criminality: Federal Bureau of Investigation (FBI) statistics showing dramatic increases in the number of women arrested for nontraditional crimes, and sensationalistic accounts of women's violence. In the 1970s, the activities of female political activists such as Leila Khaled, Bernardine Dohrn, and Susan Saxe were featured. Of course, women's involvement in political or terrorist activity is nothing new, as the activities of Joan of Arc and Charlotte Corday demonstrate.

Arrest data collected by the FBI seem to provide more objective evidence that dramatic changes in the number of women arrested were occurring during the years associated with the second wave of feminist activity. For example, between 1960 and 1975, arrests of adult women went up 60.2% and arrests of juvenile women increased a startling 253.9%. In specific, nontraditional crimes, the increases were even more astounding. For example, between 1960 and 1975, the number of women arrested for murder was up 105.7%, forcible rape arrests increased by 633.3%, and robbery arrests were up 380.5% (Federal Bureau of Investigation, 1973, p. 124; Federal Bureau of Investigation, 1976, p. 191).

Law enforcement officials were among the earliest to link these changes to the movement for female equality. "The women's liberation movement has triggered a crime wave like the world has never seen before," claimed Chief Ed Davis of the Los Angeles Police Department (Weis, 1976, p. 17). On another occasion, he expanded on his thesis by explaining that the "breakdown of motherhood" signaled by the women's movement could lead to "the use of dope, stealing, thieving and killing" (*Los Angeles Times* Service, 1975, p. B4). Other officials, such as Sheriff Peter Pritchess of California, made less inflammatory comments that echoed the same general theme: "As women emerge from their traditional roles as housewife and mother, entering the political and business fields previously dominated by males, there is no reason to believe that women will not also approach equality with men in the criminal activity field" (Roberts, 1971, p. 72).

Law enforcement officials were not alone in holding this position; academics like Adler (1975a, 1975b) also linked increases in the number of women arrested to women's struggle for social and economic equality. Adler noted, for example, that "in the middle of the twentieth century, we are witnessing the simultaneous rise and fall of women. Rosie the Riveter of World War II has become Robin the Rioter or Rhoda the Robber of the Vietnam era. Women have lost more than their chains. For better or worse, they have lost many of the restraints which kept them within the law" (Adler, 1975b, p. 24).

Such arguments, it turns out, are nothing new. The first wave of feminism also saw an attempt to link women's rights with women's crime. Smart (1976), for example, found the following comment by W I. Thomas written in 1921, the year after the ratification of the 19th Amendment guaranteeing women the right to vote:

> The modern age of girls and young men is intensely immoral, and immoral seemingly without the pressure of circumstances. At whose door we may lay the fault, we cannot tell. Is it the result of what we call "the emancipation of woman," with its concomitant freedom from chaperonage, increased intimacy between the sexes in adolescence, and a more tolerant viewpoint towards all things unclean in life? (Smart, 1976, pp. 70-71)

Students of women's crime were also quick to note that the interest in the female criminal after so many years of invisibility was ironic and questioned why the new visibility was associated with "an image of a woman with a gun in hand" (Chapman, 1980, p. 68). Chapman concluded that this attention to the female criminal was "doubly ironic" because closer assessments of the trends in women's violence did not support what might be called the "liberation hypothesis" and, more to the point, data showed that the position of women in the mainstream economy during those years was "actually worsening" (Chapman, 1980, pp. 68-69).

To be specific, although what might be called the "liberation hypothesis" or "emancipation hypothesis" met with wide public acceptance, careful analyses of changes in women's arrest rate provided little support for the notion. Using national arrest data supplied by the FBI and more localized police and court statistics, Steffensmeier (1980, p. 58) examined the pattern of female criminal behaviour for the years 1965 through 1977 (the years most heavily affected by the second wave of feminist activity). By weighting the arrest data for changes in population and comparing increases in women's arrests to increases in men's arrests, Steffensmeier concluded that "females are not catching up with males in the commission of violent, masculine, male-dominated, serious crimes (except larceny) or in white collar crimes" (1980, p. 72). He did note increases in women's arrests in the Uniform Crime Report categories of larceny, fraud, forgery, and vagrancy, but by examining these increases more carefully, he demonstrated that they were due almost totally to increases in traditionally female crimes, such as shoplifting, prostitution, and passing bad checks (fraud).

Moreover, Steffensmeier (1980) noted that forces other than changes in female behaviour were probably responsible for shifts in the numbers of adult women arrested for these traditionally female crimes. The increased willingness of stores to prosecute shoplifters, the widespread abuse of vagrancy statutes to arrest prostitutes combined with a declining use of this same arrest category to control public drunkenness, and the growing concern with "welfare fraud" were all social factors that he felt might explain changes in women's arrests without necessarily changing the numbers of women involved in these activities.

Steffensmeier's findings confirm the reservations that had been voiced earlier by Simon (1975), Rans (1975), and others about making generalizations solely from dramatic percentage increases in the number of women's arrests. These reservations are further justified by current arrest data that suggest that the sensationalistic increases of the early 1970s were not indicative of a new trend.

Between 1976 and 1979, for example, the arrests of all women rose only 7.1%, only slightly higher than the male increase of 5.8% for the same period (Chesney-Lind, 1986).

Finally, women offenders of the 1970s were unlikely targets for the messages of the largely middle-class women's movement. Women offenders tend to be poor, members of minority groups, with truncated educations and spotty employment histories. These were precisely the women whose lives were largely unaffected by the gains, such as they were, of the then white, middle-class women's rights movement (Chapman, 1980, Crites, 1976). Crites, for example, noted that, "These women rather than being recipients of expanded rights and opportunities gained by the women's movement, are, instead, witnessing declining survival options" (Crites, 1976, p. 37). Research on the orientations of women offenders to the arguments of the women's movement also indicated that, if anything, these women held very traditional attitudes about gender (see Chesney-Lind & Rodriguez, 1983, for a summary of these studies).

To summarize, careful work on the arrest trends of the 1970s provided no support for the popular liberation hypothesis of women's crime. Changes in women's arrest trends, it turned out, better fit arguments of women's economic marginalization than of her liberation (Simon & Landis, 1991).

THE REVIVAL OF THE "VIOLENT FEMALE OFFENDER"

The failure of careful research to support notions of radical shifts in the character of women's crime went almost completely unnoticed in the popular press. As a result, there was apparently nothing to prevent a recycling of a revised "liberation" hypothesis a decade and a half later

As noted in an earlier chapter, one of the first articles to use this recycled hypothesis was a 1990 article in the *Wall Street Journal* titled, "You've Come a Long Way, Moll," that focused on increases in the number of women arrested for violent crimes. This article opened with a discussion of women in the military, noting that "the armed forces already are substantially integrated" and moved from this point to observe that "we needn't look to the dramatic example of battle for proof that violence is no longer a male domain. Women are now being arrested for violent crimes—such as robbery and aggravated assault—at a higher rate than ever before recorded in the US" (Crittenden, 1990, p. A14).

As noted in Chapter 3, many of the articles to follow dealt with young women (particularly girls in gangs), but there were some exceptions. For example, the "Hand That Rocks the Cradle Is Taking Up Violent Crime," (Kahler, 1992) focused on increases in women's imprisonment and linked this pattern to "the growing number of women committing violent crimes" (Kahler, 1992, p. 1).

Comparing the arrest rates that prompted the first media surge of reporting on the "liberation" hypothesis with the arrest rates from the second wave of media interest today, it is evident that little has changed. As noted earlier in this chapter, women's share of violent crime has remained more or less stable, though arrests of women for "other assaults" did climb by 126.2% in the past decade (but the arrests of men increased by 80.7%) (Federal Bureau of Investigation, 1995). Moreover, between 1993 and 1994, the number of women arrested for serious crimes of violence increased by only 5.5% (Federal Bureau of Investigation, 1994, p. 226).

The news media were not alone in their interest in women's violence— particularly violent street crime. In a series of articles (Baskin, Sommers, & Fagan, 1993; Sommers & Baskin, 1992, 1993), the authors explore the extent and character of women's violent crime in New York. Prompted by an account in their neighborhood paper of two women who shot another woman in a robbery, the authors note that their research "has led us to the conclusion that women in New York City are becoming more and more likely to involve themselves in violent street crime" (Baskin et al., 1993, p. 401). Some of the findings that brought them to this conclusion follow.

In one study (Sommers & Baskin, 1992), they use arrest data from New York City (and arrest histories of 266 women) to argue that "black and Hispanic females exhibited high rates of offending relative to white females." They further argue that "violent offending rates of black females parallel that of white males" (Sommers & Baskin, 1992, p. 191). Included in their definition of "violent" crimes is murder, robbery, aggravated assault, and break-and-enter (apparently classified as a violent crime in New York City, but classified as a property crime by the FBI).

The authors explain that this pattern is a product of "the effects of the social and institutional transformation of the inner city" (Sommers & Baskin, 1992, p. 198). Specifically, the authors contend that "violence and drug involvement" are adaptive strategies in underclass communities that are racked by poverty and unemployment. Both men and women, they argue, move to crime as a way of coping with "extreme social and economic deprivation" (p. 198).

A second study (Sommers & Baskin, 1993) further explores women's violent offences by analyzing interview data from 23 women arrested for a violent felony offence (robbery or assault) and 65 women incarcerated for such an offence. Finding a high correlation between substance abuse and the rate of violent crime (particularly for those who committed robbery and robbery with assault), they also noted that "the women in our study who were involved in robbery were not crime specialists but also had a history of engagement in nonviolent theft, fraud, forgery, prostitution, and drug dealing" (p. 142). In fact, they comment that "these women are not roaming willy-nilly through the streets engaging in 'unprovoked' violence" (p. 154).

Just how involved these women were in more traditional forms of female crime was not apparent in the text of this article. In an appendix, however, the role played by a history of prostitution in the lives of these women offenders is particularly clear As an example, the women who reported committing both robbery and assault also had the highest rate of involvement with prostitution (77%) (Baskin & Sommers, 1993, p. 159).

In a third paper Baskin et al. (1993) explore "the political economy of street crime." This work, which appears to be based on the New York arrest data and a discussion of the explosion of crack selling in the city, explores the question, "Why do black females exhibit such relatively high rates of violence?" (Baskin et al., 1993, p. 405). Convinced that the concentration of poverty is associated positively with the level of criminal activity, regardless of race, the authors then conclude that "the growing drug markets and a marked disappearance of males" combine with other factors in underclass communities "to create social and economic opportunity structures open to women's increasing participation in violent crime" (Baskin et al, 1993, p. 406).

The authors further suggest that traditional theories of women's offences, particularly those that emphasize gender and victimization, do not adequately explain women's violent crime. Their work, they contend, "confirms our initial sense that women in inner city neighborhoods are being pulled toward violent street crime by the same forces that have been found to affect their male counterparts (e.g., peers, opportunity structures, neighborhood effects)"

(Baskin et al., 1993, p. 412). They conclude that the socioeconomic situation in the inner city, specifically as it is affected by the drug trade, creates "new dynamics of crime where gender is a far less salient factor" (Baskin et al., 1993, p. 417).

These authors argue that in economically devastated inner cities such as New York, women's violence—particularly the violence of the women of color—does not need to be considered in terms of the place of these women in patriarchal society (e.g., the effect of gender in their lives). Instead, they contend that these women (like their male counterparts) are being drawn to violence and other forms of traditionally male crimes for the same reasons as men.

This turns the "liberation" hypothesis on its head. Now it is not presumed economic gain that promoted "equality" in crime, but rather it is economic marginalization that causes women to move out of their "traditional" roles into the role of criminal. Is that really what is going on?

In this article I have hopefully already cast doubt on the notion that there has been any dramatic shift in women's share of violent crime (at least as measured by arrest statistics). This chapter has also provided evidence that women's participation in offences that sound "non-traditional" (such as embezzlement, DUI, and larceny theft) is deeply affected by the "place" of women in society. Both of these findings cast doubt on claims for the existence of a new, violent street criminal class of women—at least without first providing a more detailed exploration of trends in women's involvement in crimes such as robbery and drug selling. Because these offences, particularly drug use and sale, feature so prominently in the debate about the nature of adult women's offences, they will be explored in detail in the next chapter.

Has there been an increase in women's participation in traditionally male types of crime, such as violent crime? Does women's search for "equality" with men have a darker side, as suggested by some of the arrest statistics reviewed in this chapter? To answer this question fully, the next chapter will explore the current context of women's violence. Specifically, the chapter will explore the relationship between apparently male offences (such as robbery and drug selling) and more traditional female offences (such as prostitution).

Unit V

Gender Orientation:
Gays and Lesbians

In 1985, Kenn Zeller was attacked and killed by five teenagers in a Toronto park – the youths wanted to "beat up a fag". In 1989, a gay AIDS activist was killed on board a crowded Montreal bus by a gang of 15 youths, and in 1993 an Ottawa women was attacked by a man with a baseball bat. He broke four of her ribs because he resented the relationship she was having with another woman (EAGLE, 1994).

In December 1994 Bill-41 was submitted to the House of Commons as a measure to protect the equal rights of gays and lesbians in Canada. Section 718.2 of the Bill specifically refers to the protection of offences "motivated by bias, prejudice, or hatred based on the race, nationality, colour, religion, sex, age, mental or physical disability or sexual orientation of the victim... shall be deemed to be aggravated circumstances." However, s. 318(4) of the Criminal Code has not been amended. The section still uses the term "identifiable group" (EAGLE, 1994).

In spite of being protected under the Charter of Rights and Freedom, there is still a palatable level of fear and hostility towards gays and lesbians. The killing of Matthew Shepard, a gay Wyoming man, drew international attention in 1998. The 21-year-old was pistol-whipped, tied to a fence post in the bitter cold and left to die from exposure (Bronskill, 1998). Such stories are not isolated incidents in society and their impact has a ripple effect on other members of individuals who practice alternative lifestyles.

While lesbians and gays are allowed to parade and, in some provinces, legally marry, the justice system is still struggling to find 'their' equalitarian response. For example, the Criminal Code has provisions for sexual assault, including rape of children and women, but not for homosexual rape. Homosexual rape is excluded from the court, but some homosexual acts are subject to legal control. Why is it that where police are required to enforce laws banning homosexual practices they only do so when forced to do so? For example, a 1997 report showed that victimization of gays and lesbians were the most under-reported of minority groups targeted in hate crimes. One of the explanations being offered is the fact that these groups "think the police would lack sensitivity" to their situation (Kaufmann, 1997).

In 1998, the Conservative government of Alberta considered exercising the notwithstanding clause of the charter to nullify a Supreme Court ruling on gay rights in the province. The ruling pertained to the dismissal of Delwin Vriend, a homosexual instructor at a Christian school in Edmonton. Shortly after the Supreme Court ruling, the Alberta legislature also supported Klein's decision (Chase, 1998). So while the charter might rule in favour of protecting the rights of all Canadian citizens, it appears that the concept is not necessarily embraced across the country. In 1998, Premier Harris's Ontario government was accused of using "expensive stalling tactics and court interventions" to deny equal right for gays and lesbians. The accusation arose after a female partner was unable to receive insurance benefits after her partner had been killed in a motor vehicle accident four years earlier (Harris government..., 1998).

In 1992, in the case of *R v. Butler,* the Supreme Court ruled against the sales of published material intended for lesbian and gay consumers. It also ruled in favour of confiscating an array of political and erotic work that undermines the fundamental liberties of lesbian and gay men. The decision was allegedly inspired by a similar US anti-pornography ruling used to restrict lesbian and gay rights (Canada, 1998).

The irony is that in spite of general social attitudes towards such practices, when offenders are sentenced to prison a percentage of them resort to homosexual practices. While not condoned by prison administrators, such practices are recognized and even accepted as part of the criminal population subculture. Even so, the terms used within the prison setting to describe the various homosexual activity reflect a demeaning and derogatory connotation with such terms as "wolf," "fag," "butch," "dike" and "punk." There are reliable estimates of prison rape, a unique category of homosexual behaviour, but various studies indicate that somewhere between 5% and 20% of inmates have been the target of sexual aggressors of the same gender.

The issue of sexual orientation is compounded not only by social attitudes but moral and religious as well. Some religious leaders say that the Bible condemns same-gender relations and that such behaviour is therefore a sin. During World War II, Hitler's Germany put some 50,000 homosexuals in concentration camps and killed nearly a half million more. Yet, after the war, there was no concerted effort to acknowledge such discriminatory practices. Our intolerance is further fuelled by such heinous crimes as the gay serial killers Jeffrey Dalhmer, John Wayne Gacy and more recently Andrew Cananan alias "Da Silva." Homosexual behaviour has existed in most societies and evidence of it can be found in prehistoric art. Today there are many activist groups that campaign for the compassion of gender orientation.

In this unit, two articles are included that serve to highlight important themes of diversity and justice. (Also remember the information provided by Julian Roberts in Unit III of this volume indicated that lesbians and gays are increasingly targeted). This fact is also illustrated in the data provided by the first article in the present unit by the National Victim Center in the United States. Violence perpetrated within gay and lesbian relationships is the focus of the second article by Waterman, Dawson and Bologna.

Discussion Questions:

1. To what extent are Canadians committed to the principle of equality and respect of certain identifiable groups?
2. How might bias and prejudice against gays and lesbians be constructively resolved in the criminal justice system?
3. How might we explain the fact that homosexual practices are not uncommon in prison settings and yet not socially sanctioned?
4. Why does the criminal justice system tend to not treat acts of bias, violence and prejudice against such groups as not serious?
5. How do we explain the injustice of many men enjoying or fantasizing about sharing two women in an intimate act but yet not tolerate personal choice?
6. What does it mean when an athlete like former Olympic champion Mark Tewksbury (in December 1998) receives front-page coverage when going public about his gay sexual lifestyle? Why is it we hear so little about gay female athletes?

References

Bronskill, J. (1998, Nov. A7). Hate-crimes victims avoid courts, study reports. *Calgary Herald*, A7.

Canada. (1998). Canada: Human rights watch. (Online: www.injusticeline.com).

Chase, S. (1998, April 7). Klein ponders overruling courts on gay rights. *Calgary Herald*, A1-2.

EAGLE. (1994, December). Excerpt from the "EAGLE submission to House of Commons Standing Committee on Justice and Legal Affairs." (Online: www.ncf.carlton.ca/ip/social.services/eagle.bill41).

Harris government denies equal treatment for gays and lesbians. (1998, June 11). NDP Caucus at Queens Park, Toronto, ON. (Online).

Kaufmann, B. (1997, November 14). Minority groups targeted in hate crime. *Calgary Sun*.

Web watch: An excellent site that focuses on equality for gays and lesbians (EAGLE) can be found at: www.eagle.ca. The site offers numerous related links.

At a Glance:
Violence Against Gays and Lesbians

Infolink: National Victim Center

Although the prevalence of anti-gay and lesbian violence is not fully known on a national scale, studies are providing detailed statistics on its possible extent:

- Anti-gay and lesbian incidents increased 2% from 1993 to 1994, resulting in nine cities reporting more than two thousand incidents. Nearly half of the incidents involved physical assault with 62% of those victims sustaining injury (New York City Gay and Lesbian Anti-Violence Project, 1995).
- Approximately one-half of perpetrators are age twenty-one or younger (Comstock 1991).
- A campus survey reported that 61% of the gay/lesbian respondents feared for their safety as their orientation would be used as a reason for violence (Herek & Berrill, 1992).

OVERVIEW

The victimization of gays and lesbians based upon their sexual orientation includes harassment, vandalism, robbery, assault, rape and murder. The location

Infolink: A Program of the National Victim Center, (1992). *At a glance: Violence against gays and lesbians*. No. 25. Washington, D.C.: National Victim Center.

of these crimes is not restricted to dark streets leading from gay establishments. Violence against gays and lesbians occurs everywhere: in schools, the workplace, public places and in the home. Those who commit these acts come from all social/economic backgrounds and represent different age groups (National Gay and Lesbian Task Force, Safety and Fitness Exchange, Lance Bradley and Kevin Berrill, 1986).

THE SOCIETAL CONTEXT

The majority of violent acts tends to be committed by younger males. Berrill reports that "the general profile of a 'gay-basher' . . .is a young male, often acting together with other young males, all of whom are strangers to the victim(s)" (Herek & Berrill, 1992: 29). Gregory M. Herek provides a framework to explain the problem:

> "Heterosexism is defined...as an ideological system that denies, denigrates, and stigmatizes any non-heterosexual form of behavior, identity, relationship, or community. Like racism, sexism, and other ideologies of oppression, heterosexism is manifested both in societal customs and institutions...."

He continues by pointing out that one half of states outlaw consenting sex between adult homosexuals (Herek & Berrill, 1992: 89-91). Howard J. Ehrlich further expounds "...that three basic threats evoke a violent response: violations of territory or property, violations of the sacred, and violations of status...the victim's behavior or potential behavior is defined by the actor as leaving no choice but to respond with violence" (Herek & Berrill, 1992, p.108-109).

This learned behavior can be traced to subtle societal approval. Herek discusses views by gays and lesbians which advocate for a more positive portrayal of homosexual characters in the film industry (Herek & Berrill, 1992). Other sources indicate this effort has some momentum. "Frequently, homosexual characters are the murdering bad guys, from Will Paton in *No Way Out* and Al Pacino in *Cruising* to Elizabeth Ashley in *Windows* and Michael Caine and Christopher Reeve in *Deathtrap*. Just as often, they are filled with self-loathing and doom, suffering for their homosexuality, from Marlon Brando in *Reflections in a Golden Eye* and Rod Steiger in *The Sergeant* to Sandy Dennis in *The Fox*" (Gilbert, 1992).

Comstock reported that according to a *Wall Street Journal* survey, 66% of chief executive officers of Fortune-500 companies are reluctant to promote homosexuals to management level positions and, in his own survey, 77% of male first-year college students have been brought up to disapprove of homosexuality. Comstock also points to data which describe perpetrators and their scenarios of violence. Male adolescents require "recognizing and conforming to the cultural stereotype of masculinity..." and "high sex-role identification" (Comstock; 1991, p. 107-111). These developmental stages within the heterosexism model can have worse results than close-mindedness, especially as some social scientists explain social identification: "...anti-gay violence can help in-group members to feel more positive about their group and consequently about themselves as well" (Herek & Berrill, p. 160).

The victims may "perceive their offenders as representative of the dominant culture in society and an agent of that culture's stereotyping of the victim's culture" (*Serving Victims of Bias Crimes*, 1992). Although homosexuality in itself is not sufficient to compose a separate culture, it is easily understood why this attitude prevails when considering Herek's discussion of the roles religion, law and mass media play in subordinating gays and lesbians (Herek & Berrill, 1992). "Regardless of the attackers' motives, victims almost always are chosen for *what* they are rather than *who* they are. This is why anti-gay hate crimes are a form of terrorism. The attack is against the community as a whole" (Herek, 1991).

SPECIAL CONCERNS FOR VICTIMS

Similar to violence directed toward those for ethnic, religious or for any reasons found inherent in the victim's inner-self, anti-gay and lesbian violence may pit the victims against themselves. The feelings of vulnerability due to criminal reactions by others can lead to stress and self-dehumanization. The victim viewing himself, or herself, as perpetually vulnerable or that his or her existence is the cause of this violence is unhealthy and maladaptive. It is important that they not fall into the common trap of self-blame and recognize that their orientation did not lead to the attack, but rather consider "that this was not a random attack, but a pre-meditated, purposeful act aimed at...their community" (*Serving Victims of Bias Crimes*, 1992).

PROGRAMS TO REDUCE ANTI-GAY/LESBIAN VIOLENCE

A practical victim assistance/crime prevention measure was established after the hate-motivated murder of Paul Broussard of Houston, Texas on July 4, 1991. This community, proactive program allows police to escort gays to their cars in a large gay area in Houston (Hightower, 1992). The New York City Anti-Violence Project detected a 10% drop in the severity of anti-gay and lesbian attacks from 1990 to 1991 and attributed the decrease to community patrols. The project currently sponsors a program that examines and responds to violence toward those perceived or reportedly perceived to have HIV/AIDS. Berrill reports "all evidence suggests that AIDS has negatively affected the cultural climate in which anti-gay violence occurs" (Herek & Berrill, 1992: 38).

CONSIDERATIONS FOR VICTIMS

The victim has the right to *not* report an incident if he or she so chooses. If the attack requires hospitalization, medical service providers may be required to report the incident to the police. If so, the victim may identify the attack as hate-related or not. There are several arguments for reporting the incident as hate-related. Without documentation as to the prevalence of anti-gay or lesbian violence, there is less justification for legislation to be enacted which will hopefully decrease the frequency of these crimes. Just as legislation requires justification to be enacted, so do programs set up in response to specific problems. Without input from victims, community patrols or other programs may be suspended. On an interpersonal level, increased exposure to gays and lesbians may work toward dispelling negative stereotypes, and thus reduce a perceived threat to would-be offenders.

Sexual Coercion in Gay Male and Lesbian Relationships: Predictors and Implications for Support Services

Caroline K. Waterman, Lori J. Dawson, and Michael J. Bologna

Numerous studies have documented the prevalence of forced sex in heterosexual couples. Positive effects of this research include increases in awareness about the problem among helping professionals and the public, as well as increases in support services and prevention programs. However, no research has been done on sexual coercion in gay male and lesbian relationships, and few support services exist. Therefore, this study is an investigation of the prevalence and correlates of coercive sex in gay male and lesbian relationships. Participants were 36 women and 34 men who were in gay or lesbian relationships. The results indicated that 12% of the gay men and 31% of the lesbians reported being victims of forced sex by their current or most recent partners. The higher reporting rate among women may be due to greater awareness of issues pertaining to sexual abuse, and greater likelihood of identifying various forms of coercion as force. For men, being a victim of forced sex was generally associated with being a victim of other forms of violence. For both sexes, victims of forced sex believed that it would be relatively difficult to get counseling. Implications for support services are discussed.

A considerable amount of research and public attention has been focused on sexual coercion in heterosexual relationships, and numerous studies have documented the occurrence of forced sex in a substantial portion of heterosexual

Infolink: A Program of the National Victim Center, (1992). *At a glance: Violence against gays and lesbians.* No. 25. Washington, D.C.: National Victim Center.

couples. For example, Russell (1982) found that 14% of the wives in her San Francisco sample had been sexually assaulted by their husbands or ex-husbands. Similarly, Finkelhor and Yllo (1983) report that 10% of the women in the Boston survey who were married or in couples had been victims of unwanted sex from their partners. Additionally, it is important to note that men have been victims of relationship rape (Doron, 1980; Meuhlenhard & Cook, 1988). Furthermore, heterosexual relationship rape is often more traumatizing than rape by a stranger (Finkelhor & Yllo, 1985; Russell, 1982).

Research on heterosexual relationship rape has played a number of important roles. For example, such research has raised awareness about the problem among helping professionals and the general public; reduced victims' feelings that they are alone; and demonstrated the need for support services and prevention programs. Unfortunately, no research has been done on sexual coercion in gay and lesbian relationships, and few support services exist to deal with this problem. Thus, in an article in *The Advocate,* Califia (1986) calls for greater attention to problems connected with violence in gay and lesbian relationships.

Therefore, the present study was designed to investigate the prevalence and correlates of coercive sex in gay and lesbian relationships. In this study, participants were asked about incidents of "forced sex" rather than "rape," because research has shown that victims of heterosexual relationship rape frequently do not identify the experience as rape (Finkelhor & Yillo, 1985; Russell, 1982). However, one question was included to assess the extent to which gay men and lesbians viewed forced sex as rape.

The hypotheses and their rationales are as follows: a) Forced sex would be more common in relationships that involved other forms of violence than in relationships not characterized by violence (e.g., in heterosexual couples, battering has been found to be one of the strongest predictors of sexual assault (Browne, 1987; Frieze, 1983; Walker, 1979); b) Victims of forced sex would be in relationships of longer durations than people who were not victims of forced sex (i.e., there is greater opportunity for sexual coercion over time, and partners in relationships of longer durations may feel that they have a greater "right" to demand sex from their partners. Also, among heterosexuals, Kanin and Parcell (1977) found that length of relationship was a predictor of sexual aggression); c) Victims of forced sex would perceive themselves as having less power in their relationships, and fewer alternatives to their relationships, than people who are not victims of forced sex (e.g., power inequality and lack of alternatives for the victim are central concepts in the exchange/social control theory of domestic violence (Gelles, 1983); and d) Victims of forced sex would perceive greater difficulty in attaining counseling than people who were not victims of forced sex. (This hypothesis also follows from Gelles' exchange/social control theory).

METHOD

Subjects

Gay and lesbian students were recruited from the following places in the northeast: a state university, a state college, a private university, and a gay student activist conference at a state university. People were asked to participate in a study on "conflict resolution in gay and lesbian relationships." To participate, a person must have been involved in the past or at that time in a gay or lesbian relationship. One hundred and one students responded, but 31 did not fill out the "Conflict Tactics Scale" (described below) and omitted other questions as well. Thus, participants who provided usable data were 36 women and 34 men who ranged in age from 17-36, with a median age of 23.

Regarding the other 31 respondents, 9 women and 8 men answered the two questions about forced sex described below. The percentages of women and men who answered each question affirmatively did not differ significantly from the percentages of the 36 women and 34 men who comprised the sample.

Instruments

Forced sex. Participants were asked the following two questions: "Have you ever forced a partner to have sex against his/her will?" "Has your partner ever forced you to have sex against your will?"

Violence. The Straus (1979) "Conflict Tactics Scale" was used with the term "partner" substituted for "wife" and "spouse" to make the scale gender and sexual-affectional preference neutral. This scale is composed of 19 tactics that individuals can employ during a conflict. These tactics range from "discussed issue calmly" to "used knife or gun." For each tactic, respondents indicate how often the tactic was used. The "violence" part of the scale includes activities involving "the use of physical force against another person" (ibid.: 77) such as shoving, slapping, kicking, beating up and using a knife or gun. The "Conflict Tactics Scale" does not contain questions about sexual conflicts or sexual coercion. In the present study, participants were asked to fill out the scale once regarding their behavior toward their current or most recent partner and once regarding the behavior of their current or most recent partner toward them. Evidence pertaining to the reliability and validity of the "Conflict Tactics Scale" is contained in Straus.

Other dependent variables. Six 7-point Likert scales were used to assess respondents' perceptions of the following: their power in their relationship, their economic power in their relationship, how easy it would be to find another partner for a relationship, how a new relationship would compare with their current or most recent one, how easy it would be to get counseling to deal with physical aggression in their relationship, and how strongly they agreed that "forcing a partner to have sex against his/her will is rape."

RESULTS

Prevalence of forced sex

The percentages of men and women who were perpetrators and victims of forced sex in their current or most recent relationships are contained in Table 1. The difference between the percentages of men and women who reported that they forced their partners to have sex was not significant, $x^2(1, N = 70) = 16$, N.S. However, the difference between the percentages of men and women who reported that they were victims of forced sex in their relationships approached significance, $x^2(1, N = 69) = 3.44, p < .07$.

Table 1:   Percentages of men and women who were perpetrators and victims of forced sex

	Men (n=34)	Women (n=36)
Perpetrator	5.9%	8.3%
Victim	12.1%	30.6%

RELATIONSHIP BETWEEN FORCED SEX AND VIOLENCE

Table 2 contains the percentages of subjects who were victims and perpetrators of violence as a function of gender and whether or not the subject was a forced-sex victim. Men who were victims of forced sex were significantly more likely than men who were not victims of forced sex to be victims of violence, $x^2(1, N = 32) = 14.34 \, p < .001$, as well as perpetrators of violence, $x^2(1, N = 33), = 430, p < 05$. For women, neither of these effects attained significance, but there was a tendency for women who were victims of forced sex to be less

Table 2:   Percentages of subjects who were victims and perpetrators of
violence as a function of gender and forced sex victim

| | Men | | Women | |
| | Victim of Forced Sex (n = 4) | Not Victim of Forced Sex (n = 29) | Victim of Forced Sex (n = 11) | Not Victim of Forced Sex (n = 25) |
Variable				
Victim of Violence	100.0	10.3	18.2	50.0
Perpetrator of Violence	50.0	10.3	45.5	58.3

likely than women who were not victims of forced sex to be victims of violence, $x^2(1,N = 35) = 3.18, p < .08$. Thus, the first hypothesis was confirmed for men only.

OTHER DEPENDENT VARIABLES

Mean scores on each dependent variable, as a function of gender, and whether or not the person was a victim of forced sex are presented in Table 3. For each dependent measure, a 2 x 2 analysis of variance was performed.

Length of relationship. Hypothesis b (that forced sex victims would be in relationships of longer duration than people who were not forced sex victims) was not confirmed, $F(1,57) = .84$, N.S. However, the main effect for gender did attain significance, $F(1,57) = 4.15, p < .05$, with lesbians generally being in relationships longer than gay men. No statistically significant interaction was found between Gender and Forced Sex Victim, $F(1,57) = 1.61$, N.S.

Perceived power and alternatives. The data do not support hypothesis c about perceived power and alternatives. Analyses of variance revealed no significant effects on perceived power, economic power, ease of finding a new partner, and view of how a new relationship would compare with the current one.

Perceived ease of attaining counseling. As predicted in hypothesis d, there was a significant main effect for forced-sex victim, $F(1,57) 8.99, p <.01$, in that people who were victims of forced sex thought it would be more difficult to get counseling than those who were not victims of forced sex. For this

Table 3:   Means on dependent variables as a function of gender and
            forced sex victim

| | Men | | Women | |
| | Victim of Forced Sex | Not Victim of Forced Sex | Victim of Forced Sex | Not Victim of Forced Sex |
Variable	(n= 4)	(n = 23)	(n = 10)	(n = 24)
Length of relationship (in months)	20.75	8.37	18.70	18.54
Perceived power in relationship	4.00	4.13	5.20	4.29
Perceived economic power in relationship	3.25	3.78	4.10	4.33
Perceived ease of finding new partner	4.00	3.76	4.30	4.25
How think new relationship would compare with current one	3.50	4.24	3.70	3.46
Perceived ease of attaining counseling	3.00	4.78	3.60	5.00
Belief that forced sex is rape	6.67	6.57	6.80	6.82

Note: Nine subjects did not fill out these 7-point Likert scales. For each scale, high
scores indicate higher levels of the variable.

dependent measure, neither the interaction between Gender and Forced Sex
Victim nor the main effect for gender approached significance, $F(1,57) = .12$,
N.S. and $F(1,57) = .46$, N.S. respectively.

Belief that forced sex is rape. As can be seen in Table 3, the means on this
variable are uniformly very high. Analysis of variance revealed no significant
effects.

DISCUSSION

The results of this study suggest that sexual coercion is a problem for a
considerable number of gay men and lesbians. Thus, accessible support services
are needed, along with programs to promote public awareness of the problem
and the services.

The generalizability of the present findings are limited by the fact that the sample was composed of a small number of college students. Furthermore, respondents were asked to participate in a study on "conflict resolution." Therefore, this study may have attracted people who had high levels of conflict in their relationships. However, although future research on other populations would be very useful, the results suggest that support services are needed now.

In interpreting the data, it is important to note that respondents were asked about "forced" sex, and there may be considerable variability in the behaviors that respondents interpreted as constituting "force." In a study on "forced" sexual intercourse on dates, Struckman-Johnson (1988) found that some of her participants viewed psychological pressure as force. Furthermore, regarding marital rape, Finkelhor and Yllo (1983) identify varieties of coercion that do not involve physical force, such as "social coercion" and "interpersonal coercion" (p. 121). Thus, research on the varieties of sexual coercion in gay and lesbian couples is also needed.

Unit VI

Age:
The Elderly and Youth

In 1649 a young female was hanged for stealing food. She stole because she had no money and was hungry (Carrigan, 1998). In 1997, a 13-year-old Aboriginal girl from Australia was arrested and kept in an adult jail overnight. She was stealing food to feed herself and other neglected children she was caring for (Amnesty International, 1998). Proposed amendments to the Young Offenders Act *(to be renamed the* Criminal Youth Justice Act) *in 1999 will allow for easier transfer of youth, as young as fourteen, to adult court when they commit a serious crime.*

In 1996, an elderly couple were found by Calgary Police officers sitting weeping in their car with $5 between them. They ended up in this predicament after they sold their house and moved in with their son who overmedicated them with prescription drugs. Then after obtaining power of attorney the son dumped his parents on to the streets. It is estimated that 4% of seniors are victims of some form of abuse and injustice. (Scott, 1998)

Both the young and old of society are at risk within the criminal justice system. In Anglo-Saxon North American culture both groups are characterized by their inability to contribute to the economy. Young persons are deemed in need of guidance balanced with accountability while the elderly are generally thought to have learnt from life experience that crime does not pay.

Whenever a young person commits a violent crime they make front-page news. Their behaviour is considered counter to everything that childhood represents, and Canadian's are shocked and outraged at their violent acts. Incidents such as the killing of Ryan Garrioch, Reena Virik and Clayton McClough by other teenagers have been used as the vehicle upon which to call for tougher punishments and greater accountability within the youth justice system. To what extent do we risk becoming like our neighbours to the south?

According to Amnesty International (1998), the United States leads the world in child incarceration, and research over the years has repeatedly shown that 6% of teenage youth (primarily boys) account for more than half of all serious crimes. And given that the number of young persons is growing, we are "sitting atop a demographic crime bomb" (Paul, 1996). Yet, such views are juxtaposed to the observations of such organizations as UNICEF who point out that around the world young people are denied many of the rights and considerations of an adult in the criminal justice system. In their 1996 review on the rights of children, Canada was among the countries identified as requiring additional legal reforms relating to the administration and handling of young offenders (Justice for Juveniles, 1996).

Although young persons are entitled to the same rights as adults under the charter, they are treated differently when it comes to punishment. Unlike adults, young persons are not entitled to early parole nor are they entitled to a jury trial. Yet, in many cases they receive longer sentences for crimes similar to those committed by adults. Much has been said and written about the convoluted nature of the principles reflected in the Young Offenders Act. Several years ago, Susan Reid and Marge Reitsma-Street examined the act and identified four different models of juvenile justice in the declaration of principles. The sociologist James Hackler (1996) once described the act as the most complex piece of legislation in the world. Why are standards of responsibility so divergent when examined internationally. For example, Winterdyk (1997) examines six different juvenile justice models from around the world and based on his review found the minimum and maximum age of responsibility varies considerably between countries. This calls into question the social and political rationales for setting age limits.

A relatively new area of interest and concern to criminologists is the elderly. Demographic data inform us that within a few years the elderly will represent the largest segment of Canadian society. However, the criminal justice system is ill equipped to address their needs when they come into conflict with the law. As of early 1999, the last *Justice Service Bulletin* to report on crimes against the elderly dates back to 1992, Vol. 12(15)—"Elderly Victims of Violent Crime." A sad commentary given that criminals often regard older persons as easy targets for a variety of crimes (e.g., medical fraud, mail fraud schemes, retirement estates, home improvement scams and various other 'confidence' scams). In fact, the Criminal Intelligence Service of Ontario reports that many offenders have been well established and date back to the early 1950s. Some of the scam artists have set up a "family business" of sorts involving wives, sons and daughters! Yet, very little has been done to protect the elderly (Strategic intelligence…, 1998). This is, in part, complicated by the 'victim of choice' for this targeted group. Arrest and prosecution are complicated by a reluctance to report and in many cases failure to realize they have been defrauded.

Not only are we witnessing a growing number of elderly but also their numbers are rapidly increasing in the criminal justice system—in particular within prisons. One American study estimates that within a few years, nearly 10% of the inmate population will consist of offenders aged 50 or over (Bradley, 1990). Given its appeal to retirees, provinces like British Columbia might see this trend earlier. In 1992, CSC reported that a significant number of inmates aged 50 and older met the criteria for organic disorder (i.e., a mental organic brain syndrome) while the younger inmates tended to experience problems of depression, antisocial, substance or alcohol disorder (The prevalence..., 1992). Currently, there are no provisions to protect the older inmate from being exploited by younger inmates, and the system is ill equipped to address their special health and nutritional needs (Bradley, 1990). Finally, research shows that the elderly offender is more likely to commit murder and sexual offences than theft or break-and-enter. Given that the sentences for these types of crimes tend to be longer, the criminal justice system has not yet considered the financial and ethical implications of punishing the older offender.

In this unit, the first article by McKie illustrates that Canadian society is aging. This fact means that issues of elder abuse will likely become more significant. The short Infolink piece from the National Victim Center in the United States gives a quick summary of the different types of elder abuse. The report from Health Canada documents the extent of elder abuse in Canadian society and sociological factors which are correlated with it. The final article in this unit relates to youth crime issues. It investigates questions about the possible myths surrounding the notion that young crime is on the increase and that a punitive response is the answer.

Discussion Questions:

1. How is diversity among the young and old represented in the criminal justice system?
2. Are the different handling and processing orientations justified? Clarify.
3. The 1984 Beijing Rules and 1995 Riyadh Guidelines (from the United Nations International Covenant on Civil and Political Rights) say the primary aim of juvenile justice is rehabilitation and reintegration of youth into society. How has the Canadian young offender system respected/neglected this mandate?
4. Although we have always had people at both end of the age spectrum, why has the CJS been slow to respond to their respective needs?
5. What unique problems does the older offender pose for the CJS? Should they be given special considerations?

References

Amnesty International—juveniles. (1998). (Online: www.amnesty.org/ailib/intcam/juvenile/feature.htm).

Bradley, S. (1990, March). Graying of inmate population spurs corrections challenges. *On the line*, 13:5.

Carrigan, D.O. (1998). *Juvenile delinquency in Canada: A history.* Toronto: Irwin.

Hackler, J. (1996). Anglophone juvenile justice: Why Canada, England, the United States, and Australia are behind other developed countries. In J. Winterdyk (Ed.), *Issues and perspectives on young offenders in Canada.* Toronto: Harcourt Brace. (Ch. 12).

Justice for juveniles. (1996). UNICEF - The Convention of the Rights of the Child. (Online: www.unicef.org.pon96/cojustic.htm).

Paul, D. (1996, June 17). Violence with a youthful face. *Alberta Report* newsmagazine. (Online).

"The prevalence, nature and severity of mental health problems among Federal male inmates in Canadian penitentiaries." (1992). Ottawa: Correctional Service Canada.

Scott, S. (1998). Many seniors suffer some kind of abuse. (Online—www.cadvision.com/moorec/abuse.htm).

Strategic intelligence assessment on "crimes against the elderly." (1998). Criminal Intelligence Service Ontario. (Online).

Winterdyk, J. (Ed.). (1997). *Juvenile justice system: International perspectives.* Toronto: Canadian Scholars' Press. (Introduction).

Web watch: For an excellent overview into a wide variety of issues pertaining to young offenders see "The Great Young Offenders Act Debate" website at www.peelbarristers.com/~biss/pages/tgyad.htm . Relevant sites for seniors are more difficult to locate. However, the following two sites offer some interesting information: the Senior's Information Exchange at www.hc-sc.gc.ca/seniors-aines and the Canadian Association of Independent Living Centre (CAILC) at www.cailc.ca/.

The homepage for UNICEF and where one can locate links to UNICEF documents relating to the rights of young people is www.unicef.org.

Population Aging: Baby Boomers into the 21st Century

Craig McKie

Canada's population characteristics are changing rapidly and will continue to do so well into the future. The median age is higher than ever before and Canadians are becoming increasingly concentrated in older age groups. Because of this aging pattern, Canada already changed from a child-centered society to one focused on the needs, health concerns and spending priorities of baby boomers, the middle-aged majority.

Baby boomers will continue to be the largest cohort of the population until about the middle of the next century. As they get older, baby boomers will exert additional pressures on social institutions, whose services are determined, to a large extent, by the age of the public they serve.

MEDIAN AGE RISING

The median age of the population—the point at which half the population is below that age and half above—is much higher now than at the beginning of the century. In 1992, the median age of Canadians was 33.8 years, compared with 23.9 years in 1921. The only period of decline in median age over this time

McKie, C. (1993). Population aging: Baby boomers into the 21st century. *Canadian Social Trends, Catalogue No. 11-008*, (Summer), 2-6. Statistics Canada information is used with the permission of the Minister of Industry, as Minister responsible for Statistics Canada. Information on the availability of the wide range of data from Statistics Canada can be obtained from Statistics Canada's Regional Offices, its World Wide Web site at http://www.statcan.ca, and its toll-free access number 1-800-263-1136.

was between 1952 and 1966, when it dropped from 27.7 years to a postwar low of 25.4 years. Since 1970, however, the median age has climbed sharply and, at current low birthrates and moderate net migration levels, this trend is expected to continue well into the next decade.

In 1992, the median age of women (34.6 years) was 1.7 years higher than that of men (32.9 years). For the first half of the century, however, the median age of women had been lower than that of men. This was due to relatively high mortality rates among young women, who often died during childbirth. In 1921, the median age of women was 23.2 years, compared with 24.7 years for men. In 1953, the median ages of men and women were equal (27.6 years). By 1968, the median age of women had surpassed that of men by one year. Since then, the gap has been growing.

LOW FERTILITY RATE CONTRIBUTES TO RISING MEDIAN

Many factors have contributed to the rising median age in Canada. Medical and technological advances have all but eliminated most infectious diseases responsible for high mortality rates among children earlier in the century. In addition, health care has improved, in general, and has become more accessible to the public. During the past two decades, however, one of the major factors contributing to the increase in the median age has been a low fertility rate among women. In 1970, the year that Canada's median age started climbing sharply again, women's total fertility rate (the average number of children born to a woman in her lifetime) fell below replacement level. (The replacement level is the fertility rate necessary to maintain the current size of the population without immigration). For the past 22 years, the fertility rate has remained below replacement level (2.1), averaging about 1.7 births per woman of child-bearing age. Low fertility rates are likely to continue, despite a modest echo of the baby boom during the late 1980s and early 1990s as baby boomers had their own children. Between 1988 and 1992, the annual number of births was about 35,000 above the previous 10-year average. It is not likely that this mini-boom will last much longer: a similar mini-boom occurred in the United States, but has already passed its peak.

PROVINCIAL MEDIAN AGES CONVERGING

While all provincial populations are aging, there are differences in the speed of the change and in the current provincial median ages. These differences are, in large part, the legacy of past immigration and migration trends, as well as lifestyle, environmental and health care experiences. During the past 22 years, however, the lowest and highest provincial median ages have converged. By 1992, the gap had fallen to 4.0 years from 7.4 years in 1970.

Newfoundland residents had the lowest median age of any province in 1992 (31.0 years). The median was also relatively low in Alberta, at 31.7 years. Provinces with the highest median ages were British Columbia (35.0 years) and Quebec (34.5 years).

Twenty-two years earlier, Newfoundland also had the lowest median age (20.4 years), and British Columbia, the highest (27.8 years). Between 1970 and 1992, however, the provincial median ages increased by varying amounts. Without exception, increases were relatively high in the Atlantic provinces and Quebec compared to Ontario and the Western provinces. For example, over the 22 years, Newfoundland's median age rose almost 11 years, the largest provincial increase. The median age climbed by 10 years in New Brunswick and by just over 8 years in Prince Edward Island and Nova Scotia. In comparison, the median age in Manitoba increased 6.4 years and the median ages in the other three Western provinces rose about 7 years.

In Ontario, the median age of the population rose 6.9 years from 1970 to 1992, a reflection, in part, of high immigration levels. Quebec's median age rose sharply from 1970 to 1992 (9.3 years), mainly because of a very rapid reduction in the birthrate in that province. Until the mid-1980s, Quebec's median age always had been lower than Ontario's. By 1987 however, the median age of Quebec residents exceeded that of Ontario residents. In just 22 years, Quebec's median age went to 6 months higher than Ontario's from about 2 years lower.

MEDIAN AGE WILL GET EVEN HIGHER

All current Statistics Canada's population projections suggest a continuation of the rapid aging process. The median age of the population will continue to rise sharply and will reach 49.9 years in 2036.

According to all projections, women's median age will continue to be higher than men's, a reflection of women's higher life expectancy. In addition, the gap between women's and men's median ages will widen. The median age of women in 2036 is 52.1 years, compared with 47.8 years for men (a gap of 4.3 years, compared with 1.7 years in 1992).

AGING OF THE BABY BOOMERS

The process of aging, and the longer life expectancy of women compared to men, has already produced dramatic changes in the age and gender distribution of the Canadian population. The number of working-age people as a proportion of the total population in particular, has almost reached an historic high. Unprecedented growth in the number of seniors, however, is projected to occur in the future.

In 1991, of the total population of about 27 million, 21% were under age 15, 48% were aged 15-44, 20% were aged 45-64 and 12% were seniors aged 65 and over. This contrasts sharply with the 1961 distribution. That year, 34% of the population were children under age 15, while just 8% were seniors.

Furthermore, according to projections, modified to include the most recent data (a 1991 total fertility rate of 1.84, a 1992 immigration level of 250,000 and emigration of 86,886), the age distribution will continue to change dramatically. In 2036, 16% of the population will be under age 15 and 37% will be aged 15-44. In contrast, older people of working age (45-64) will account for 24% of the population by 2036, while those aged 65 and over will make up 22%.

The number of seniors is projected to increase much more rapidly than the number of younger people. Between 1992 and 2036, the number of children under age 15 and the number of young working-age people (15-44) will remain about the same (6.4 million and 14.3 million). The number of older people of working age (45-64), however, will increase to 9.4 million. As a result, the working-age population (aged 15-64) is expected to increase 28% between 1992 and 2036. This increase is small compared with expected growth in the senior population (those aged 65 and over). From 1992 to 2036, the number of seniors will increase 168% to 8.7 million. Among people aged 90 and over, the growth rate will be even faster. Between 1992 and 2036, their numbers are projected to multiply almost five times to 480,000 (362,000 women and 118,000 men).

IMPLICATIONS OF THE CHANGING DISTRIBUTION

As the baby-boom generation ages and the size of the population of young people remains constant or declines, many aspects of our society and economy will change. The needs and priorities of the dominant age group will likely shift the focus of public policy, alter the composition of the labour force, and change the nature of privately and publicly provided goods and services.

Pension plans will likely be more stressed in the future because a large number of baby boomers will reach retirement age at about the same time. By 2010, the oldest baby boomers will have reached age 65, the conventional age of retirement. Unlike members of earlier generations, both men and women of the baby-boom generation have high labour force participation rates. Consequently, by the time they retire, many will have large public pension plan entitlements, as well as employment pensions and Registered Retirement Savings Plans. Pressure on pension plans will be further exacerbated by a decline, or stagnation, in the number of contributors to these plans.

As the population ages, the future supply of people for the labour force may be limited, especially for some occupations. The younger working-age population will be depended upon to provide many services for the rapidly increasing senior population. Some of these services, such as those provided by police, fire fighters or construction workers, require a level of physical strength and agility that is most prevalent in young people. It is possible, therefore, that labour shortages could occur in these types of occupations.

Finding caregivers for seniors will become a more pressing problem as the population ages. Today's small families may find their capacity to provide care for elderly relatives severely limited, both because of family size and the geographic dispersion of family members. Thus, additional institutional facilities, as well as new approaches to care for seniors may be required in the future.

Also, interprovincial migration associated with retirement has begun and is anticipated to increase. British Columbia, for example, has already become a popular destination for seniors. Concentrations of older people in specific areas would require very age-specific services from both public and private sectors.

At a Glance:
Elder Abuse

Infolink: National Victim Center

- According to the U.S. Census, 20.2 million people—or 12 percent of all Americans—are over 65 years of age. Approximately one out of every 25 elderly persons is victimized annually. (Heisler, C. J., 1991)
- Elders are more likely than younger victims to be victimized by offenders with guns or other weapons, and to be victims of violent crimes at the hands of strangers. In addition, elders are twice as likely as younger persons to be victimized at or near their homes. (Commonwealth of Pennsylvania, 1988)

BACKGROUND

According to the Attorney General's Family Violence Task Force, references to elder abuse can be traced throughout Greek mythology, the writings of Shakespeare and modern literature. Yet, it has only been in the last twenty years that serious attention has been given to family violence and elder abuse. Perhaps, at least in part, this elevated consciousness can be attributed to the increasing numbers of aging Americans (Pennsylvania Attorney General's Family Violence Task Force Report, 1988).

Infolink: A Program of the National Victim Center, (1992). *At a glance: Elder abuse.* No. 18.

An important step towards recognizing elder abuse occurred in 1978 when Suzanne Steinmetz presented her research on the abuse of the elderly to the Congressional Subcommittee hearings on domestic violence. Her testimony prompted the House Select Committee on Aging, chaired by the late U.S. Representative Claude Pepper, to further examine the mistreatment of the elderly. The "Pepper Committee" subsequently introduced the term "elder abuse," and alerted the nation to the widespread severity of this problem (Pennsylvania Attorney General's Family Violence Task Force Report, 1988).

OVERVIEW

The effects of the baby boom and increased life expectancy have both contributed to the immediate and projected increase in the number of elderly Americans. It is estimated that by the year 2000, those over the age of 50 will account for one-half of the population. Medical advances and the implementation of "protective legislation" have greatly increased the length of life for many Americans (Griffin & Williams, 1992: 19).

Yet, other simultaneous societal changes may have contributed to the predisposition of some individuals to become abusive towards the elderly. In previous generations extended family members could share the responsibility of caring for the aging. However, increased mobility, strained economic times and smaller nuclear families have limited familial resources. Currently, the responsibility of elder care usually falls on a select few (Griffin & Williams, 1992: 20).

The definitions and statistics regarding elder abuse vary. They range from estimates that one out of ten persons living with a family member is subject to abuse—approximately 2.5 million a year (Griffin & Williams, 1992: 20)—to 1 in 25 elderly persons being victimized annually (Heiser, 1991). Still others conclude that 3.6 percent of our nation's elderly citizens are victims of abuse each year (Pennsylvania Attorney General's Family Violence Task Force Report, 1988). Most researchers agree that the abuse of the elderly fall within the five following categories: *physical abuse, sexual abuse, psychological abuse, financial abuse* and *neglect*.

PHYSICAL ABUSE

"Non-accidental physical force that results in injury" (Pennsylvania Attorney General's Family Violence Task Force Report, 1988).

Indicators:

- fractures and dislocations;
- lacerations and abrasions;
- burns;
- injuries to the head, scalp, face; and/or
- bruises—on upper arms (from shaking), around wrists or ankles (from being tied down), in shapes similar to objects, inside of thighs or arms (Bloom, 1989: 41).

Physical frailty, decreased physical ability, and vision and audio impairments make older persons especially susceptible to physical abuse (NOVA, 1985).

Sexual Abuse

"Non-consensual sexual contact" (Pennsylvania Attorney General's Family Violence Task Force Report, 1988).
Indicators:

- sexually transmitted diseases; and/or
- pain, itching, bleeding or bruising in the genital area.

As elderly victims are less physically able, often all that is needed to subdue them during a sexual assault is intimidation by physical force (Muram, Miller, & Cutler, 1992).

Psychological Abuse

"Infliction of mental anguish by threat, intimidation, humiliation, or other such conduct" (Pennsylvania Attorney General's Family Violence Task Force Report, 1988).
Indicators:

- low self-esteem;
- overly anxious or withdrawn;
- extreme changes in mood;
- depression;
- suicidal behavior; and/or
- confusion or disorientation (Bloom, 1989:41).

Diminished ability to cope with stress, termed a "decrease in homeostatic capacity," as well as the state of "chronic loss" that often accompanies aging (i.e., loss of one's home, peers, spouse, etc.), renders elders susceptible to psychological abuse.

FINANCIAL ABUSE

"Unauthorized use of funds or property" (Pennsylvania Attorney General's Family Violence Task Force Report, 1988).

Financial abuse or exploitation involves the theft or conversion of money or property belonging to an elder, accomplished by force, misrepresentation, or other illegal means often by taking advantage of the elder's partial or total lack of legal competency (Hyman, 1990: 6).

The loss of what may appear to be a minimal amount of money to some may account for a substantial loss for an elder person. It may result in the elder having to go without food, medication, or possibly his or her apartment.

NEGLECT

"Failure to fulfill a caretaking obligation" (Pennsylvania Attorney General's Family Violence Task Force Report, 1988).

Indicators:

- poor personal hygiene;
- signs of overmedication, undermedication,
- and/or misuse of medication (Bloom, 1989: 42);
- incontinent elder dressed in soiled clothing;
- elder left alone and deprived of stimulation and affection (Skeates and Douglas, 1990); and/or
- malnutrition (Bloom, 1989: 42).

The different types of neglect include the following:

Active Neglect. willful failure to provide care.

Passive Neglect: inadequate knowledge or infirmity of caretaker, resulting in non-willful failure to provide care.

Self-neglect: failure of elder to care for her or himself (Pennsylvania Attorney General's Family Violence Task Force Report, 1988).

In addition to the abuse that elderly persons are subject to by relatives and/or caretakers in their homes or in institutions, they may also become targets for criminal victimization. Contrary to popular assumptions that elderly citizens are disproportionately victims of crime as a result of their physical limitations, in reality, they are the *least* victimized age group. Yet, further examination does reveal that elderly persons may be subject to more severe crimes, and that they are more fearful of crime; thus the consequences of victimization are often more detrimental (Pennsylvania Attorney General's Family Violence Task Force Report, 1988).

The low victimization rate for elderly persons may be explained by their lifestyles, which limit the amount of time they spend out in the evening and their contact with likely offenders. However, this does not safeguard them from becoming victims of serious crimes. Research indicates that personal larceny with contact (pocket-picking, purse snatching), a significant and dangerous crime as it involves both theft and personal contact, is the most common crime against elderly Americans. Robbery, inclusive of both theft and assault, is second in frequency. In addition, the following are further aspects that characterize the severity of crimes against the elderly:

- Elders are twice as likely as younger persons to be victimized in or near their homes.
- Elders are more often victimized by offenders with weapons, including firearms.
- Elders are more likely than younger persons to be victims of violent crime perpetrated by strangers.
- Elders suffer greater physical, psychological, and financial loss when victimized.
- Elders are more easily injured, heal more slowly, are less resilient emotionally, and are less financially stable than younger victims (Pennsylvania Attorney General's Family Violence Task Force Report, 1988).

As the number of aging Americans continues to increase, the abuse and victimization of the elderly will become a national problem of even greater proportion. Effective programs to detect elder abuse and to treat its victims are necessary and should be established in every community.

Intergenerational Conflict and the Prevention of Abuse Against Older Persons: Final Report to Health Canada

J.A. Tindale, J.E. Norris, R. Berman, and S. Kuiack

INTRODUCTION

In this report the literature on elder abuse has been examined to ask two pointed questions. Is it likely that the social construction of parent-child relationships over the family life cycle is associated with child-to-parent elder abuse later on? If so, are there preventive strategies that families and practitioners can consider? The answer to both questions is yes. These questions stem from the literature that looks at what happens when adult children continue to need support beyond the point where both generations might have expected it (Norris & Tindale, 1994). This literature has been extended in the current study. Areas of potential conflict were explored within typical families, and consideration was given to how such conflicts might be resolved. The assumption, based on available research (Norris & Tindale, 1994), was that most families manage their differences non-abusively. The link between family relationship history and present or future developments in those relationships has not been seriously considered in the literature on adult parent-child relations (Whitbeck, Hoyt & Huck, 1994). This lapse is particularly important in the area of elder abuse.

Tindale, J., Norris, J., Berman, R., & Kuiack, S. (1994). *Intergenerational conflict and the prevention of abuse against older persons: A final report to Health Canada*. Ottawa: Minster of Supply and Services Canada.

The data analysed here extend the analysis to those families who find intergenerational support difficult. When the relationship circumstances of those families are explored, it can be argued that perceived inequities in the exchange of support are likely to be important contributors when there is family violence. Within an intergenerational context, this violence is likely to manifest itself in elder abuse.

Society expects that parents will nurture their young children and that these children will reciprocate with affection. Society also expects that children will become increasingly autonomous, and will not require the active nurturance of their parents beyond late adolescence. Love is expected to remain; significant contributions of tangible assistance are not. Nevertheless, as several authors have noted recently (e.g., Norris & Tindale, 1994), children often become only semi-autonomous, relying upon their parents for help well into their young adulthood and beyond. Various factors have contributed to this situation: the international economic recession that has lasted several years and been accompanied by significant job losses; an increase in the number of students extending their education beyond high school; high divorce rates; and more single mothers.

Asking and giving among adult generations requires negotiation between parents and children and between spouses. This is particularly important when families have not anticipated that such a situation would come about, and are unsure as to how it can be managed. Even with open communication, however, strain can still result and sometimes that strain produces conflict. Nevertheless, within normally functioning families, characterized by strong attachment relations, strain and conflict are resolved in the course of the family learning mutual, and thereby sustainable, interaction patterns (Patterson, 1982; 1986).

The analyses that follow:

- explore the status of current theorizing on elder abuse;
- suggest that this literature neglects the importance of the ways in which parent-child relationships are constructed;
- review the scant literature available that places elder abuse in a cross-cultural context;
- discuss data which do suggest links between the evolution of the parent-child relationship and the possibility of subsequent abusive relations;
- look further at these data to lend credence to the notion that cultural variations in the meanings families give to their expectations regarding

parent-child relations can shed light on why these relationships sometimes become abusive; and

- present suggestions for professional practitioners, families and those engaged in advocacy which are a beginning in the process of prevention.

A Familial Context for Literature on Elder Abuse

According to a recent national survey, four percent of the elderly are maltreated in Canada (Podnieks, Pillemer, Nicholson, Shillington, & Frizzell, 1989). Some of these abused elderly are mistreated by a son or daughter. What leads an adult child to abuse his or her parent(s)? While a number of theories/ factors have been used to explain elder abuse, the ones that focus on family relationships, in particular those that consider the parent-child relationship history, will be presented here.

Relationship Crises

The evidence to support the intergenerational transmission of family violence is limited, especially with respect to adult children retaliating against their now elderly parents. Griffin and Williams (1992), however, do point out that Steinmetz (1978) found that only one child out of 400 raised in a non-abusive home was abusive to his or her parent after reaching adulthood, while one of every two adults who were abused as children abused their elderly parents when they became adults.

What is the history of such abusive parent-child relationships? The term "filial crisis" is designed to convey the sense that parent-child conflicts that began in adolescence often continue into later life. This kind of relationship history has not received much research attention that carries the phenomenon forward into old age. Nevertheless, Godkin, Wolf and Pillemer (1989) suggest that complex and long-term family problems and unresolved conflicts are likely tied up with elder abuse. These researchers found that families in which abuse occurs are more likely to have emotional problems that contribute to interpersonal difficulties. They state that "given the emotional and interpersonal problems of both parties, it is perhaps likely that a shared living arrangement becomes a 'pressure-cooker' situation that leads to abuse" (p. 223).

SOCIAL EXCHANGE/WEB OF DEPENDENCIES

Griffin and Williams (1992) suggest that the most commonly cited risk factor for elder maltreatment is stress on caregivers created by dependent elderly people. Godkin and colleagues (1989), however, argue that it is in fact the dependencies on part of the abuser that may lead to abuse. Abusers have been found to be financially and emotionally dependent on their victims (Godkin and colleagues, 1989; Pillemer, 1985). And while Ward and Spitze (1992) assert that, generally, co-residence does not have a negative effect on parent-adult child relations, housing dependence was found by Pillemer (1985) to be a factor that contributed to abuse. It is important to emphasize at this point that it is not simply co-residency that leads to abuse but, rather, the problem may lie in the fact that, people with a poor relationship history are living under the same roof.

Godkin and colleagues (1989) note that perceived power is intrinsic to the concept of exchange and offer that attempts by the dependent caretaker to restore the power balance may result in this adult child using violence. Pillemer (1991) argues that while the available evidence cannot accurately discern who is dependent on whom, it does appear that a serious imbalance of power in either direction may lead to a risk of abuse. If we are to know why a power imbalance has arisen in a parent-child relationship, we must have a grasp of the meanings people give to their family relationships.

SYMBOLIC INTERACTIONISM AND THE CONSTRUCTION OF RELATIONSHIPS

Symbolic interactionism can be applied to the issue of violence to shed light on the different meanings of violence that people hold and the consequences these meanings have in various situations (McDonald, Hornick, Robertson, & Wallace, 1991 citing Gelles, 1979). These meanings emerge as family members construct their relationships with each other (Cheal, 1991). The Symbolic Interactionist framework encompasses relationship development and the meanings that those who are involved construct. In this framework, the meaning of the relationship will determine the importance attributed to any particular behaviour. For example, it is more important to know whether parents perceive their relationship with their children to be equitable (and vice versa), than it is to know that the two generations are co-residing.

While the meaning of family relationships has been briefly conceptualized in the elder abuse literature, not very much work has been done that links the construction of those relationships to the possibility of later life conflict and abuse.

ATTACHMENT IN THE PARENT-CHILD RELATIONSHIP

The parent-child relationship is normally characterized by feelings of attachment that mediate the multitudinous exchanges that occur between the generations on an ongoing basis (Bowlby, 1969). A secure attachment allows the child to create a mental representation or "working model" of a good relationship. This model guides choices about how to manage interactions with others, both within families, and in the broader social world (Main, Kaplan, & Cassidy, 1985). It should be remembered that the majority of individuals of any age has had secure attachment experiences as children, and manage their current relationships in a manner that generally can be considered to be functionally sound.

One very significant outcome of strong bonds of attachment within the family is the capacity to negotiate and exchange support when it is required. Within such families, there is open communication about differences and a sense that, in the long run, help given and received are balanced. This is the essence of the conceptualization of global reciprocity in well functioning intergenerational families.

Attachment theory has not been considered in the literature on elder abuse, although it has been mentioned in connection with child abuse. Children raised by abusive parents are likely to show evidence of insecure relationships as adults (Goldberg, 1991). As well, they are more likely than securely attached adults to have problems in parenting their own children (Main, Kaplan, & Cassidy, 1985). This suggests that attachment problems may predispose families to a pattern of abuse that is transmitted down through the generations.

These findings suggest that an attachment perspective may be a useful way of understanding the history of the parent-child relationship. For example, it may be that some caregivers become abusive whereas others do not because there is a weak bond of attachment between parent and child. Cicirelli's (1983; 1991) research on caregiving children provides support for this perspective. He has found that feelings of secure attachment on the part of children are likely to lead to protective (i.e., caregiving) behaviours if parents become dependent (Cicirelli, 1983). Presumably, these protective behaviours would guard against the potential for abuse even when other factors might predict it.

A critical feature of intergenerational family relationships, and a dimension generally ignored in the literature on elder abuse, relates to the relationship children have with their siblings and the conditions under which perceptions of inequity between brothers and sisters can be contributing factors to abusive behaviour directed at parents.

THE SIBLING RELATIONSHIP

Siblings bonds have been shown to be important influences on children's development. As well, they may provide the most long-lasting attachment experiences that anyone may have: sibs share ties and experiences from birth or early childhood through until old age and death (Norris & Tindale, 1994). Nevertheless, sibling issues have not received any attention within the literature on elder abuse. Recent work on the "non-shared environment" of siblings, for example, may be instructive (Dunn & Plomin, 1991). This work notes that, despite what parents may say, they treat each of their children differently. This suggests that children who feel they have never been favoured by their parents may be more likely to mistreat them in old age than would their favoured sibs. When there are step-, half- or adoptive siblings within the same family, all attempting to manage the care of parents, the situation may be complicated further. In talking about the various interrelationships within parent-child relations, much of the literature assumes majority cultural settings. The fact that there has not been much research into ethnic variations in the occurrence of elder abuse does not diminish the fact that the evidence to date suggests cultural meanings in relationships are important.

ETHNIC VARIATIONS

There is a lack of research on ethnic differences in patterns of elder neglect and abuse in Canada. McDonald and co-workers (1991) mention ethnicity only twice: once to assert that elder abuse occurs across ethnic, social and socioeconomic strata, and for a second time when they cite Phillips and Rempusheski (1985) surrounding reasons why practitioners do not label a situation as abusive; cultural stereotypes influence their definitions. While some large survey studies on ethnicity and elder abuse are under way in both Canada (Canadian Association of Social Workers, 1993), and the United States (Griffen & Williams, 1992), authors Ogg and Munn-Giddings (1993) lament that "ethnicity is rarely mentioned in any [elder abuse] studies, indicating an almost total lack of knowledge."

It is even more rare when ethnicity is a specific focus of a study on abusive adult children. One example of such research (Anetzberger, 1987) considered the history of family violence among Americans sharing an Appalachian background. Appalachian communities typically are not well off economically, their people are often not well educated, and they live in isolated rural and mountainous settings in and near the state of Tennessee. Two important dimensions of this research are particularly relevant to this study. Parental abuse of children greatly increased the likelihood that the children, in turn, would later abuse their parents. Such relationship histories were common among study participants and this contributed to a culturally defined acceptance of elder abuse as expected, even if not desirable. And secondly, the likelihood that children would abuse parents was increased when there was long-term adult co-residency between parents and children.

Although these research findings are important, there are far too few studies involving both relationship histories and cultural variations. Indeed, comparative literature on family relationships is impeded as a significant body of research does not exist. As well, there is a need for longitudinal studies of relationship histories, and sensitivity in interpreting culturally diverse data (Cicirelli, 1994). Clearly, the areas of relationship patterns over time and ethnic variability in the meaning given to those relationships deserve much more attention.

REDIRECTING RESEARCH EFFORTS

A major reason for the lack of extensive research on elder abuse is the reluctance of victims to report their mistreatment. As Wahl and Purdy (1991) have noted, there are five possible reasons for older persons' hesitancy in disclosing abuse: they fear retaliation from the abuser; they are dependent upon the abuser for care; they fear institutionalization; they are ashamed to report that a family member is abusing them; and they believe that police and social agencies cannot help them. Such strong feelings make it unlikely that older victims will be willing to discuss abuse with researchers, even when confidentiality or anonymity is assured.

A possible solution to this problem is to move the focus of research into elder abuse to an earlier period in the family life cycle. Most studies of elder abuse have examined currently abusive situations and identified correlates (e.g., frailty of the elder, dependency of the abuser). An alternative strategy is to consider predictors and potential risk factors as they emerge in developing families. This would link the research to the large, and overlapping, bodies of literature on child abuse and spousal assault which gerontological researchers usually overlook. Perhaps more importantly, a life-span view of elder abuse would encourage researchers to examine areas of conflict which, in well-functioning families, are managed successfully and do not lead to abuse. Determining problematic issues and "homegrown" strategies for dealing with them could be quite valuable in the identification of older families at risk for abuse as well as suggesting methods of re-mediation where abuse already occurs. The research reported here reflects a first attempt at this redirection of efforts.

CONFLICT AND THE POTENTIAL FOR ABUSE

Statistics indicate that most families are not abusive. Indeed, intergenerational families typically provide a great deal of support for their members (Norris & Tindale, 1994; Seniors Secretariat, 1993). This is not to say, however, that support never requires negotiation, or never has strings attached. There are areas of strain and conflict within even the most supportive of families. One goal of the research reported here was to examine these potentially problematic areas and determine within a group of well-functioning families with young adult children:

1. why serious conflict does not normally occur;
2. the relationship circumstances where conflict does emerge; and
3. the conditions under which conflict could escalate rather than lead to resolution.

To explore possible differences among ethnic groups on any of these issues, this study included a sample of 10 Italian-Canadian and 10 Anglo Canadian families (Tindale, Norris, Kuiack, & Humphrey, 1993). These families met the following inclusion criteria: parents in an intact relationship with at least one child over the age of 18 and under the age of 40. Interviews with both generations of the 20 families yielded 70 completed responses. These interviews were carried out in the respondents' homes and probed the type, extent and impact of assistance exchanged by adult children and their parents. The support discussed could be either tangible (e.g., money) or intangible (e.g., advice).

All 20 families reported the extension of tangible aid in each direction. As it was extended from parents to children, tangible aid included shelter, school tuition, car repair and financial loans. Intangible support primarily involved advice and moral support. Children, in turn, reported giving their parents tangible help in the form of labour, such as house or pet sitting and yard work. Unique to the Italian sample was assistance given in the translation of English documents. Interestingly, there was only one notable gender difference for help extended by either generation: unlike Anglo fathers, mothers and daughters, the sons in this group did not report providing any intangible support. This suggests one source of strain within Anglo families.

In the great majority of families, conflict was not reported. Only 2 of 9 young adult daughters reported that assistance had had a negative impact on the relationship. Similarly, when asked, only 4 of 28 young adult children reported that their giving help to parents resulted in conflict. The sources of conflict can be characterized as relating to:

- co-residency,
- gender and intangible support,
- perceived parent-child inequities, and
- perceived sibling inequities.

Co-residency

One marker of the transition to adulthood in Western society is achieving residential independence. Moving away from home evokes changes in family dynamics. Social roles and relationships of parents and their adult offspring are challenged and altered. Studies of the impact of gaining autonomy from parents, or alternatively from children, have been conducted. Researchers have good understanding of the impact of the 'empty-nest' on parents as well as the impact of children's autonomy on parent-adult child interaction, relationship quality and individual well-being. Returning home, however, although it also creates changing family dynamics, has not been well researched.

The phenomenon of returning home after attempting residential autonomy is becoming more common (see Norris & Tindale, 1994, for a more detailed discussion). The current social and economic climate with increased marital dissolution, poor job prospects and increased enrolment in higher education has led many offspring to choose to return home in order to recover from an ill-fated first attempt. When adult offspring move back into the parental home after what seemed to be a successful launching, this can place a strain on the parent-child relationship. Research has indicated that, although co-residence of parents and adult children is not rare, it is not the preferred living situation for any family member (Ward & Spitze, 1992). Nevertheless, there is not enough research into the impact of co-residence on family relationships to conclude that this living arrangement can in itself lead to abuse, or even to increased conflict.

One interesting finding in the current analysis of 20 families was that the impact of co-residence is affected by both the gender and the generation of family members. The majority of both Anglo and Italian fathers did not report feeling that having a previously launched child return home was particularly stressful. In addition, all the Italian mothers who experienced the return of an adult child reported that it was a positive experience. Anglo mothers, however, did feel that having "boomerang" children was difficult. These women noted that it was stressful to have to change parenting style or expectations to accommodate an adult child. The ethnic and family role variation in the experience of co-residence indicates that it is the nature of, or the expectations for, the family relationship which is the key to understanding how co-residence can cause strain within the family.

Boomerang children are also semi-autonomous adults. Returning home means that parents, the child and any other significant others (i.e., peers of the child and the parents) all have to reassess the level of autonomy that should be accorded this child. Differences of opinion on this point between parent and child can be a source of stress. Nevertheless, these data underscore the point that even those family members who find the situation particularly stressful (i.e., Anglo mothers) generally accommodate themselves to the new arrangement.

The source of the stress also has a bearing on how difficult it is to manage. Is it the shared home and reduced privacy which cause unease or is it the character of the parent-child relationship? The results of this study suggest the latter may be most important. As one Anglo parent commented: "For our youngest one to come back it was often more of a burden. He tended to be rather dependent, and he didn't always come back because we asked him to."

Another Anglo parent held a similar view: "The youngest child, it was a bit more difficult having him home. Having an adult living at home who behaves like a child still, that complicates things."

There are insufficient data to argue that birth order is a critical issue, although this may indeed be the case. The central point here is that parents can manage co-residency more easily with some of their children than they can with others.

Although other research indicates that living away from one's parents is the preferred arrangement for adult offspring, this study indicated that there are ethnic variations in the circumstances surrounding the decision to leave home in the first place. Two Italian parents, for example, indicated the difficulty they had in coming to terms with their children leaving home:

She's my first born and I think the first person to make the
adjustment to leave home. That was kind of an emotional trauma,
I think, for the entire family. If I had forbidden her to do it, she
would not have done it. In your mind you can balance it, but your
heart sometimes doesn't always see it the same way.

None have moved back, because if they move out once they no
come back no more. That's that, before they move out they got to
think about it, that's that.

One Italian daughter explained why she chose to remain living at home: "If
I moved out, my mom would cry."

Likewise, there is ethnic variation in response to the decision to return
home. One Italian father saw his child's decision to move home as a sign that
they had provided a good home: "At least we know that we are in touch or else
they won't come back. A person won't come back to me or to anybody unless
there is some love there."

The interesting contrast in the experience of co-residence for the Anglo
and Italian parents provides insight into the reasons why co-residence in itself
cannot be identified as leading to abuse. For the Anglo sample, mothers
indicated that having an adult child move home was a source of stress. The
Italian parents noted, however, that an adult child considering moving out can
cause family stress while his or her return can confirm the parents' view that
they have a loving home. The Italian children may respond to their parents'
views by feeling that they have little choice but to remain at home. For the
offspring as a group (i.e., both Anglos and Italians), stressors can result from
the decision to leave home, from a sense that one cannot leave home, or from
a belief that one cannot return home. Thus, the nature of the parent-adult child
relationship and the quality of family communication provide insights into
how stressors related to co-residence can be managed successfully.

Consider co-residency from the perspective of the children. Of the Anglo
offspring in this study who moved back into the parental home, all reported the
experience as having a negative impact on the relationship with the parents.
Areas of conflict included losing one's adult status and privacy, and
experiencing guilt for intruding on the parents. As did their parents, the offspring
stated that these situations had been resolved in such a way that there were no
long-term consequences for their relationships. One Anglo child made the
point that he had moved back home, and they needed to make it work: "I think
we realized it was sink or swim. I mean, we either found some compromise or
ruin everything for good."

For the Italian offspring, only 2 of the 13 who moved out and then returned home reported that the experience was negative. For one daughter, returning to a busy household after having been on her own required some adjustment: "When I came back home I found that there are so many voices and the phone's ringing off the hook and I was just used to being by myself. Actually, I am having a hard time."

Another Italian daughter found renegotiating her autonomy while in her parents' home the source of difficulty: "When I came back home, I was never really home very often in the evening. So I think (my father) found that really difficult, because he didn't understand why I wasn't in."

One Italian daughter reported that her relationship with her parents did not change with her returning home, but this in itself created a problem. Speaking for herself and other adult offspring in the home, she indicated that the lack of change in the parents' expectations was a source of stress: "They still complain about us coming in after a certain time and we don't think they should. You know, they really don't have the right because we're all adults now, but they still do."

A unique problem associated with moving back home was raised by another Italian daughter. Her role prior to moving out was to translate English documents for her parents. Despite demonstrating their ability to manage without her assistance, upon her return home the parents expected her to resume this role. Providing this assistance to her parents led the daughter to question her decision to come back:

> Sometimes I feel that my father, realizing that I am living here, it's really easy now for him to be less independent. I'm sometimes questioning. Are you asking me to do this because you really don't understand? Or is it because I can get it done in half the time. In that respect I wonder if I'm doing him a favour, am I doing the right thing?

In high-functioning families, stressors such as co-residence have negative, although not permanent, implications for the relationship. These data suggest, however, that families with poor communication skills or dysfunctional parent-child relations may not be able to resolve the conflict caused by co-residence. In such cases, there is an increased likelihood that the conflict could fester, and escalate: elder abuse then could be one possible outcome.

GENDER AND THE GIVING OF EMOTIONAL SUPPORT

This study revealed an interesting relationship between gender and intangible support. As noted above, no Anglo son reported providing intangible support to the parents. This has been well supported in the literature (although no attention has been given to the effects of ethnicity): sons provide tangible support to their parents while distancing themselves emotionally. One daughter in our study noted: "I am there if they need to talk to me (my brother) is there as well, but he helps out in other ways, like helping my father with building things."

It has been speculated that this distancing is a buffer to stress and burnout for sons when parents become more dependent on their offspring for assistance in their later years. Daughters, on the other hand, often do not have this buffer and are deeply involved with their parents' emotional care (Myles, 1991).

To the degree that some sons are distanced and daughters are involved, the risk of greater strain on female caregivers is increased. If the source of this strain is not addressed and resolved, either in a re-negotiation of the parent-child relationship, or by outside intervention, then the distancing of sons could contribute to an increase in the risk of abuse by the daughter. This situation also points to potential conflict among siblings regarding care for their parents.

For the Italian sample, no gender differences in the provision of intangible support were found. There is no literature that helps to explain this difference between ethnic groups. Nevertheless, a recurrent theme in the comments of the Italian families was that both tangible and intangible types of support were expected and received by all within the Italian network. This was articulated best by one Italian daughter: "It's never been, 'No, I can't do it because I don't have the time.' There's no such thing as never having time to help the family in any way."

There was a strong identification that the Anglo daughters or daughters-in-law gave more of all kinds of help to parents than did sons. The views of two daughters illustrate this point: "Well, personally, I think daughters do more. Mind you my sister-in-law is similarly inclined the way that I am. I will probably get more assistance from her than my brother." "I probably do more because I'm a girl and girls always seem to do more."

For the Italian sample, on the other hand, the offspring indicated that they felt the giving and receiving of assistance was equal across siblings. Nevertheless, they did identify a traditional gender division in the areas which a son or daughter was expected to contribute the most. This division is demonstrated in the comments of two daughters: "Because we're more a traditional family so, for the outdoor stuff, it's more the guy stuff, and the indoor stuff it's more the woman's thing." "For my sisters, we all help out in the house."

Likewise, Italian sons indicated a gender division in expectation for assistance: "Right now it's more my sisters (they rely on) for the responsible stuff." "Mostly I am asked to do long trips, the driving, like to Chicago. On a day-to-day thing, they rely on my sisters."

Anglo fathers did not recognize that they received intangible support from their children, either sons or daughters, although they reported giving it to their children. This is a potentially problematic situation. It may be, for example, that the lack of recognition by these fathers of the emotion expressed in a gesture of helping may lead children to feel unappreciated. On the other side of the relationship, the inability of these fathers to recognize emotional input may cause them to feel there is little affection expressed by their adult children and lead them to feel unloved. The results of such inadequate communication may have consequences for the parent-child relationship when the parents are middle-aged and the children young adults, and again when the parents are considerably older. At this later point, chronic and severe communication blocks could serve to diminish the parent-child relationship in a way that could increase the likelihood of elder abuse.

PERCEIVED INEQUITIES IN SUPPORT BETWEEN PARENTS AND CHILDREN

This study indicated differences between Anglo parents and their children in the perceived extent of assistance required by the older generation. These differing perceptions are a likely key to understanding how family relationships may deteriorate to the point where there is a risk of abuse.

When adult children with busy lives and children of their own feel obligated to assist parents, this can cause hard feelings and frustration. A sense of obligation may lead to having to choose between assisting the parents or pursuing other interests. As one of the children remarked:

> I had an awful lot of work to do and I would always find myself in a, well, it wouldn't be overt emotional blackmail, but I would always feel that I've got this paper to get off but if I don't till the garden (my father) is going to put his back out.

Another indicated that more than the labour required, it was a lack of appreciation that was resented: "Sometimes I feel unappreciated for all I do."

The Italian sample did not indicate that the expectation or obligation to assist parents presented any difficulties within the parent-adult child relationship. On the other hand, the comments of both groups of families suggested parents' provision of help to their children can cause strain. A breakdown in parent-child communication can lead to situations where parents give too much to an adult child who wishes to be recognized as autonomous and capable. The result can be conflict in the relationship, especially so when the adult child is married and a parent. This is indicated clearly by one Anglo daughter whose parents continued to treat her like a child while she struggled to see herself in the marital context as an independent adult:

> ...(my parents) are always here and some things happen between a husband and wife, or with a new mom, and you want to work it out yourselves. But (mom and dad) are there with ages of wisdom and sometimes it is hard to tell them, look, I usually love having your input, but right now leave me alone.

One unmarried Anglo child remarked that the support beyond what she asked for or expected is a denial of her impending adulthood:

> Sometimes it does feel a bit like, well I'm the youngest and as I grow up it's like 'Oh, the baby is getting older now,' and the odd time I feel like they are trying to hold me back a little. They don't want the baby to grow up.

An Italian son observed that his parents' assistance had a negative impact on their relationship because it left him desiring more autonomy: "I don't feel guilty that I am borrowing the money. But it makes me want to have a job and pay for things myself. I want to do as much as I can on my own."

In a situation where adult children feel they are being denied autonomy, the relationship normally is renegotiated. The situation is manageable, if not resolved, and both generations carry on. Where the relationship is flawed, and/or the communication patterns are seriously impaired, the resentment may well create pressures that get expressed in abusive ways.

SIBLING PERCEPTIONS OF INEQUITABLE SUPPORT FOR PARENTS

A sense of imbalance in how much help is provided to the parents by the adult siblings is another possible area of conflict. This study revealed that many of the adult offspring thought there were inequities in the levels of support extended to the parents. One Anglo daughter remarked: "I often feel that I do more. I feel sometimes (my sister) can be very self-centred."

One Anglo son, while complaining that he felt his older brother did not help out as much with the parents as the other siblings, in fact, identified that it was his wife, the daughter-in-law, who provided the assistance to his parents rather than himself:

> I would say my older brother, because he was first born, is the favoured child. He doesn't bust his butt to get over to help do any work. You know he's got to do his 9 to 5 thing and he's got two kids. My wife says, 'Too bad, I work 13 hours a day and I still get over there, why can't he?'"

Support to parents by the siblings was not identified by the Italian sample as an area of inequity. Yet, gender differences in the type of assistance Italian parents expected from their children were identified by a sister and brother as cause for difficulty:

> My brother gives them a lot of financial advice. I think it comes back to the situation with my father, my brother being the eldest child and being male. I really feel that has something to do with it. I think he is looked upon as having the ideal solution to everything. You know, whatever I say doesn't matter sometimes.

> It's tough. Not so much as the relationship with our parents as maybe it is between her and I. I don't know, maybe we've gone off in our own little directions or you know, come across some new ideas. Maybe it's something traditional with my being the oldest and being male, I don't know.

One Italian mother indicated that this expectation for the role played by the eldest son within the family can cause sibling conflict: "Yeah, typical little Italian boy. I hate to say it but it's causing problems with the younger brother and sister because they see that he doesn't pull his weight."

The expectations for the role of the eldest daughter within the family can also be a source of strain between siblings. One Italian daughter remarked: "Now there are several people that I have to look over even though I'm not the oldest. But like I said, my older sister is not around that much."

A sense that one adult child does more than his or her siblings may lead to an extended familial conflict. Its resolution may well be more complex because it depends upon the quality of peer as much as parent-child relations and communication. The extended family context widens the range of possible sources for abusive behaviour to originate.

CONCLUSIONS: CONFLICT AND PREVENTION IN PARENT-ADULT CHILD RELATIONS

Every family can identify situations that have caused strain. The study data discussed in this report indicate that families are usually able to resolve these issues with communication and patience. When this happens, there are no long-term negative consequences for the relationships. Thus, circumstances that cause conflict are not rare for families and may not be the key for understanding what leads to elder abuse. The history and nature of communication patterns within the family, the affectionate quality of relationships and even problem-solving skills are more likely to improve understanding of how situations such as co-residence and sibling rivalry can help build a simmering pot that one day boils over as abuse.

These research conclusions can be translated into concrete suggestions for practice. The list is not exhaustive, merely suggestive.

PROFESSIONALS

- Understand what your client families consider conflict and what they consider a resolved conflict.
- More attention needs to be paid to dysfunctional relations as potentially abusive. There likely is a link between parent-child relations across the family life cycle.
- Respect the needs of adult children to buffer whatever frustrations they may feel toward their parents.
- Reports of elder abuse should be treated on a case-by-case basis considering gender, ethnicity and relationship histories.
- Child abuse workers, spousal abuse workers and elder abuse workers need to talk to each other.
- Civility is universal even while cultural expression may vary.
- Front-line professionals can develop role play scenarios that focus on intergenerational differences in expectations.

FAMILY

- Something as simple as civility is an extremely important value. Look for this and demand it in interpersonal communication.
- Families with adult children who need continued support have to talk about the expectations of each generation. For example, do parents and children agree on what independence means?
- Realize that a child co-residing with a parent has compromised autonomy.
- Siblings who felt treated equally as young dependents may harbour resentment toward each other as young adults if they perceive differential support and sense of autonomy in the relationship to their parents.
- Some points of friction within families fall along intergenerational lines, others have their source in gender differences, and others represent variations in relations parents have with different children.
- Poor parent-child relations with young children can return to haunt parents in their later years.
- Seek professional help as soon as parent-child relations deteriorate, whatever the age of children.
- As circumstances change, expectations need to be renegotiated.

ADVOCACY

- Treat the cause, not the symptom. Elder abuse may be symptomatic of a larger social problem (e.g., youth unemployment may well be the issue).
- Prevention is the key: raise awareness of the link between family relationships and elder abuse.

Youth Crime in Canada: Public Perception vs. Statistical Information: 1997

John Howard Society of Alberta

EXECUTIVE SUMMARY

This paper explores public misconceptions about the nature and extent of youth crime and the youth justice system's response to youthful offending.

A number of public misconceptions about youth crime are identified. It is shown that the public believes that youth crime is increasing dramatically, as is the seriousness of the crimes committed. The official statistics respecting the nature and extent of youth crime are then presented. It is concluded that public perceptions that youth crime is increasing in number and seriousness are not supported by the official data.

It is also shown that the public perceives the Young Offenders Act to be lenient and unable to effectively control the behaviour of young people. Official statistics respecting youth court dispositions are presented and the justice system's handling of young offenders is compared to that of adult offenders. It is concluded that the youth justice system is, in fact, highly punitive.

Reasons for the discrepancy between public perceptions and what the official statistics tell us about youth crime are explored. The role of the media and professional groups in shaping public attitudes is addressed.

The damaging effects of public misconceptions of youth crime are also explored. Among the detrimental effects of false public perceptions of youth

John Howard Society of Alberta (1997). Youth crime in Canada: Public perceptions vs. statistical information (On-line: www.acjnet.org/doc.y1paper.htm). Reprinted with permission from the John Howard Society of Alberta.

crime are public intolerance, unnecessary legislation changes and inappropriate programming choices for young offenders.

The paper concludes with some suggestions for bridging the gap between public misconceptions about youth crime and the official statistics on youth crime. It is recommended, first, that public knowledge of the criminal justice system be improved, second, that the media become better informed about youth justice issues and more accurately report youth crime and third, that the fears which accompany public misconceptions about youth crime be respected and addressed.

INTRODUCTION

The Young Offenders Act (YOA) was enacted in 1984 to reconcile issues of responsibility and accountability with respect to young offenders. However, extensive coverage of youth crime in the media may initially lead one to conclude that present policies are ineffective given that crimes committed by youths appear to be increasing in number and seriousness. Indeed, youth crime in Canada has come to the fore as a public concern fuelled by beliefs that rates of youthful offending are escalating and that youth justice responses need to become harsher to deal effectively with this problem. Has youth crime seen a dramatic rise in numbers in recent years? Are the YOA and its enforcers too lenient with youth?

The proceeding pages will attempt to address these questions by looking first at the degree to which the public feels youth crime is a problem, as well as the popularity of the "get tough" mentality. Then, youth crime trends and youth court dispositions will be examined. It will be shown that the perception that youth crime is reaching epidemic proportions is not supported by the official statistics and research. As well, it will be seen that the YOA and its administrators are actually "tough" on youthful offenders, relative to adult offender treatment and considering the severity of punishments available in Canadian criminal law. Several explanations will be offered with respect to the discrepancy between the official statistics and public opinion and some suggestions will be made to address this situation.

IS YOUTH CRIME OUT OF CONTROL?

The Perceptions

Based on the number and content of media reports on youth crime, it can be inferred that the public is being led to believe that youth crime is increasing in vast and unmanageable numbers, as is the seriousness of the crimes committed. Indeed, as Doob, Marinos, and Varma (1995: 22) point out:

> There is, very roughly speaking, one young person charged every week to ten days for a homicide offence. To the extent that our media report these events on a national basis, it means that the public has enormous opportunities to hear about homicides committed by youth. Thus, as University of Ottawa criminologist Julian Roberts points out, it is completely understandable, if the media are reporting these quite regularly, for people to believe that there is an increase. We remember these recent reports, and assume that it must not have been "like that" a few years ago.

Although it has been noted that studies on public perceptions of youth crime are not plentiful (Hartnagel, personal communication, June, 1995), those that have been conducted suggest a public perception that youth crime is rising. A Calgary study of 464 residents, for example, found that roughly 30% of its respondents listed youth gangs or youth violence as the primary crime problem in the city (Collins, 1992). The yearly *Macleans*/CTV polls show a consistently high and increasing number of Canadians claiming youth behaviour in their neighbourhoods has been getting worse: from 47% in 1990 to 79% in 1994 ("*Macleans*/CTV poll," 1993; McDonald, 1995). The polls also reveal that 76% of respondents felt youth behaviour in general is in decline, up from the 1992 figure of 64%. A critical question to ask, then, is whether the criminal activities of the young have, in fact, been getting worse and becoming more frequent, which can be answered, in part, by looking at trends in youthful offending.

The Statistics

Trends in the frequency and seriousness of youth crime can be charted from Canadian Centre for Justice Statistics' (CCJS) reports. Youth crime in these reports is measured by the number of charges laid against young offenders (aged 12-17 years), and/or by the number of cases processed in youth court. At first glance, the statistics appear to show significant increases in youth crime from 1986/87 to 1992/93; the 1992/93 statistics indicate a 27% increase in charges since 1986/87 and a 32% increase in cases heard at court (CCJS, 1994, August). There are a number of important considerations in interpreting these statistics. First, it is important to note that the increase in charges against youth and cases in youth court correspond with a simultaneous increase in the size of the Canadian youth population. In addition, 81% of the charges that comprise the 27% increase are "administrative offences," including failures to appear in court, comply with terms of probation or complete community service orders in the time allotted. These offences consistently represented approximately one-quarter of all offences over the period. Further, Carrington (1995) has warned that 1986/87 statistics should be approached with caution when being compared to later statistics. This is because the YOA came into effect in 1984, and the statistics from the few years immediately following its enactment might not be reliable, considering the new inclusion of 16 and 17-year-old youths who typically commit more crimes than younger offenders 12-15 years of age. Given that 16 and 17-year-olds were gradually brought into the youth justice system over the first few years of the YOA's enactment, the statistics for the years 1986 and 1987 may have been affected by this transition. Another important trend to consider is the number of youths charged for each criminal incident (Carrington, 1995). In his 1995 study, Carrington found that though the number of suspects for youth criminal charges between 1986 and 1992 remained relatively stable, the police had developed a propensity to charge more young suspects for each crime. Thus, the number of youth crimes did not necessarily increase but, rather, the number of young persons charged for each criminal incident had apparently risen.

Along with the belief that youth crime is widespread go the perceptions that youth crime is increasing in seriousness and in proportion to all crime (youth and adult crime combined). Again, however, the official statistics do not support such a belief. In terms of proportions, homicide rates are deemed to be among the most accurate indicators of crime trends. This is because the offence of murder affords little opportunity at any point in the criminal justice process for outside factors to bias a case's handling (i.e., the seriousness of murder means reporting or charging rates for this crime should not change over time). National statistics show youths are responsible for approximately 47 murders each year (CCJS, 1996, July) or roughly 8% of all homicides, a proportion that has remained unchanged for at least a decade (CCJS, 1995, August).

Other national statistics also refute the belief that youth crime is growing in seriousness. Property crime comprises almost half of all youth court cases while violent offences represent only 21% of youth court cases (CCJS, 1996, March). While the portion of youth court cases involving violent offences increased between 1986/87 (13%) and 1994/95 (2 1%), the increase has been largely attributed to a significant increase in minor assault cases (CCJS, 1996, March; CCJS, 1995, January). Others (Hackler, cited in Jeffs, 1993; Carrington, 1995) also attribute the increase in violent offence cases in youth court to increased reporting to police of such incidents as minor school yard scuffles, or of any unwanted touching of one youth by another that is legal grounds for an assault charge. This reporting increase can be attributed to society's growing intolerance for undesirable youth behaviour. Therefore, the data do not clearly indicate that youth crime is increasing in severity or becoming a larger proportion of all crime.

While meaningful conclusions can be drawn from justice statistics (Church Council on Justice and Corrections, 1995), the limitations and biases that are present in such data must be noted. First, localized reports on crime rates are usually compiled by area police. As several authors point out (Fulton & Fisher, 1992; Jeffs, 1993), the decisions to lay charges, the severity of charges and even the data compilation itself are subject to possible police bias. Certain districts, for example, may be suffering from budgetary restrictions that could lead them to exaggerate a crime problem or lay more charges. This may be done in the hopes that the apparent increase in crime will lead to more financial support in future budgets. It is also well known that police tend occasionally to focus on a specific type of crime and concentrate their efforts on it (Jeffs, 1993). Such a concentration of efforts in any given year may seriously affect youth crime statistics for that year. Further, it has been found that the police tend to lay more serious charges against young offenders than may be expected in a given incident (Jeffs, 1993). This is done in anticipation of leniency and lesser-charges (i.e., a plea bargain) at a later point in the justice process.

Is the YOA too Lenient? Is There a Need to Get Tough?

Perceptions that the YOA is lenient and does not effectively control youth behaviour are as popular as the belief that youth crime is rising dramatically. The next few paragraphs will outline manifestations of the belief that the YOA is lenient, and will examine the number and severity of dispositions that official statistics indicate young offenders are receiving.

The Perceptions

Since the introduction of the Young Offenders Act, many Canadians have been frustrated due to a perceived leniency in the act and its enforcement. A recent study conducted by Sprott (1996) found that 88% of respondents felt that youth court sentences were too lenient. Two studies by Hartnagel and Baron (1994, 1995) also reveal the public's perception of a lenient YOA. Members of both rural and urban communities in Manitoba and Alberta (approximately 1250 in each province) were asked to agree or disagree, on a seven-point scale, with three statements: (1) "A curfew for children under 16 is a good idea", (2) "Young offenders who commit a second offence should be tried in adult courts", and (3) "Youth courts have become too lenient with young offenders" (Hartnagel & Baron, 1994: 5; Hartnagel & Baron, 1995: 10). In response to the curfew statement, Albertans were 69.8% in agreement (with roughly half of all respondents strongly agreeing). In Manitoba, 67.5% agreed with the curfew (approximately two-thirds of these in strong agreement). Eighty-three percent of Albertans agreed with moving youths to adult court for repeat offences (about two-thirds of which strongly agreed), and 66.9% of Manitobans agreed (over half of which strongly agreed). Finally, the statement of the courts' leniency was supported by 86.9% of Albertans (two-thirds strongly agreeing) and 78.3% of Manitobans (approximately two-thirds strongly in agreement). These results clearly support a strong favouring of more punitive approaches towards young offenders.

Other activities also suggest the public's wish to "get tough" with young offenders. Alberta Chief Justice Ed Wachowich states that several studies he has reviewed show that members of the public feel judges are far too indulgent with young people (Teele, 1994). This sentiment even extends to schools in their handling of youth crime: 56% of those surveyed in an Ottawa-Carleton study thought school boards were not punitive enough in their treatment of youthful offenders (Dube, 1994). With respect to the YOA, there have been several community forums in Edmonton and Calgary that have called for a lowering of the minimum age of criminal responsibility and more regular transferring of young offenders to adult court (Jeffs, 1994). Further, the murder of Barb Danelesko in Edmonton led to a 64,000-name petition urging for a more punitive YOA (Grace, 1994). Public efforts to amend the Young Offenders Act sharply contrast the official data on youth crime.

PROBLEMS RESULTING FROM FALSE PUBLIC PERCEPTIONS

As alluded to in the foregoing discussion, the public intolerance that results from punitive attitudes may surface in several ways. For example, it may spur individuals to band together into lobby groups or initiate letter writing campaigns. More commonly, however, it will surface in individuals' reactions to undesirable youth behaviour. Informal methods of dealing with youths will continue to be put aside in the belief that they are ineffective, leading to heightened police intervention and more charges laid for otherwise minor incidents that historically would never see a courtroom. As previously noted, the increase in charges will give the appearance of a drastic increase in youth crime. This apparent increase is made public by the media, fuelling more anger and calls for actions. In response, judges are more punitive with youths, perceiving a need to reflect the will of the public in their sentencing practices (Roberts, 1992). As well, politicians are compelled to make unneeded changes to youth crime laws ("Toughen youth sentences," 1994). This governmental response is exemplified in the YOA reforms recently passed by the federal government. They include an increase of the maximum custodial disposition from 5 years to 10 and automatic transfer of youths aged 16 and 17 years to adult court if charged with a serious offence ("Rock pushes crackdown," 1994). Such measures, it has been documented, can open new doors for even more negative public attitudes by supporting the perception that youth crime is serious enough to change laws and that punitive measures will indeed prevent young persons from offending.

A more pragmatic problem associated with public misconceptions of youth crime is the effects these misconceptions can have on programming choices. A public that perceives an increase in youth crime and a youth justice system too lenient to deal with the apparent problem will be inclined to demand tougher sanctions for young offenders. A public better informed about youth crime and successful responses to youthful offending will be inclined towards making more enlightened demands, such as alleviating the conditions which promote offending behaviour among young people. In an era of fiscal restraint, it is particularly important to ensure that money is not spent on programs for young offenders that are unnecessary:

> We cannot afford to be manipulated into promoting harsh solutions
> for fictional problems. Panic-free social policy would use resources,
> largely wasted in enforcement and punishment systems, to promote
> healthier environments and hopeful opportunities for our youth.
> (The John Howard Society of Ontario, 1994: 4)

The key tool with which false public perceptions can be dispelled is the dissemination of accurate crime statistics. Yet, persons with strong attitudes in opposition to the statistics have been known to merely become confused and anxious once they are presented with official statistics (Doob, cited in Church Council on Justice and Corrections, 1995). Even worse, such persons often conclude that the data is inaccurate, or that it can be manipulated to support whichever view one wishes to present. This will discourage efforts to change public attitudes by publicizing accurate youth crime statistics to dispel myths.

Thus, negative public perceptions of youth crime can do serious damage in terms of widening the gap between fact and opinion, as well as discouraging the use of youth crime statistics. The question that remains is how to address this dilemma.

Discussion

Although data on public perceptions of youth crime are not readily available, the studies that do exist can be generalized into two common views: (1) the number of youthful offenders in Canada is on the rise relatively and absolutely, especially in terms of violent offences, and (2) the YOA is not punitive enough to deal effectively with youths, leading to the conclusion that harsher measures must be undertaken. National statistical data lend no support to these views, and smaller scale studies are inconclusive. Both types of data are subject to biases and methodological flaws. Many experts agree that the media are primarily to blame for creating distorted perceptions and keeping the public ill-informed, given the public's reliance upon them. Government and police responses perpetuate the myth of the seriousness of youth crime through, for example, efforts to amend the Young Offenders Act and introduce tougher sanctions for young offenders. The continuation of these beliefs can serve to frustrate attempts to educate the public and bring views in line with the official statistics. Evidence exists that members of Canadian society can become better informed and make more enlightened decisions. This can be accomplished through, first, improved public knowledge of the criminal justice system, second, a better informed media accompanied by more accurate media reports and third, efforts to respect and address the very real fears that accompany public misconceptions about youth crime.

Unit VII
Mental and Physical Disabilities

It was not until May of 1995 that amendments to the Criminal Code *and* Canada Evidence Act *were introduced to acknowledge the rights of persons with disabilities.*

In 1996 Prime Minister Chretian was attacked by man who was found not criminally responsible because he suffered from schizophrenia. Rather than being sent to prison he was placed in a mental health facility. Similarly, in 1995, a prominent Ottawa television personality was fatally shot. His assailant, Jeffrey Arenburg was a known paranoid schizophrenic with a history of violence against media members. Prior to the shooting he had spent four years in a psychiatric hospital.

In 1988, Correctional Service of Canada commissioned a mental health survey of federally sentenced inmates. The survey revealed that nearly 75% of inmates displayed antisocial personality characteristics, approximately 70% suffered from alcohol abuse/dependence and nearly 56% displayed anxiety disorder symptoms (Motiuk & Porpozino, 1992). A more recent survey in 1998 revealed that little has changed. The percentage of inmates with mental health problems remains at nearly 75%. And as one researcher observed, the developmentally challenged tend to have higher rates of involvement in violent crime than those less challenged (Finn, 1992) and they are treated more restrictively when it comes to conditional release than offenders without mental disorders (Conditional release…, 1993). Other than these reports noting that mental health represents a major challenge facing (federal) corrections, there is little indication that much is being done for these inmates.

The mentally ill and physically (and developmentally) challenged inmates are a challenging population. Before the Middle Ages we use to care for them within our own family and society. Then in the Middle Ages we began to consider them repulsive and subjected them to barbaric treatment (e.g., banishing, branding and other fear-based treatment). The first insane asylum was built in the early 1400s where insane offenders could be held indefinitely. This general practice did not change much in Canada until became signature of the human rights' agreement during the mid-1900s. Yet, as recently as 1995, after the fatal shooting of a popular Ontario journalist, Brian Smith, a coroner's jury called for changes to the Mental Health Act of the province that would limit the rights of "potentially dangerous mentally ill people from living in the community." The jury also recommended forced hospitalization of the seriously mentally ill (Coroner's jury…, 1997).

Today, their treatment, as indicated by their representation in the inmate population, should be seen as important to policy-makers, our courts and the public at large. To date, most institutions are ill equipped to address the wide range of mental health problems inmates display. In 1982, Toch described their treatment as "bus therapy"—a process in which inmates are simply shuffled through the system without receiving any specialized care. In fact, Sommers and Baskin (1990) report that "chemical straitjacketing" (i.e., the use of psychotropic drugs) is commonly used to simply keep disturbed inmates docile.

In 1995, the law reform division of the Department of Justice reviewed the Criminal Code and the Canada Evidence Act in relation to persons with disabilities having improved access to the criminal justice system. At the time of preparing this section, no noteworthy steps have been taken to ensure this group of offenders is guaranteed special consideration at all levels of the criminal justice system.

Although s. 672 of the Criminal Code pertains to whether the accused is "fit to stand trial," the courts are ill equipped to address issues of mental health. The insanity plea is limited to but a few cases a year, and based on the criteria few inmates would truly qualify for such classification. However, mental health problems do not necessarily involve a mental illness but they may involve compromised cognitive skills. Therefore, in accordance with our crime control and just deserts models of justice, inmates are processed through a system that is not designed and ill equipped to address the needs of those experiencing mental health problems. As the eminent psychiatrist Karl Menninger once said: "society gets the crime [criminals] it deserves."

Two articles are included to highlight the relation between individuals with disabilities and justice in Canada. Katherine Nessner's article provides statistical data on the number of individual's with disabilities in Canadian society. Richard Sobsey's unique work explores the consequences of being disabled and the impact that has on justice.

DISCUSSION QUESTIONS:

1. Why do we insist on viewing offenders as "bad" and deserving of punishment?

2. What steps need to be taken to ensure that those suffering from mental and/or physical challenges are fairly dealt with by the criminal justice system?
3. To what extent might other forms of offenders such as the developmentally challenged, sex offender and offenders with AIDS, among others, be discriminated within the criminal justice system?
4. To what extent might fiscal restraints compromise the fair and equitable processing and handling of these marginalized groups?
5. Currently, inmates have a constitutional right to treatment but the CJS is not required to provide specialized services simple because their clients are criminal. How do you feel about this?

REFERENCES

Conditional release and offenders with mental disorders. (1993, December). *Forum.* (Online).

Coroner's jury makes recommendations regarding treatment of mentally ill individuals two after murder of journal Brian Smith. (1997, December). (Online: www.ccjp.actfile/1997/smithd12.html).

Finn, M.A. (1992). Prison misconduct among developmentally challenged inmates. *Criminal Justice and Mental Health*, 2(3): 287-299.

Motiuk, L.L. and Porporino, F.J. (1992). The prevalence, nature and severity of mental health problems among federal male inmates in Canadian penitentiaries. Research report. Ottawa: Research and Statistics Branch, Correctional Service Canada.

Toch, H. (1982). The disturbed disruptive inmate: Where does the bus stop? *Journal of Psychiatry and Law*, 10: 327-349.

Sommers, I. and Baskin, D. (1990). The prescription of psychiatric mediation in prison. *Justice Quarterly*, 7: 739-755.

Web watch: As this unit covers a broad spectrum there is no one website that covers the various groups. Of general interest, visit the Canadian Mental Health Association homepage at www.icomm.ca/cmhacan/english/homeeng.htm.

Profile of Canadians with Disabilities

Katherine Nessner

The integration of Canadians with disabilities into mainstream society remains one of this country's major social objectives. In 1986, disabled people numbered 3.3 million and made up 13% of Canada's population.

ONE IN FOUR SEVERELY DISABLED

A relatively large proportion of people with disabilities are severely impaired. In 1986, 23% of the disabled population had a severe disability. Most people with disabilities, though, had a condition that was less than severe: 32 % had a moderate disability, while 45% had a mild disability.

RESTRICTED MOVEMENT

The most common disabilities involve some restriction of movement. In 1986, 66% of the disabled population aged 15 and over had mobility problems. These included limitations in their ability to walk, move from room to room, carry an object a short distance, or stand for a long time. Another 58% of people with disabilities reported difficulty in performing activities such as bending, reaching, dressing themselves, getting in and out of bed, or grasping objects.

Nessner, K. (1990). Profile of Canadians with disabilities. *Canadian Social Trends*, (August): 2-5.

Hearing problems were the next most common disability, affecting 32% of disabled people. Another 18% were visually impaired, while 8% had difficulty speaking. A variety of other conditions, such as psychiatric problems or developmental delay, affected over 30% of people with disabilities.

NUMBER OF DISABILITIES

Most adults who reported that they were disabled had more than one disability. In fact, in 1986, this was the case for 64% of disabled people: 31% had two types of disability, and 33% had three or more.

MOST PREVALENT AMONG ELDERLY

Elderly people are the most likely to be disabled (see Figure 1). In 1986, nearly half (46%) of the population aged 65 and over reported having some form of disability. Furthermore, among those aged 85 and over, 82% were disabled.

In contrast, 16% of 35-64-year-olds, 6% of people aged 15-34, and 5% of children under age 15 had a disability.

As well, older people are more likely than those in younger age groups to have a severe disability. In 1986, 35% of disabled people aged 65 and over had a severe condition. This compared with 16% of the disabled population aged 15-64, and 9% of disabled children.

Multiple disabilities also tend to be more common among elderly people. In 1986, 75% of the disabled population aged 65 and over reported more than one disability, whereas the proportion for those aged 15-64 was 56%.

Women aged 65 and over are slightly more likely than men in this age range to be disabled. While 47% of elderly women reported some form of disability in 1986, the corresponding figure for men was 44%. At younger ages, the proportions of males and females with a disability were almost identical.

FEW IN INSTITUTIONS

Although most people with disabilities live in private households, a significant minority are in institutions. In 1986, 7% of the disabled population lived in facilities such as special care homes and institutions for the elderly and chronically ill; general hospitals; psychiatric treatment centres; institutions for the physically handicapped; and orphanages and children's homes.

Figure 1:   People with disabilities as a percentage of population, by age,
1986

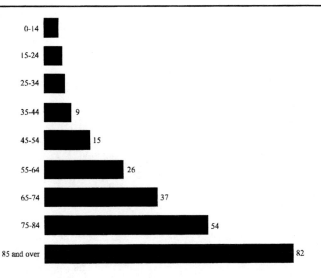

Source: Statistics Canada, Catalogue 82-602.

The elderly account for the vast majority of disabled people living in institutions (see Table 1). In 1986, 79% of all institutionalized people with disabilities were aged 65 and over.

Table 1:   Percentage of people with disabilities living in institutions, by age group and sex, 1986

Age Group	Males	Females
0-14 years	1%	1%
15-34	4%	3%
35-64	3%	2%
65-74	5%	6%
75-84	16%	21%
85 and over	34%	46%

Source: Statistics Canada, Catalogue 82-602.

Disabled elderly women are more likely than their male counterparts to live in institutions. In 1986, 19% of disabled women aged 65 and older were in institutions, compared with 11% of elderly men. In addition, for both women and men, the rate of institutionalization climbs sharply at progressively older ages. Among those aged 85 and over, for example, 46% of disabled women and 34% of disabled men were in institutions.

In contrast, fewer than 5% of disabled men and women aged 15-64 lived in institutions, and among children, the proportion was less than 1%.

Not surprisingly, the more severe the disability, the more likely the disabled person is to be in an institution. In 1986, 24% of people with severe disabilities were in institutions, whereas the figure was 4% for those who were moderately disabled, and just 1% for those with mild disabilities.

LIVING ALONE

At all ages, a relatively high proportion of people with disabilities live alone. In 1986, 12% of non-institutionalized disabled people aged 15-64 lived alone, compared with 7% of the non-disabled in this age range. As well, 30% of disabled people aged 65 and over lived alone, compared with 26% of those without disabilities.

Still, most non-institutionalized disabled people live in a family setting, although the proportion is less than for non-disabled people. In 1986, 78% of disabled people aged 15-64 were living in families as husbands, wives, lone parents, or children. The corresponding figure for the non-disabled population was 86%.

The remainder of both people with (9%) and without (7%) disabilities were living with other family members such as brothers, sisters, aunts and uncles, or with non-relatives.

MARITAL STATUS

As is the case for the non-disabled population, most adults with disabilities are married. In 1986, 62% of both disabled and non-disabled 15-64-year-olds were married. Among people aged 65 and over, 52% with disabilities were married, while the figure for the non-disabled was 61%.

Disabled adults, however, are more likely than people without disabilities to be divorced, separated, or widowed. At ages 15-64, 11% of disabled people were divorced or separated, compared with 6% of their non-disabled contemporaries. As well, 6% of the disabled population aged 15-64 were widowed, in contrast to 2% of non-disabled people.

On the other hand, non-institutionalized disabled adults are less likely than their non-disabled counterparts to be single. In 1986, 22% of people aged 15-64 with disabilities were single, compared with 31% of those without disabilities.

Differences in marital status, however, are largely a reflection of the age distribution of these two populations, with the disabled more concentrated in older age groups.

LESS FORMAL EDUCATION

Disabled people tend to have less formal education than non-disabled Canadians (see Table 2). For example, in 1986, 5% of non-institutionalized disabled people aged 15-64 were university graduates, whereas the corresponding figure for the non-disabled population was 11%. Similarly, 10% of people with disabilities had earned a postsecondary certificate or diploma, compared with 14% of those without disabilities.

Table 2: Educational attainment of disabled and non-disabled population aged 15-64, 1986

	Disabled	Non-disabled
University degree	5%	11%
Certificate or diploma	10%	14%
Some postsecondary	16%	20%
Some or completed secondary	40%	44%
Less than Grade 9	29%	11%

Source: Statistics Canada, Catalogues 82-602 and 93-110.

At the same time, people with disabilities are much more likely than other Canadians to have low levels of education. In 1986, 29% of non-institutionalized disabled people aged 15-64 had less than Grade 9, while the figure was 11% for other people in this age group.

Some of these differences in educational attainment, though, may be due to the fact that the disabled population is older, on average, than the non-disabled population, and older people generally have lower levels of education.

LOWER LABOUR FORCE PARTICIPATION

In recent years, the role of disabled workers in the Canadian labour force has expanded. Technology has allowed many more disabled people to perform in a wide variety of jobs, and special training has become more readily available. Still, compared with non-disabled adults, a much smaller proportion of the disabled population is employed.

In 1986, only 40% of the 1.8 million disabled people aged 15-64 were employed. This compared with 70% of non-disabled adults.

This discrepancy holds among both men and women. While 50% of disabled men aged 15-64 were employed, the figure was 80% for non-disabled men.

Similarly, only 31% of disabled women had jobs, in contrast to 60% of non-disabled women. Employment rates for disabled people are low, not because their unemployment rates are high, but rather because a large proportion of them do not participate in the labour force. In 1986, 51% of people with disabilities were not in the labour force: 40% of men and 61% of women. By contrast, just 22% of non-disabled people did not participate in the labour force: 12% of men and 32% of women.

OCCUPATIONS

While disabled people are employed in most fields, they are less likely than other workers to have managerial or professional jobs, and are more likely to work in skilled and semi-skilled trades or manual jobs.

In 1986, workers with disabilities accounted for 6% of total employment. However, they made up just 5% of senior managers, middle managers, and professionals.

On the other hand, 10% of people in skilled crafts and trades were disabled, as were 12% of semi-skilled workers and 14% of other manual workers.

INCOME GAP

Disabled adults generally have lower incomes than other Canadians. In 1985, disabled men aged 15 and over had a median income of $13,000, compared with $20,900 for non-disabled men. The difference was not as great among women: disabled women had a median income of $8,200 in 1985, compared with $10,000 for those without disabilities.

The income gap between people with and without disabilities narrows after retirement age. At age 65 and over, 8% of the disabled and 10% of the non-disabled population had 1985 incomes less than $5,000. However, 52% of disabled elderly people received $5,000 to $10,000, compared with 41% of their non-disabled counterparts. At the other end of the income scale, 7% of elderly disabled people had 1985 incomes greater than $25,000, whereas the figure for those without disabilities was 13%.

Only a minority of the disabled population receive disability-related pensions. Moreover, disabled people in the 15-64 age range are more likely than those aged 65 and over to have some income in this form. In 1985, such payments were made to 23% of disabled 15-64-year-olds, while the proportion among those aged 65 and over was just 7%.

Sexual Abuse and Exploitation of Disabled Individuals

Dick Sobsey and Connie Varnhagen

PURPOSE AND METHODOLOGY

Canada's national initiative against child sexual abuse is now underway. A number of studies have been undertaken to determine more specific targets for this program. The purpose of this study was to provide additional information on the nature and extent of risk for abuse among people with disabilities, and to determine if current prevention and treatment services meet their needs adequately.

The primary method for gathering relevant evidence was through review of existing literature. This included a number of electronic database searches in education, law, psychology, medicine, social work, and related disciplines. Since much of the information required was not categorized by a few simple descriptors, an intensive conventional library search and consultation with service providers and other researchers was required to locate essential information.

Two pilot studies were undertaken to supplement the literature review These were intended to: determine reliability of previously published data, determine the extent of generalization of non-Canadian data to Canada, and to

Sobsey, D. and Varnhagen, C. (1991). Sexual abuse, assault and exploitation of Canadians with disabilities. From *Child Sex Abuse: Critical Perspectives on Prevention, Intervention, and Treatment*. Edited by C. Bagley and R.J. Thompson. Reprinted with permission of the publisher, Wall & Emerson, Inc., Toronto.

provide initial data relevant to some essential issues that are not addressed in published material. One of these studies surveyed agencies serving victims of sexual abuse to determine how they served people with disabilities. The other collected some basic information about incidents of sexual abuse involving victims with disabilities. Studies were conducted in English and French.

Due to some issues that may generalize across age groups, and a tendency for some previous investigators to treat child sexual abuse and sexual assault and exploitation of adults as a single concern, this study addresses both groups of victims. Care should be taken in applying results across populations, and it is essential that the distinct needs of children and adults with disabilities be recognized.

LITERATURE REVIEW

More than 50% of 200 publications on sexual abuse and people with disabilities were published in the last four years. The number of relevant publications appears to be increasing substantially each year, and this effect will likely appear even more dramatic after the remainder of publications from the 1987 publication year are indexed and accessible. There is also a clear change in the content of these publications. Earlier articles focus on philosophy, theoretical issues sex education, and humanistic concerns but provide little data. More recent publications continue to emphasize these areas, but provide incidence and prevalence data to support them. Space here would not allow a complete review of the literature and a more comprehensive annotated bibliography on this topic is available from the authors (Sobsey & Varnhagen, 1988).

STUDIES ON DISABILITIES AND RISK FOR SEXUAL ABUSE

The majority of cases of sexual abuse are likely never reported; using FBI statistics and data collected by the Seattle Rape Relief Disabilities Project, Ryerson (1981) estimates that only 20% of the cases of sexual abuse involving disabled people are ever reported to the police, community service agencies, or other authorities. Thus, it is very difficult to compile accurate statistics concerning the incidence of sexual abuse among the disabled population.

There are two reasonable approaches to compiling incidence statistics. In the first, wide-scale samples of disabled people are obtained and their history of sexual abuse elicited. The incidence is then recorded and compared with the incidence for the general population. This procedure is used to determine whether there is a greater incidence of sexual abuse among the disabled sample in comparison with the general population. Incidence statistics are difficult to obtain using this direct approach; there are few data banks devoted generally to disabled people that include incidence of sexual abuse. Most often, records from specialized agencies, such as birth control counselling group sheltered workshops, or group homes, are examined for incidence of sexual abuse.

In the second approach, wide-scale samples of victims of sexual abuse are identified. Representation of different disabilities within the sample is compiled and compared with representation within the general population. Using this procedure, it is determined whether people with certain disabilities are under- or over-represented as victims of sexual abuse. This approach leads to more stable statistics than does the former approach. It may be a better indicator of prevalence than of incidence since active case files usually reflect people victimized in a relatively fixed time interval.

Neither approach can determine if the disability reported is a result of the abuse rather than a prior condition that possibly put the victim at greater risk. This is particularly important when considering that sexual abuse may be accompanied by physical abuse. Even when physical abuse is not present, regression, withdrawal, and other behavioural changes often result from sexual abuse. To minimize this ambiguity, studies that clearly report prior disabilities are examined first. However, it should be remembered that even where disability results from abuse, any special needs of those victims must be considered in providing appropriate treatment services.

DISABILITIES AMONG ABUSE VICTIMS

Table 1 summarizes statistics concerning prevalence of prior disabilities obtained from studies of child sexual abuse. The data were obtained through medical centre records of children who had been treated in emergency or outpatient departments over 12 to 18 month periods. Computing weighted averages, 5% of the sexually abused children had some form of intellectual impairment, 3% had a physical or sensory impairment, and 5% were psychiatrically impaired prior to the abuse. Differences in the percentages that appear in various categories are partly the result of differences in categorical definitions, but intellectually and physically impaired children are certainly over-represented in these samples. The prevalence of intellectual impairment in the general population ranges from 1% to 3% (Tarjan, Wright, Eyman, & Keeran, 1973). A comparable percentage of physical and sensory disabilities in the general population is difficult to identify since the authors' definitions were not adequately clear.

Table 1: Prevalence of prior disabilities in studies of victims of child sexual abuse

	n	Impairment	Intellectual Impairment	Physical Impairment	Psychiatric Other
Tilelli, Turek & Jaffe (1980)	113	5%	2%	5%	2%
Shah, Holloway & Valkil (1982)	174	4%	not reported	not reported	not reported
Browning & Boatman (1977)	14	14%	14%	0	0

Table 2 summarizes statistics concerning child abuse. These may or may not have included sexual abuse. The Gil (1970) and Lebsack studies (cited in Soeffing, 1975) examined nationwide data banks of child abuse, and the Hawkins and Duncan (1985) study considered statistics within one state; all reports were collected for a 12-month period. Weighted averages of the representation of the different types of disabilities are comparable to those obtained with cases of explicit sexual abuse; three percent of the children were intellectually impaired, three percent were physically impaired, and five percent were psychiatrically impaired. Again, precise comparisons with non-abused populations are difficult to make due to inadequate specifications of criteria for inclusion in categories and differences in criteria across studies.

In spite of methodological differences and concerns, the general consistency of these studies suggests that children with disabilities experience significant risk for sexual and physical abuse. This risk appears to be

Table 2: Prevalence of disabilities in studies of physical abuse

	n	Impairment	Intellectual Impairment	Physical Impairment	Psychiatric Other
Gil (1970)	1,380	8%	14%	included in other	29%
Lebsack (1975)	14,083	2%	2%	5%	6%
Hawkins & Duncan (1985)	126	9%	not reported	10%	not reported

substantially greater than the risk for their nondisabled age-peers, although the difficulty in gathering accurate statistical information about either group suggests some caution in making this comparison. There is good reason to believe that these studies under-represent children with disabilities because these children are often rejected from services or served by specialized agencies and therefore do not appear in the case files reviewed for these studies. For example, Schilling, Kirkham, and Schinke (1986) found that although 82% of the child protection workers believed that developmental disabilities increased risk of abuse, 84% could not recall a single case that they had served, 12% had served only one, and only 4% had served two developmentally disabled clients. Even if children with disabilities experience only the same risk, they make up a very significant proportion of child sexual abuse victims and appropriate services are required. Currently, we can expect to encounter significant disabilities in about one of every seven victims of child sexual abuse. The proportion of children with disabilities in this group can be expected to increase as case reporting for children with disabilities improves (Senn, 1988).

SEXUAL ABUSE AMONG PEOPLE WITH DISABILITIES

Although not comparable, specialized, direct approaches to tabulating incidence of sexual abuse support these studies demonstrating that disabled children are at risk for sexual abuse. In a study of 87 mentally retarded females between 11 to 23 years of age referred for birth control, Chamberlain, Rauh, Passer, McGrath, and Burket (1984) found that 25% had been sexually abused. In a study of 164 children with cerebral palsy receiving regular medical attention at the University of Chicago Hospital, Jaudes and Diamond (1985) discovered that 14% of the children had been abused and/or neglected, including 2% of reported cases of sexual abuse. Finally, in a study of 55 hearing impaired, multiply handicapped children examined by otolaryngologists (i.e., the study of ears, nose, and larynx) through the Boys Town Centre for Abused Handicapped Children, Brookhouser, Sullivan, Scanlan, and Garbarino (1986) reported that 96% of the children had been sexually abused.

OTHER STUDIES

Studies that have not controlled for preexistence of the disability present an even more dramatic picture. Davies (1979) found abnormal EEG readings and active epilepsy in three to four times as many incest victims as in a matched control group. Chotiner and Lehr (1976) report a Parents Anonymous study that showed 58% of members' abused children had developmental disabilities prior to abuse problems, and a Denver Department of Welfare study indicated that 70% of abused children exhibited a "mental or physical deviation" prior to the reported abuse. Schilling, Kirkham, and Schinke (1986) found that the great majority of child protection workers believed that children with developmental disabilities were at greater risk. While the perceptions of service providers do not comprise direct empirical evidence of increased incidence, they do offer social validation for the data presented above. Finally, our own (following) pilot data similarly suggest that people actively involved in providing services to sexual abuse victims believe that people with disabilities are at greater risk.

Considered as a whole, these data strongly support a relationship between disabilities and sexual abuse. The nature and extent of that relationship may be important to understanding factors that are associated with risk of abuse for all children, and understanding the mechanism of this relationship may provide information useful in designing more effective treatment programs. Regardless of the precise mechanism of this relationship, the needs of these victims must be considered.

POTENTIAL RELATIONSHIPS BETWEEN SEXUAL ABUSE AND DISABILITY

Why children with disabilities are more likely to be found among victims of sexual abuse is not entirely clear. A number of potential relationships have been suggested. None of these has been adequately verified through empirical research, but indirect evidence is available.

SAMPLING BIAS AND CASEFINDING FACTORS

With small samples used in some of the reported studies, two factors may increase the apparent extent of disabilities among victims of abuse. First, potential investigators who happened to be working with groups that included higher proportions of disabilities may have been more likely to identify this area of concern, and likely to choose a sample from the same higher incidence population with which they worked. Second, studies that show no effects are less likely to be published. Thus, in spite of the apparent consistency of results indicating a higher proportion than expected of disabilities among victims of abuse, some caution should be exercised in this conclusion.

DISABILITY INCREASES PROBABILITY OF SEXUAL ABUSE

A number of factors have been suggested that link disabilities to sexual and physical abuse. In many cases it is not the actual impairment of the individual that contributes to increased risk; rather, society's expectations and treatment of people with disabilities appear to increase risk.

Zirpoli, Snell, and Loyd (1987) found that the severity of disability and the extent of maladaptive behaviour contributed significantly to risk of abuse among mentally retarded residents of state training centers. This suggests that the degree, as well as the nature, of the impairment may be an important factor.

Skinner (1953) presented a model of counter control in which power and authority must be restrained by individual or social counter controls to prevent abuse. People with disabilities often lack counter control. A major factor in this limitation is impaired communication. They often lack the ability or opportunity to protest effectively. Deficits in communication among developmentally disabled adolescents (Cirrin & Rowland, 1985), physically disabled children (Light, Collier & Parnes, 1985), multiple disabled children (Orelove & Sobsey, 1987), and deaf children not only reduce the amount of communication but also heavily influence the content and circumstances of communication. All children who experience significant communication deficits show very low rates of initiation and often communicate only when responding to others. These individuals would be unlikely to report abuse, particularly if not explicitly asked.

An inability to physically defend oneself may also be a factor. Physical, sensory, and intellectual impairments all are likely to interfere with the individual's abilities to escape or resist abuse. This inability is powerfully described in a disabled victim's account of sexual assault by a "caregiver" (Sexual assaults, 1988).

Our own pilot data (following) and published accounts also suggest that even when abuse is reported, police, courts, and social agencies are often unwilling to pursue charges when the victim is disabled (Senn, 1988). Hebert (1986, August) described a court experience of a victim where the judge interpreted the manifestation of the victim's cerebral palsy as disrespect for the court proceedings. The issues that surround the acceptability of testimony of a child witness and of an intellectually impaired or emotionally disturbed witness are equally complex (Robertson, 1987), and the combined circumstance most often puts the victim at an insurmountable disadvantage in our court system.

In considering the ways in which disability may lead to sexual abuse it is important to recognize that it is often not the disability that appears to increase risk—it may be society's treatment of that disability. Children with disabilities are more likely to live outside their natural families, and there is some reason to believe that this increases risk. (Rindfleisch & Rabb, 1984). In comparing the risk for abuse in a very large sample of children living in institutions with children in family environments, concluded that the risk is at least doubled in institutional settings. Van Dusen's (1987) report of 250 charges of sexual abuse against 14 staff members in a Quebec group home is, unfortunately, not a rare occurrence. The apparent increase in risk when a child is placed outside the natural family likely results from exposure to a larger number of caregivers and settings. Children removed from their homes are often moved through a number of settings, each with a number of caregivers. Assuming the same risk from each caregiver, the greater the number a child is exposed to, the greater the risk.

While victims of sexual abuse and exploitation are often disabled, the offender is also disabled in some cases. Intellectually impaired people are more likely to be institutionalized if they are unable to protect themselves, or if they are perceived as a threat to others (Robertson, 1987). This means that institutions commonly cluster sexually aggressive and assaultive individuals with defenseless victims.

Parental demoralization, family isolation, chronic parental anxiety, and family stress are among the factors identified by Meier (1978) as increasing risk for abuse. These same factors have been identified as typical effects on families of children with severe disabilities. Thus, it would appear that parental response to the child's disability may create a family environment with increased risk for abuse.

Finally, many of our current training strategies in special education may increase the potential vulnerability of disabled students. The current focus on compliance and generalization provide reasons for concern. It is interesting to note that the cumulative index for the *Journal of Applied Behavior Analysis* (Cumulative index, 1987) lists over 80 articles published over the past 20 years on the importance of teaching generalization (most with disabled subjects). Only four focus on discrimination skills. This means that disabled children are typically trained to comply with the instructions of any adult and that protest or resistance is punished. Such a student becomes the perfect target for abuse.

SEXUAL ABUSE INCREASES THE RISK OF DISABILITY

Physical abuse has often been the direct cause of disabilities in children. For example, Buchanan and Oliver (1977) found that 3% of the 140 mentally retarded children that they studied had definitely become disabled as a result of abuse. Abuse was a possible cause for mental handicap in another 8% and neglect appeared to be a major factor for 24%. Sexual abuse as a cause of disability may appear much less likely; however, the regression, withdrawal, and emotional reaction that commonly follow sexual abuse may aggravate or mimic intellectual and behavioural problems. As a result, some of these children may be diagnosed or regarded as disabled who would not be, prior to experiencing sexual abuse.

THIRD FACTOR INFLUENCES RISK OF DISABILITY AND SEXUAL ABUSE

A hypothesis of mutual causation implies that some third factor increases the probability of both disability and sexual abuse. For example, Browning and Boatman (1977) point out the role of paternal alcoholism in increased risk for incest. A study was conducted, reviewing 14 incest cases that constituted 3.8% of new cases over a 14-month period. Four of the children were disabled, physically or mentally. Excessively high rates of depression in mothers and alcoholism in fathers were cited as contributing to incest. The possibility that the existence of disabilities among some of the children increases their vulnerability is seen from a psychiatric viewpoint: such children may seek physical affection from parents as an assurance that they are loved.

COMMUNITY SERVICES SURVEY

A survey was developed to determine whether community services for the treatment and prevention of sexual abuse are available and/or appropriate for disabled victims. There were four major components of the survey: type of service provided, client characteristics, self-evaluation of services provided to disabled individuals, and risk factors for sexual abuse as a function of type of disability. The survey was four pages in length and contained eleven forced-choice and open-ended questions.

As a preliminary step in a planned, extensive service availability and needs assessment project, the survey was mailed to community service agencies dealing directly and/or indirectly with sexual abuse. These agencies included rape crisis centers, groups dealing with victims of crime, and sex education groups. Sources for these agencies were the Services to Victims and Witnesses of Crime in Canada (Norquay & Weiler, 1981), the Directory of Canadian Associations (Land & Gallagher, 1986), and initial listings in the national directory of community sexual abuse service agencies being compiled by the Developmental Disabilities Centre.

The survey sample consisted of a cross section of national community service agencies representing all provinces and both territories. Seventy-five surveys were mailed; 10 were returned as undeliverable. The recipients were instructed to complete the survey and return it anonymously. The surveys were not coded as to location of the agency, and no accounting of agency response was attempted. Because of the nature of the sampling process and survey research methods, the results of the survey must be considered to be preliminary and only tentatively indicative of national availability of treatment and prevention programs; the proposed extensive survey will follow more conventional survey research methods and procedures.

Nineteen (29%) of the surveys were returned in reasonably complete form. Eight (11%) additional agencies responded with letters indicating that their record keeping did not adequately categorize the information that we requested or that the retrieval of the information requested would be too difficult and so they were unable to respond. Finally, several agencies telephoned to express their inability to respond. Due to the limited number of complete responses, rank order analyses rather than raw numbers or percentages are presented.

TYPE OF SERVICE PROVIDED

Multiple services are provided by all but one respondent agency. Counselling (individual and family) is the most common service provided, followed by advocacy and education (sex education, public education, self-defence), which are provided with approximately equal frequencies. Eighteen of the agencies estimated the number of clients they serve each year; in total, these agencies served over 55,000 clients in the past year. Of those agencies that specified the nature of their client contact, the majority of their clients receive education, followed by counseling, referrals, and/or informational services, and crisis intervention. At first, the ranks for the nature of client contact seem to contradict the ranks for the type of services provided. However, educational programs are much less labour-intensive than counseling services; hence, many more clients can be served through educational services.

CLIENT CHARACTERISTICS

Approximately one-half of the clients served by the respondent agencies in the past year were over 21 years of age (51%). Adult clients are followed in frequency by adolescents between the ages of 13 and 21 years (41%); nonadolescent children represented a small minority of the clients (5%). The clients were predominantly female (86%).

Fourteen of the agencies have served disabled individuals in the past year; these clients generally account for a significant proportion of their clients, ranging from 1-70% with a median of 13% disabled clients. Representation of physical, intellectual, and psychiatric impairments was approximately the same across the responding agencies; this is consistent with the literature (e.g., Tilelli, Turek & Jaffe, 1980; Shah, Holloway & Valkil, 1982; Browning & Boatman, 1977) citing approximately equal incidence of sexual abuse among the three classes of disability. One of the agencies reported that they had been in contact with, but unable to provide services to, a number of severely and profoundly retarded victims.

SELF-EVALUATION OF SERVICES PROVIDED TO DISABLED INDIVIDUALS

The community service agencies generally responded that the services they provide are sometimes or often appropriate to hearing impaired, visually impaired, psychiatrically impaired, physically disabled, or mildly retarded clients. Several agencies provide services that are sometimes appropriate for moderately mentally retarded individuals. Most agencies responded that they either do not serve, or do not provide services that are appropriate for severely or profoundly mentally retarded individuals.

Those agencies that do serve disabled people are likely to make modifications to their service programs that maximize either accessibility (e.g., wheelchair accessible offices for physically disabled clients, telecommunication devices for the deaf or sign language interpreters for hearing impaired clients) or communication (e.g., visual or art therapy for hearing impaired clients, audiotapes for visually impaired clients, simple language and materials for mildly and moderately mentally retarded clients). Those agencies which experience difficulty serving disabled people cited the same factors (i.e., accessibility and communication) as problems that limit their ability to serve disabled persons.

Even though they experienced difficulties serving disabled clients, most of the respondents believed hearing impaired, visually impaired, psychiatrically impaired, physically disabled, and mildly mentally retarded individuals should be served by the same agencies that provide services to individuals without disabilities rather than by specialized agencies. The respondents were equally split on whether moderately, severely, and profoundly mentally retarded people should be served by the same or by specialized community agencies. These beliefs in service responsibilities, depending on type of disability, generally mirror the agencies' abilities to serve disabled people. Respondents were more likely to believe that a particular type of disabled individual is best served by a mainstream community agency if their own agency serves that type of person without too many difficulties or modifications.

RISK FACTORS AS A FUNCTION OF TYPE OF DISABILITY

Although very few disabled clients were served by the community service agencies in the past year, the respondents were almost unanimous in their belief that all disabled individuals are at greater risk for sexual abuse than the general population. Two respondents believed that hearing and visually impaired individuals were at the same risk for sexual abuse compared with the general population, and two respondents felt that moderately, severely, and profoundly mentally retarded individuals experienced less risk.

The beliefs about increased risk factors obtained from the survey are entirely consistent with the data on incidence (see Table 1 above). However, the client contact results obtained from the preliminary survey are not consistent with perceived prevalence. Compared to the incidence statistics discussed in the previous section, and as is demonstrated by the results of the victim survey discussed in the next section, many disabled victims are simply not receiving any community assistance.

SEXUAL ABUSE AND SERVICE PROVISION SURVEY

A survey was developed to investigate services provided to disabled victims of sexual abuse. There were four major concerns addressed by the survey: (1) characteristics of the victims, offender, and, offence, (2) whether and how the victim's disability contributed to the victim's vulnerability to sexual abuse, (3) whether the offender was charged and/or convicted of the offence and, if the offender was not charged, whether the victim's disability was a contributing factor, and (4) the nature of and satisfaction with any community services obtained to treat and/or support the victim. The survey was two pages in length and consisted of 19 open-ended and forced-choice questions.

The survey was sent to a cross section, national sample of 170 agencies that aid disabled people, including community mental retardation groups, community cerebral palsy organizations, educational, vocational, and community living agencies, and groups dedicated to supporting and treating disabled victims of violence. The names and addresses of the agencies were obtained from directories and the national directory of community sexual abuse service agencies being compiled by the University of Alberta Developmental Disabilities Centre. A brief description of the project was provided to assist agencies in requesting reports.

The recipients of the survey were instructed to disseminate the survey to any individual or group that was involved in or aware of any situation involving sexual abuse. The respondents were instructed not to include any information that would identify the victims, offender, reporter, or city and province of a criminal act; this was done to ensure confidentiality. Ninety-one completed reports have been received to date, with 88 providing usable data, and additional reports are still coming in.

CHARACTERISTICS OF THE VICTIM, OFFENDER, AND OFFENCE

Victims of sexual abuse were most commonly 18 years of age and over (47%). Children aged 0-12 comprised 34% of the victims, while 13-17 year olds made up 16% of the victims. In comparison with the community services survey, however, the victims' survey reveals a greater percentage of child victims of sexual abuse than have been served by community agencies (18% victims as opposed to 8% served). Victims were predominantly female (85%).

Sixty-seven percent of the victims were intellectually impaired; 18% of the victims had a physical impairment (generally cerebral palsy or paralysis); 14% had a hearing impairment (with an additional 5% having a hearing impairment and another disability); and a few (6%) were psychiatrically impaired. Of the total sample, 19% were multiply disabled. The victims' survey indicates many more mentally retarded victims than reported in the literature or served through the community services survey (with each source reporting intellectual impairment as representing an average of 33% of disabled victims).

Victims who were mentally retarded were most often 18 and over (52%), followed by 0-12 years old (31%), or between 13 and 17 years old (17%); this breakdown mirrors the general age findings. Breaking down the three variables of age, sex, and disability, the results reveal that the disabled person most at risk for sexual abuse is an intellectually impaired adult female.

In cases where the offenders' age was reported, offenders were most often 18 and over (63%), followed by 13-17 year olds (15%), and 0-12 year olds (2%). Offenders were predominantly male (93%). Nineteen percent of offenders were intellectually impaired, and 13% had other disabilities.

Offenders were most frequently members of the victim's natural family, or disability based service providers (20% for each group); followed by family friends (13%); strangers (12%); other disabled individuals receiving services in the same setting as the victim (11%); step-relatives (7%); boyfriend/girlfriend or transportation provider (6% for each group); foster family members (2%); and nondisability based service providers (1%). Child victims were most often sexually abused by relatives (44%), followed by disability service providers (19%); adolescent victims were generally abused by either disability service providers (25%) or neighbours/family friends (19%); and adult victims were most often abused by disability service providers or co-disability recipients (18% for each category), followed by neighbours/family friends or strangers (16% for each category). These results are consistent with the findings of Brookhouser, Sullivan, Scanlan, and Garbarino (1986); Shah, Holloway, and Valkil (1982); and Tilelli, Turek, and Jaffe (1980) and demonstrate that those people in greatest contact with the victims are the most likely offenders.

Where specific information was given about the type of abuse, intercourse was involved in 41% of the cases. Fondling (31%) was the next most frequent form of abuse. Oral sex performed on the offender was reported in 3% of the cases and oral sex performed on the victim was reported in 2% of cases. An additional 2% of cases involved forced participation, in which the offender forced the victims to engage in sexual behaviour with each other. Other types of abuse (e.g., undressing, masturbation) were reported by 15% of respondents. Six percent of respondents did not specify what form the abuse took. There were no differences in type of offence as a function of age; across all three age groups, intercourse and fondling were the most common forms of abuse. Relatives were slightly more likely to engage in fondling and intercourse than were other known or authority figure offenders.

The offence most often occurred in a private home (54%); followed by a public place (11%); a vehicle (10%); group homes or other disability service location (8% for each category); an institution (5%); and hospitals or other location (3% for each category). In the 0-12 age group, the offence was most likely to have occurred in a private home (70%) or a group home (11%). In the 13-17 age group, the offence most often occurred in a private home (36%). followed by a public place and other disability service location (21% for each category). In the 18 and over age group, the offence was most likely to occur in a private home (53%) or in a vehicle (18%). Younger and/or more disabled victims were more likely to be abused in a location associated with themselves; older and/or less disabled victims were more likely to be abused in a location associated with the offender. Again, these findings make sense; younger and more disabled people are more likely to remain in their own location, whereas older and less disabled people are more mobile and therefore at greater risk for abuse outside of their home location. The results are also supported by the general findings reported in the literature (Chamberlain, Rauh, Passer, McGrath & Burket, 1984; Zirpoli, Snell & Loyd, 1987).

CONTRIBUTION OF VICTIM'S DISABILITY TO VULNERABILITY

There were 70 responses to the questions considering whether the victim's disability might have contributed to being at greater risk for the sexual abuse. The predominant comment, comprising 35% of the responses, had to do with the victim not having enough knowledge about appropriate sexual behaviours and/or having poor judgement. Although this lack of knowledge may be common among mentally retarded and/or sheltered individuals, it can potentially be corrected through education. Overcompliance was cited by 24% of respondents, suggesting that the current focus of compliance training in special education may be harmful to students and a greater focus on assertiveness may be needed. Twenty-three percent of the respondents cited physical inability to defend oneself as a factor: this was noted by all of the reporters for physically disabled victims; and 11% cited communication deficits. In both types of situations, the victims were at least relatively helpless in either preventing or reporting the offence. Respondents also mentioned need for approval (6%), trusting the offender (5%), and that the disability placed the victim in the environment where the abuse occurred (5%). Other responses that did not fit these categories were given in 6% of reports.

CONTRIBUTION OF VICTIM'S DISABILITY TO LEGAL ACTION

Twenty charges were laid (representing 23% of reported incidents), resulting in seven convictions (representing 8% of reported incidents), one unknown result, with four cases currently unresolved. There were 54 responses as to why no charges were laid. In 67% of the cases, the incident was never reported to police. In 22% of cases, police declined to press charges, generally citing the victim as an incompetent witness. In 6% of cases, the prosecutor refused to pursue charges, and in another 6% of cases, the offender was never found. Many of the respondents were dissatisfied with the legal action taken or denied.

Community Service Contact and Evaluation

Sixty-five percent of respondents reported that treatment and/or support services were sought for the victim. Of these, 67% sought counseling, 44% sought help from the victim's current family or school, 14% sought legal services, 12% sought medical services, and 2% sought educational services. In addition, in 19% of cases the victim received protective services (removal from home).

Sixty-one respondents evaluated the services that had been contacted and/or received. Seven percent of responses indicated that the victim received the same services as nondisabled clients and no special services were required, and 26% indicated that the services received met the special needs of the victim's disabilities. In 30% of cases services were altered to meet the special needs of the victim, but the alterations were not adequate, while 38% of respondents indicated that no special services were provided, but that they would have been helpful. Older and/or less disabled victims were more likely to receive appropriate services; younger and/or more disabled victims were less likely to receive appropriate, or even any, services from community agencies.

Conclusions and Recommendations

In spite of the limitations of individual studies, there is little doubt that people with disabilities are at greater risk for sexual abuse. Although most of the reviewed data came from outside of Canada, the consistency of our pilot data with the findings of the non-Canadian studies suggests that the findings reported elsewhere can be expected to generalize well to Canada. The extent of increased risk remains unclear, and although a number of factors appear as likely contributors, the mechanism for increased risk is uncertain. While recommending that research should move to more applied topics of prevention and victims' services, some further investigation of the mechanisms of increased risk may be helpful for accomplishing these ends and for increasing our understanding of risk factors for all children. Even if people with disabilities were at no greater risk than others in our society, it is imperative that appropriate prevention and treatment services be developed to meet the needs of this group of children and adults.

The literature reviewed here and our own pilot studies suggest that current prevention efforts and treatment services often fail to meet the needs of people with disabilities and that failure becomes increasingly common as a function of the severity of the disability. It is time for researchers and clinicians to switch their focus from documenting the existence of this problem to developing the appropriate prevention and treatment services for people with disabilities.

In establishing appropriate services for children with disabilities, it is important to recognize general trends in service delivery for people with disabilities. Prevention and victims' services should be fully integrated with those services provided to nondisabled children and adults whenever possible. Efforts should be directed toward identification of resources and training required to enable generic community services to serve this population, not toward establishing separate services.

Special educators need to review the philosophy of curricula to increase focus on assertiveness, choice, discrimination of appropriate and inappropriate requests, and improved sex education. Legal safeguards, including standards for caregivers and improved legal rights for disabled victims of abuse, are also required.

Unit VIII

Prevention and Intervention Strategies

*In 1998, while visiting the Far-East, Prime Minister Jean Chretian spoke ut
against human rights violations while at home he was having to contend with
the APEC inquiry, tainted-blood scandal and a host of other social issues. In
1997, Amnesty International reported that in spite of public outcry, China
executed more 'criminals' than any other country in the world.*

*In 1957 Prime Minister (1963-1968) Lester B. Pearson won the Noble prize
for his diplomatic peace initiative in proposing to send UN peacekeeping
forces to the Suez Canal area. In 1994 the Lester B. Pearson Canadian
International Peacekeeping Training Centre was established in Annapolis,
Nova Scotia.*

For many years Canada has been hailed as a supporter of human rights. Our armed forces have served on numerous United Nations peace missions. We have had Canadian's hold high positions within the United Nations crime prevention and human rights tribunals. On the surface Canada has much to be proud of. However, on the fiftieth anniversary of the Universal Declaration of Human Rights, the UN accused Canada of failing to live up to its covenant commitments.

The year 1998 marked the fiftieth anniversary of the declaration. Yet, in spite of the fact that as a civilization humans have been around for considerably longer, human rights are touted as something we should all strive to achieve. What does it mean that as human beings we need to be reminded and given direction in how to promote human rights, be law abiding and strive to enhance our quality of life? As Ole Ingstrup, Commissioner of Correctional Service Canada (CSC), recently noted, we all need to reflect on and respect the significance of human rights issues (Ingstrup, 1998). Yet, as we have seen in previous sections of this reader, our history and our justice system has a less than impeccable record. John Peters Humphrey (a Canadian diplomat), one of the key authors of the human rights declaration, summarized the philosophy of the declaration by suggesting "all human being are born free and equal in dignity and rights" (Scott, 1998:2). Yet, we continue to incarcerate people for life, we continue to discriminate against women, various racial and ethnic groups, and even the physically and mentally challenged in our society. How can the Canadian justice system protect society while respecting the rights of all citizens? Is the concept logistically an impossibility? In recent years we have been witness to a plea for better handling of offenders and better methods to reintegrate them into the society. Yet, our incarcerations have increased in the 1990s. 'Minority' groups continue to be disproportionately over-represented in our criminal justice system. The proposed amendments to the Young Offenders Act (see Unit VI) reflect a conservative and punitive approach to the handling of young offenders.

Even though official accounts tell us that crime has decreased throughout most of the 1990s, it still remains considerably higher than in the 1960s when we started using the current data collection methodology. Furthermore, public perceptions of crime have not declined. And as we have seen throughout this reader, certain groups are more prone to being victimized in spite of politicians promising order, law and security for all Canadians.

Universally, people look to their governments to provide quality of life through protection from crime and enforcement of human rights. However, it would appear that our criminal justice system (and other public institutions) is unable to provide such protections.

In this unit we offer several articles that speak to various efforts that have been made to offer institutionalized conflict resolution mechanisms as well as measures by which to construct a criminal justice system that is both fair and effective in its objectives. For example, we saw that accessibility to justice is not equal for all Canadians, the plights of many groups continue to receive token attention from the criminal justice system. We continue to have an over-reliance on imprisonment; the majority of those charged and sentenced come from the ranks of the economically and socially marginalized groups. Even HIV infection rates and incidence of AIDS among Canadian offenders exceeds the rates of the general population (Zinger, 1998). Ironically, these and other points have also been expressed in Latin American countries—a part of the world that is commonly thought of as third world and punitive with its administration of justice (Dandurand and Paris-Steffens, 1998). Is it realistic to expect Canadians to provide service and advise to other "less developed" nations when the issues we offer advise for are often the same we must contend with at home?

DISCUSSION QUESTIONS:

1. How is it possible for offenders to attempt to speak out against injustices when criminal justice politics are attuned to suppressing 'insurrections'?
2. In the new restorative justice and/or reintegrative shaming approaches, what are the implications should the offender not wish to participate?

3. What other aspects of humanity might we want to explore?
4. How do we begin to prevent or intervene in something that was never right to begin with?
5. Is it realistic to expect the system to teach honesty, respect and caring characteristics?

References

Dandurand, Y. and Paris-Steffens, R. (1998). "Beyond wishful thinking: Canadian/Latin American cooperation in criminal law reform and criminal justice." The Focal Papers. Vancouver, BC: Canadian Foundation for the Americas.

Ingstrup, O. (1998, November). Respect and human rights. *Let's Talk,* p. 1.

Scott, A. (1998, November). Human rights and corrections. *Let's Talk,* pp. 2-3.

Zinger, I. (1998, November). Human rights for all. *Let's Talk,* pp. 4-6.

Web watch: www.unac.org offers an overview of what Canadians are doing for a better UN. It also provides useful links to a variety of human rights issues.

www.crime-prevention.org/ncpc/ is the site of the National Crime Prevention Council of Canada and includes information on national strategies, a search engine and access to related publications.

www.bconnex.net/~cspcc/crime_prevention/ contains a varied collection of articles and commentary on how to prevent and reduce crime in Canada.

Should Victims
Participate in Sentencing

Wayne Renke

An innocent voice cut through the rank atmosphere of the Bernardo sentencing proceedings. Eleven-year-old Ryan Mahaffy wept as he addressed Bernardo: "Because you murdered my sister, you have changed my life in so many ways.... Because of you I am an only child... some people have called you a monster and evil and I agree."

Some might wonder whether Ryan's evidence should have been admitted. Why should the impression of victims—those who have been harmed or their survivors—form any part of sentencing proceedings?

Victim participation in sentencing seems objectionable on many grounds. It opens up another front against which an offender must defend. It compromises judicial independence—how could a judge resist the emotional and political pressure exerted by victims before the bench? It yields evidence irrelevant to offenders' culpability "Punishment," wrote George Fletcher in *With Justice for Some: Victim's Rights in Criminal Trials,* "responds to the wrong the offender commits, but not to the particular wrong as measured by victims willing to testify.... It hardly makes sense to think of life as sacred if its value is a function of how much others love or need the person killed," or, one might add, if it is a function of the eloquence of a survivor or his or her family. Victim participation is prejudicial to offenders since victims may encourage excessive sentences to achieve vengeance, typically not an accepted purpose of sentencing. It is unfair to offenders since those who have harmed eloquent victims may face stiffer sentences.

But despite these objections and despite the high value accorded offenders' interests in the criminal law, victims like Ryan Mahaffy should have the right to participate in sentencing hearings. Victim participation promotes both the accountability of sentencing proceedings to the public and the accountability of offenders to their victims. Current governing legal rules permit restrained victim participation while preserving offenders' procedural protections. Nor does victim participation seriously compromise the equal treatment of offenders.

THE BURDEN OF PROOF

As a matter of policy, even apart from charter concerns, the interests of accuseds or offenders should have presumptive priority over competing interests in the criminal justice process. A trial is not a rally, public inquiry or parliamentary committee hearing. A trial determines guilt or innocence. Punishment is imposed on the offender and none other. Generally, the state, with its large aggregations of power, should not be permitted to limit individuals' liberties without justification. Therefore, advocates of measures that limit offenders' interests through state power should bear the burden of proof.

Victim participation in sentencing may be considered a form of state action since the state facilitates it through both legislation and assistance programs. It may also be considered to limit offenders' interests by, at least, increasing offenders' legal and practical burdens and by threatening increased sentences. Nevertheless, compelling interests are served by victim participation in sentencing, and offenders' interests are not necessarily impaired unduly by the promotion of these interests.

INTERESTS SERVED BY VICTIM PARTICIPATION IN SENTENCING

The practical result of victim participation in sentencing is that a victim is permitted to speak for him or herself. The victim may make a statement in writing, in accordance with a victim impact statement program, or orally, upon the ruling of the sentencing judge. The victim's words are not words of a lawyer but the words of ordinary experience. Why one might wonder, is this recovery of the victim's voice important? It might benefit a victim personally by providing catharsis, but what public interests does it serve?

Victim participation promotes the openness, intelligibility and accountability of criminal processes to the public. Victim participation reinscribes sentencing in ordinary experience. When a victim is permitted to describe the effects of an offence in his or her own words, private grief is expressed in ordinary language. The words used, the emotions conveyed, and the message given to the offender are comprehensible. The victim's speech opens the court room. The victim's speech does matter to sentencing; this shows that the criminal justice process reflects, to a degree, the perspectives of citizens, the victim's speech is a small sign of the court's accountability. Victim participation, then, should enhance the public's regard for the administration of justice, itself a worthy objective.

Moreover, victim participation takes back victimhood and punishment from their professionalized redefinitions. Legal discourse is not necessary to define or comprehend victims' injuries, and the pursuit of remedies for criminal injuries does not require the substitution of legal professionals for victims. We should keep in mind that the appropriation of criminal prosecutions by the legal profession is a relatively recent (19th century) development in Anglo-Canadian law. Victim participation in sentencing is also a small sign that the criminal law is not the sole province of an autonomous guild. But if sentencing is open to victim participation and if victims wish to see that justice is done, they cannot rely only on lawyers. They must act, they must participate. Sentencing becomes accountable to the public in the sense that the public bears some responsibility for its functioning; it becomes more the public's institution.

One might suggest that a crime, in contrast to a private wrong, harms society rather than the individual. Punishment, then, should reflect the social significance of the crime, not its impact on the victim. This suggestion is too baldly put. Evidence concerning the magnitude and impact of a crime on a victim has traditionally been considered in the calculation of sentences.

A benefit of the legislative and policy focus on victims might be the increased awareness and use of such evidence. Victim participation of the type we are considering, however, seems to serve some further purposes; it is not merely a new or improved version of what was always previously admissible. A further interest victim participation promotes is the accountability of offenders.

According to Bill C-41, one of the objectives of sentencing is "to promote a sense of responsibility in offenders, and acknowledgement of the harm done to victims and to the community." Accountability moves in two directions—from the offender to the community and from the offender to the victim. This point turns on the rejection of the view that crime is only a violation of the relation between the offender and society. An offence is also, primarily and directly, a violation of the relation between the offender and his or her victim. Without victims, there would be no crimes. Outside the law, a common technique for encouraging an offender to take responsibility is to show the offender the precise consequences of his or her actions, to show how others have been hurt, to show the losses caused by those actions. Victim participation imports this technique into sentencing. Exposing an offender to the harm he or she has inflicted on another person may elicit remorse and accountability more effectively than advising an offender that he or she has transgressed against some abstract community.

If victim participation is understood within the framework of accountability, it has no necessary connection to increased punitiveness. Accountability is concerned less with the quantity of the sentence than with the quality of the sentencing procedure, less with the judge's impression of the gravity of the offence than with communication between the victim and offender. Understood in this way, victim participation in sentencing avoids many of its criticisms. It does not provide a measure of injury that varies with victims' literary skills. A compelling statement should not be an aggravating factor in sentencing; a poorly written statement or the absence of a statement should not be a mitigating factor in sentencing. Rather, an expression of victim impact exposes the meaning of the criminal act to the offender ("look, this is what you have done").

Even if one concedes that victim participation in sentencing serves compelling interests, its governing legal rules must not unduly impair offenders' interests.

CURRENT LAW

Victims may put statements before sentencing courts pursuant to legislation or judges' rulings. Under current legislation, for the purpose of determining a sentence, the judge may (not must) consider an unsworn statement prepared by a "victim" in a provincially prescribed form. "Victim" means the person to whom harm was done or who suffered physical or emotional loss as a result of the commission of the offence; or, where this person is dead or incapacitated, the spouse or any relative of that person, anyone who has custody of that person or anyone who is responsible for the care, or support, of that person or any of that person's dependants. The statement is to describe the harm done to or the loss suffered by the victim as a result of the offence. The statement is filed with the court and a copy is provided to the accused and the prosecutor.

Victims' participation through this procedure is circumscribed. The statement is to concern only a victim's loss, not other matters such as sentencing recommendations or the victim's reflections on the substantive offence. The statement is reduced to writing, so the court is guarded against emotional outbursts during viva voce testimony. The judge has the ordinary power to disregard any prejudicial or scandalous portions of the statement. The judge has the discretion to disregard the statement entirely.

The offender maintains due process protections. The mere fact that the statement is unsworn should cause no alarm. Sentencing hearings tend to be relatively informal and evidence is frequently accepted simply through the unsworn submissions of counsel. If the offender challenges some allegation in the statement, he or she may call evidence to contradict the allegation. The victim may be called as a witness for the Crown, provide sworn testimony and be subject to cross-examination.

The victim impact statement provisions do not exhaust the means by which victims may participate in sentencing. Victims generally lack standing in criminal cases, though, and so cannot claim to be heard as of right. If Crown counsel cooperates, the victim may be called as a witness so that he or she may testify; or, as in the Bernardo case, the Crown may proffer videotaped or other documentary evidence prepared by the victim. The offender may or may not challenge the admissibility of the evidence. Generally the judge is entitled to consider any credible and trustworthy evidence.

The last and overriding protection for the offender is the judiciary. Judges are subject to myriad influences and pressures. Yet, they are generally considered to maintain their independence and impartiality. If judges are not swayed by pickets, editorials, or condemnations by hostile politicians, they should be expected to maintain their independence in the face of victims and determine fit sentences. Furthermore, a judge's sentence is reviewable by the provincial court of appeal (in practice, the court of last resort in most sentencing matters), which can correct a sentence falling outside the established range of punishment.

The law as it now stands adequately constrains victim participation in sentencing. Victim participation, however, could be modestly enhanced without diminishing offenders' protections.

PROSPECTIVE DEVELOPMENTS

The law might be developed in two directions. First, victims could be extended the right to make oral unsworn statements respecting the impact of the offence. This would be the equivalent of the offender's ability to offer unsworn evidence at sentencing. If the victim were properly briefed, his or her evidence would not stray into improper areas; the judge, in any event, could maintain control over the proceedings. The oral statement would give the victim a greater sense of participation in the sentencing. A victim might also find an oral statement advantageous if he or she has difficulty expressing himself or herself in writing. Oral statements pose advantages and disadvantages for the offender. The offender may obtain less complete disclosure of the contents of the oral statement before the hearing; but if the statement is contentious, the victim will be present to be called as a witness. Otherwise, the oral statement would be on the same footing as a written statement. The oral statement appears to be an acceptable development.

Second, the scope of statements could be expanded. Victims could be permitted to make sentence recommendations or to reflect on the circumstances of offences. Victims, I suggest, should not make sentencing recommendations. The purpose of victim participation is to inject ordinary experience into the court, not to transform victims into another set of lawyers with another set of legal submissions. Crown prosecutors, not victims, may best oppose offenders' positions on sentence. Furthermore, insofar as offender accountability is the target of victim participation, sentence quantum should not be the concern of victims. Victims should also not comment on the circumstances of offences. Again, it is the prosecutor's job to marshal this evidence. The victim should be given no special forum in which to provide an unsworn version of what may well be controversial facts. The victim's version of events should be adduced in the ordinary course of trial or sentencing proceedings. To permit this evidence to be given unsworn in sentencing proceedings would violate the offender's due process rights.

EQUALITY ISSUES

The mere fact that different offenders face different types of victim participation does not raise equality concerns. Offenders embrace contingency when they engage in crime. Some victims die; others miraculously survive. Some victims attend trial; others may not. Some victims give compelling testimony; others may not. Harming an eloquent victim is simply one of the risks run by the offender. Moreover, if, as I have suggested, the focus of victim participation is offender accountability rather than sentence increase, offenders may not be materially prejudiced by even eloquent victim participation.

In any event, the distinction between eloquent and non-eloquent victims is frequently exaggerated. Money and a higher education are not prerequisites for expressing pain. Witness Ryan Mahaffy's remarks: they would not have been improved by a ghost-writer.

The real equality issues in the victim participation context concern the information provided to victims and the assistance available to them. All victims should be informed of the ways in which they may participate in sentencing and should have access to assistance if they desire to participate. Provincial victims' assistance programs, police departments, RCMP detachments, and victim assistance units attached to policing services do attempt to inform and assist victims. Unfortunately, limited resources in our difficult economic times leave the scope of victim assistance programs at less than an ideal level. Not all victims receive the information or assistance they might need. This, however, is a political grievance of victims, not a ground for eliminating the good that the present system can accomplish.

CONCLUSION

Sentencing should become neither spectacle, nor occasion for the Crown and victims to "gang up" on offenders, nor space for the displacement of law by emotion. The interests of victims may be recognized in sentencing, however, without producing these results. In sentencing, legal reality and victims' reality should merge; victims should be allowed to reach offenders through ordinary language, and show offenders that reality of the effects of their acts. Perhaps the belief that offenders will be prompted to take responsibility for their actions is unrealistically optimistic. This belief, I suppose, is no more unrealistically optimistic than the beliefs that offenders will be rehabilitated or that prospective offenders will be deterred by punishment.

Criminal Trial and Punishment: Protection of Rights under the Charter

Marilyn Pilon

ISSUE DEFINITION

The *Canadian Charter of Rights and Freedoms* came into force on 17 April 1982. The legal rights guaranteed by the *Charter* are contained in sections 7 to 14 inclusive. They deal with such matters as the right to life, liberty and security; the right to be secure against unreasonable search and seizure; the rights of an accused upon arrest; the right of an accused to certain proceedings in criminal and penal matters; and the right not to be subject to cruel and unusual punishment.

The purpose of this analysis is to determine what effect sections 11, 12 and 13 of the *Charter* have had on existing criminal law since then. As there are now a great number of decided cases dealing with these sections, this paper will concentrate on significant decisions of the provincial courts of appeal and the Supreme Court of Canada.

BACKGROUND AND ANALYSIS

The Interpretation of an Entrenched *Charter*

When analyzing the decisions of the courts with respect to these sections, it is important to remember that the *Charter* is entrenched within the Constitution

Pilon, M (1995). *Criminal trials and punishments: Protections in Canada* -Background Paper BP-91-8E. Ottawa: Research Branch Library of Parliament. Reproduced with the permission of the Minister of Public Works and Government Services Canada, 1998.

of Canada and that, by virtue of section 52(1) of the *Constitution Act*, 1982, "the Constitution of Canada is the supreme law of Canada, and any law that is inconsistent with the provisions of the Constitution is, to the extent of the inconsistency, of no force or effect."

It could be argued that two sections of the *Charter* illustrate a conscious attempt by its framers to restrain the Canadian courts from achieving the level of judicial activism which has been prevalent in the United States and to continue in some measure the Canadian heritage of parliamentary supremacy. Section 1 allows legislatures to impose reasonable limits upon rights and freedoms, while s. 33 allows the legislatures to expressly declare that a statute may operate notwithstanding certain sections of the *Charter*.

In its decision in the *Southam* case, the Supreme Court of Canada indicated that "the task of expounding a constitution is crucially different from that of construing a statute." As outlined in Southam, the *Charter* is a purposive document; that is, "its purpose is to guarantee and to protect within the limits of reason, the enjoyment of the rights and freedoms it enshrines. It is intended to constrain governmental action inconsistent with those rights and freedoms; it is not in itself an authorization for governmental action."

It is in this context of the contrast between the concepts underlying the *Charter* and the American *Bill of Rights* that this paper examines the legal rights protected by sections 11, 12 and 13 and discusses recent court decisions showing the impact of those sections on the criminal justice system.

Specific Rights: Section 11

This section states:

11. Any person charged with an offence has the right:
    (a) to be informed without unreasonable delay of the specific offence;
    (b) to be tried within a reasonable time;
    (c) not to be compelled to be a witness in proceedings against that person in respect of the offence;
    (d) to be presumed innocent until proven guilty according to law in a fair and public hearing by an independent and impartial tribunal;
    (e) not to be denied reasonable bail without just cause;
    (f) except in the case of an offence under military law tried before a military tribunal, to the benefit of trial by jury where the maximum punishment for the offence is imprisonment for five years or a more severe punishment;

(g) not to be found guilty on account of any act or omission unless, at the time of the act or omission, it constituted an offence under Canadian or international law or was criminal according to the general principles of law recognized by the community of nations;

(h) if finally acquitted of the offence, not to be tried for it again and, if finally found guilty and punished for the offence, not to be tried or punished for it again; and

(i) if found guilty of the offence and if the punishment for the offence has been varied between the time of commission and the time of sentencing, to the benefit of the lesser punishment.

1. "Charged with an Offence"—The Application of Section 11

In *R. v. Wigglesworth,* the Supreme Court of Canada held that s. 11 rights "are available to persons prosecuted by the State for public offences involving punitive sanctions, i.e., criminal, quasi-criminal and regulatory offences, either federally or provincially enacted." Thus, even though a minor traffic offence may carry slight consequences, the criminal or quasi-criminal nature of the proceedings would bring it within s. 11.

The Court also held that section 11 applies to proceedings that carry a true penal consequence. The possibility of a year of imprisonment for officers found guilty of a major service offence in R.C.M.P. Service Court was held to attract s. 11 guarantees, even though the proceedings were found to be disciplinary rather than criminal or quasi-criminal in nature.

2. Informed of Specific Offence—Section 11(a)

The courts have interpreted "the right to be informed without unreasonable delay of the specific offence" as arising when the information is laid; that is, when the person is "charged with the offence". It has also been held that this section does not offend the right to lay alternate charges.

An example of the operation of this subsection can be seen in the *Ryan* case, in which the court quashed an information laid two months after the accused had received an appearance notice. The courts have interpreted the phrase "informed ... of the specific offence" pragmatically, implying the right to be informed of the substantive offense and the acts of conduct that allegedly form the basis of the charge.

3. Tried Within a Reasonable Time—Section 11(b)

In the 18 October 1990 *Askov* decision of the Supreme Court of Canada, Mr. Justice Cory, for the unanimous Court, held that the right to be tried within a reasonable time, like other specific s. 11 guarantees, is primarily concerned with an aspect of fundamental justice guaranteed by s. 7. The primary aim of s. 11(b), he said, is to protect the individual's rights and to protect fundamental justice for the accused. There is a need to treat those on trial fairly and justly. There is also a practical benefit to be derived from resolving charges quickly since memories fade with time and witnesses may move, become ill or die. Victims of crime also have an interest in whether or not criminal trials take place within a reasonable time.

Mr. Justice Cory argued that the failure of the criminal justice system to work "fairly, efficiently and with reasonable dispatch ... inevitably leads to community frustration with the judicial system and eventually to a feeling of contempt for Court procedures." The judge went on to say that in determining whether the delay in bringing the accused to trial has been unreasonable, the court should consider a number of factors, such as: (1) the length of the delay; (2) the explanation for the delay; (3) the accused's waiver of the right to be tried expeditiously (i.e., through requests for, or agreement with, adjournments or failure to demand as early a date as possible for trial); and (4) prejudice to the accused. The longer the delay, the more difficult it should be for a court to excuse it and "very lengthy delays may be such that they cannot be justified for any reason." Those delays that will weigh in favour of the accused, he continued, are those attributable to the Crown or to systemic or institutional delays; in complex cases, longer delays will, to a point, be acceptable.

Mr. Justice Cory held that when considering delays occasioned by inadequate institutional resources, essentially the reason for the two-year trial delay in *Askov,* the court may compare the jurisdiction in question (i.e., Ontario) with other, "better" jurisdictions in the rest of the country. In all cases, the Crown will have the burden of showing that the institutional delay in question is justified. A waiver of rights by the accused will justify delay, but, to be valid, such a waiver must be informed, unequivocal and freely given.

The *Askov* decision generated considerable confusion in Canadian criminal courts. From the date of the decision until April 12, 1991, more than 34,495 charges in Ontario alone were stayed, dismissed or withdrawn on the basis of the judgment. This appeared to have a serious impact on the public's confidence in the administration of justice. Mr. Justice Cory, who wrote the judgment, was so "shocked" by its effects that he told a legal conference that the Court had not been made aware of the potential impact of the decision at the hearing. He suggested that the ruling may have been misinterpreted by lower courts and defence counsel.

In order to ensure that the *Askov* decision was "properly understood and applied throughout Ontario", the Ontario Court of Appeal heard and determined six special cases. In *R.* v. *Bennett,* the lead case, the Court concluded that a large number of cases had been stayed because *Askov* had been erroneously interpreted as meaning that a systemic delay beyond six to eight months in bringing an accused to trial should automatically result in a stay or dismissal of charges. The Court of Appeal held that the assessment of the delay should not be reduced to a simplistic computation of time; courts must carefully balance the four factors noted above. Further, the case puts a heavy burden on defendants to submit "sophisticated" statistical information concerning systemic delay in particular jurisdictions in support of their motions for a stay. These conclusions were expected to reduce the number of charges stayed and withdrawn on the basis of s. 11(b).

In the subsequent case of *R.* v. *Morin,* in an appeal from the Ontario Court of Appeal, the Supreme Court of Canada was asked to consider whether delay caused by systemic factors could be excused during a transition period of reform aimed at providing trials within a reasonable time. On March 26, 1992, the majority held that an institutional delay of approximately 12 months was not unreasonable, given the absence of any significant prejudice to the accused and the strain on institutional resources brought about by a 70% increase in adult court caseloads over a five-year period in the district in question.

The Supreme Court of Canada has also held that persons charged with an offence "in the context of s. 11(b) of the *Charter*" includes corporations. In *R.* v. *CIP Inc.,* however, the Court found that a corporation could not rely on a presumption of prejudice arising out of excessive delay; that presumption is based on an accused's right as an individual to liberty and security of the person (s. 7) and these rights do not extend to corporations. Instead, an accused corporation would have to establish that its fair trial interest had been "irremediably prejudiced." Because the appellant in this instance had not argued that its ability to make full answer and defence had been impaired, the Court dismissed the appeal, holding that the initial charge ought not to be stayed.

In *R.* v. *Kalanj,* the Supreme Court of Canada held that s. 11(b) does not apply to pre-charge delay since the accused were not "persons charged" until a formal charge had been laid. In *R.* v. *L. (W.K.),* the Supreme Court applied that judgment "to rule out review of precharge delay unless the accused can establish a breach under s. 7."

In *R.* v. *Potvin,* the Supreme Court of Canada was subsequently called on to consider the application of s. 11(b) to appellate delays. A six to three majority of the court held that s. 11(b) does not apply in respect of an appeal from conviction by the accused or from an acquittal or stay by the Crown. Their reasoning was that the term "any person charged" does not, as a general rule, include an accused person who is party to an appeal. The court also said, however, that the criminal appellant or respondent is not without a remedy if delay of the appeal process affects the fairness of the trial; as a principle of fundamental justice enshrined in s. 7, the court has the power to remedy such an abuse of process.

4. Right Not to be a Compellable Witness Against Oneself—Section 11(c)

This section is worded widely and on this basis, Professor Martin Friedland argues that it may prevent the enactment of a law compelling the accused to give evidence at a preliminary hearing and to give evidence to a police officer.

An Ontario Court of Appeal decision in the *Crooks* case indicates that this paragraph does not prevent the Crown from calling, as a witness on a preliminary inquiry, an accused separately charged with the same offence.

The Quebec Court of Appeal considered the issue in *R. v. Zurlo,* where the accused and his wife were each separately charged and compelled to testify at the other's preliminary inquiry. At a subsequent joint trial the accused was prevented from cross-examining his wife and denied a motion for a separate trial. Concluding that the couple had been separately charged for the sole purpose of circumventing their right to silence, the Court set aside the conviction and entered a stay of proceedings, finding that the accused had been denied the right to a fair trial.

It should also be noted that this section has been interpreted as not impinging upon the taking of breath samples. In the *Stasiuk* case, it was decided that "the privilege against self-incrimination is a limited one that applies to an accused *qua* witness and is restricted to a testimonial compulsion. A breath test is not in the nature of a statement or a testimonial utterance."

In *Caisse Populaire Laurier d 'Ottawa Ltée* v. *Guertin et al.,* a civil remedy was sought while there were outstanding criminal charges connected with the same situation. It was decided that s. 11(c) of the *Charter* does not mean that a person who chooses to defend a civil action is not compellable in a civil proceeding arising from facts that are the subject of simultaneous criminal proceedings. The Ontario High Court added that neither s. 11(c) nor s. 13 of the *Charter* gave "any hint of support for the proposition" that the privilege against self-incrimination includes an individual's right to remain silent in parallel civil proceedings.

5. Presumption of Innocence—Section 11(d)

This section is composed of several elements, of which the presumption of innocence has been the one most considered in the case law. A major issue has been the constitutionality of statutes with a "reverse onus" clause requiring the accused to disprove an element of the offence or to prove an excuse or the existence of a fact that will avoid conviction. The Supreme Court of Canada has considered this issue in several cases (beginning with *R.* v. *Oakes* and, more recently, in *R.* v. *Whyte, R.* v. *Keegstra* and *R.* v. *Chaulk),* in which it was held that such clauses violate s. 11(d). Where an onus is put on the accused to prove something in order to escape conviction, the general presumption of innocence in the criminal law is effectively displaced by a presumption of guilt. The Supreme Court, in *Whyte* and *Keegstra,* ruled that such clauses are unconstitutional because they raise the possibility that the accused might be convicted in spite of the existence of a reasonable doubt; that is, the accused might fail to prove the existence of the exonerating element, which may, in fact, exist.

While the statutes in question may abridge the s. 11(d) right, they may still be upheld as a reasonable limitation of that right pursuant to section 1, where the legislature or Parliament has a legitimate objective for the limitation.

In *Keegstra,* the Court considered the hate propaganda provisions of the *Criminal Code.* A majority held that s. 11(d) was violated by the provision exonerating the accused from liability where he or she proves that the impugned statements were true. Nevertheless, the provision was held to be a reasonable limitation under s. 1 because otherwise the Crown would have had to prove the falsity of the accused's statements beyond a reasonable doubt. This would have excused much of the "harmful expressive activity."

Likewise, in *Chaulk,* a majority held that s. 11(d) was violated by the provision of the *Criminal Code* that raises a presumption of sanity, thereby requiring the accused to prove insanity on the balance of probabilities in order to raise the insanity defence. A majority held that this provision was a reasonable limitation on s. 11(d) because the alternative—requiring the Crown to disprove insanity—would be unduly onerous.

In *R.* v. *Downey,* the Supreme Court of Canada considered s. 195(2) (now s. 212(3)) of the *Criminal Code,* which provides that "evidence that a person lives with or is habitually in the company of a prostitute... is, in the absence of evidence to the contrary, proof that the person lives on the avails of prostitution." According to *Criminal Code* s. 212(1)(j), living "wholly or in part on the avails of prostitution of another person" is an indictable offence carrying a maximum penalty of 10 years' imprisonment. All seven judges who heard the case agreed that the impugned section infringed the accused's right to be presumed innocent (section 11(d)). A majority of four, however, held that such infringement was a reasonable limit under section 1 of the *Charter of*

Rights and Freedoms; the objective of addressing the "cruel and pervasive social evil" of exploitation by pimps was sufficiently important to warrant overriding a *Charter* right. Furthermore, the *Charter* limitation was proportionate to the legislative objective, given "the reluctance of prostitutes to testify against pimps" and the fact that the innocent "need only point to evidence capable of raising a reasonable doubt" on the issue in order to avoid conviction.

In *R.* v. *Osolin,* the Supreme Court of Canada was called upon to consider whether section 265(4) of the *Criminal Code* had infringed the appellant's right to be presumed innocent in his trial for sexual assault. Section 265(4) codifies the defence of mistaken belief in consent; it has long been interpreted as requiring the accused to provide sufficient evidence, in support of his or her claim of an honestly held belief in consent, to impart an "air of reality" to the defence. The accused's bare assertion of a mistaken belief in consent, would not on its own be enough to enable or oblige a trial judge to put the defence of mistaken belief to the jury. The appellant in *R.* v. *Osolin* argued that the evidentiary burden imposed by s. 265(4) infringed his right to be presumed innocent. Because the trial judge had refused to charge the jury with respect to the defence of mistaken belief in consent, the appellant also argued that the "air of reality" threshold operated to deny him of his right to trial by jury under s. 11(f) of the *Charter.*

In rejecting both arguments, Mr. Justice Cory found that "the mere fact of the air of reality requirement does not displace the presumption of innocence." Although it does place an evidentiary burden on the accused to "raise sufficient evidence to give the defence an air of reality to justify its presentation to the jury, the burden of proving all of the elements of the offence beyond a reasonable doubt rests squarely with the Crown." Furthermore, there was no violation of the appellant's right to trial by jury since the sufficiency of evidence in such a case is a question of law and "therefore is properly in the domain of the judge."

In the subsequent case of *R.* v. *Laba,* the Supreme Court of Canada substituted a similar evidentiary burden for a provision in s. 394(1)(b) of the *Criminal Code* making it an offence for anyone to sell or purchase precious metal ores "unless he establishes that he is the owner or agent or is acting under lawful authority." Because an accused would have to prove ownership or authority on the balance of probabilities, thereby making it possible for a person to be convicted despite the presence of a reasonable doubt as to guilt, the Crown had conceded that s. 394(1)(b) offended s. 11(d) but argued that it was a reasonable limit under s. 1 of the *Charter.* Although deterring the theft of precious metal ores was found to be a sufficiently important objective to warrant overriding a constitutionally protected right, the Court held that s. 394(1)(b) did not impair as little as reasonably possible an accused's right to be presumed innocent. Finding that Parliament's purpose would be "effectively served by the imposition of an evidential burden," the Supreme Court of Canada rewrote the impugned section to allow conviction only "in the absence of evidence which raises a reasonable doubt" that the person is an owner or agent or acting under lawful authority.

In *R. v. Ellis-Don Ltd.,* the Ontario Court of Appeal declared unconstitutional the due diligence defence as applied to a provincial regulatory offence. The case concerned a section of the *Occupational Health and Safety Act* requiring the general contractor of a project to ensure that safety measures are followed. Both the statute and the common law provided a defence of due diligence, which required an accused to prove on a balance of probabilities that he or she had taken all reasonable measures to avoid an accident. Unless this was done, the Court was required to convict the accused, even though it had a reasonable doubt about guilt. In its s. 1 analysis, the Court of Appeal held that the provision did not violate s. 11(d) to the minimum extent possible.

R. v. Ellis Don Ltd. was subsequently reversed by the Supreme Court of Canada, relying on its reasoning in *The Wholesale Travel Group Inc. v. The Queen.* In that 1991 decision, the Court had upheld reverse onus provisions in the *Competition Act* by a five to four majority; two of the five had held that requiring an accused to establish due diligence on a balance of probabilities did not infringe s. 11(d), while the remaining three found that the provision did so, but was justified under s. 1 of the *Charter of Rights and Freedoms.*

6. Fair Hearing—Independent and Impartial Tribunal—Section 11(d)

The Supreme Court of Canada ruled in the *Corbett* case that allowing prior criminal convictions into evidence does not deprive an accused of the right to a fair trial under s. 11 of the *Charter.* The section of the *Canada Evidence Act* that allows this permits an accused who is testifying on his or her own behalf to be cross-examined with respect to prior convictions. The rationale is that prior convictions can bear on the witness's credibility.

In the *Vermette* case, the Supreme Court held that statements in the National Assembly by the Premier of Quebec had not necessarily resulted in the denial of the accused's right to a fair trial due to bias in the jury. The existence of such bias would have to be determined at the time of jury selection, but statements by politicians could not frustrate the whole criminal process.

In *R. v. Valente,* the Supreme Court considered that the trial by an independent and impartial tribunal requires the tribunal's individual independence (as reflected in security of tenure and financial security) and institutional independence (as reflected in its administrative relationship to the legislative or executive branches of government). The tribunal must not only enjoy these characteristics but must be perceived to do so.

The Court Martial Appeal Court of Canada has applied the *Valente* tests for independence to both Standing and General Courts Martial. In *R.* v. *Ingebrigtson,* the Court found that Standing Courts Martial presidents lacked financial independence because the Chief of Defence Staff had authority to fix their salaries on the basis of merit. Conversely, in *R.* v. *Généreux,* General Courts Martial tribunals, appointed ad hoc for a single case, were found to be independent because their members had no reason to fear any loss of salary or rank.

On 13 February 1992, the Supreme Court of Canada overturned the decision in *R.* v. *Généreux* and ordered a new trial on the basis that the structure of the General Court Martial had infringed the accused's right to be tried by an independent and impartial tribunal as guaranteed by s. 1(d) of the *Charter of Rights and Freedoms.* Of the majority of eight, five judges found that the procedure for appointment and evaluation of judge advocates had failed to meet the tests for security of tenure or financial security set out in *Valente.* Furthermore, aspects of the system had also cast doubt on the institutional independence of General Courts Martial. Because it could not be claimed that the accused's s.11(d) rights had been impaired as little as possible, there could be no justification under section 1. At the same time, the Court indicated that recent amendments to the *Queen's Regulations and Orders for the Canadian Forces* had effectively alleviated the deficiencies relating to security of tenure and financial security.

On 6 May 1992, Bill C-77, An Act to amend the National Defence Act was passed by the House of Commons after consideration by Committee of the Whole. The bill contained provisions to alleviate the apparent lack of institutional independence identified by the Supreme Court in *Généreux.* Under amendments to the Act, the prosecutor and members of the court martial who serve as triers of fact will no longer both be appointed by the same convening authority; instead, the president and other members will be appointed by an officer designated by regulation. Prior to the Supreme Court decision in *Généreux,* authority to appoint judge advocates had been removed from the Judge Advocate General (an agent of the executive) and given to the Chief Military Trial Judge, a step that had addressed the Court's other serious reservation concerning the lack of institutional independence.

Even though allegations of bias or partiality are usually assessed on an individual case-by-case basis, the objective status of a tribunal may be relevant to impartiality just as it is to independence. When discussing the s.11(d) requirement for impartiality, in *R. v. Lippé,* the Supreme Court of Canada accepted that a reasonable apprehension of bias could arise on an institutional or structural level. For example, the Court found that the practice of law by some part-time Municipal Court judges raised a reasonable apprehension of bias. However, that apprehension had been alleviated by various safeguards that had been implemented to address the issue.

On 23 January 1992, a four to three majority of the Supreme Court of Canada found *Criminal Code* sections 634(1) and (2) inconsistent with s. 11(d) of the *Charter of Rights and Freedoms,* insofar as they provided the Crown in the jury selection process with a combination of peremptory challenges and standbys that exceeded the number of peremptory challenges available to an accused. Under the impugned *Criminal Code* provisions, the prosecutor was entitled not only to challenge four jurors peremptorily, but also to direct as many as 48 to stand by. In contrast, the accused was entitled to 20, 12 or four peremptory challenges, depending upon the nature of the charge or the maximum penalty available. Writing for three of the majority in *R. v. Bain,* Mr. Justice Cory found that the prosecutor's "overwhelming numerical superiority of choice," in the jury selection process, would give the reasonable person an apprehension of bias. Likewise, Mr. Justice Stevenson held that the Crown's "substantial advantage in the ability to shape and fashion the jury" severely impaired the appearance of fairness and impartiality. The Court found that the legislation could not be justified under s.1, but "suspended" a declaration of invalidity for a period of six months in order to give Parliament an opportunity to enact new legislation.

Bill C-70 was introduced on 6 April 1992 to fill the void created by the decision in *R. v. Bain.* In addition to abolishing the Crown's right to "stand by" prospective jurors, Bill C-70 gave the Crown and the accused an equal number of peremptory challenges and changed the order in which they would be declared. The bill also repealed provisions allowing a jury of only six persons in the Yukon and Northwest Territories and codified aspects of jury selection previously endorsed by the courts. The existing procedure on challenges for cause remained unchanged.

7. Reasonable Bail—Section 11(e)

Ordinarily, the *Criminal Code* requires the prosecution to justify the detention of an accused, pending trial. Bail will be granted unless the Crown establishes that detention is necessary, either to ensure the accused's attendance in court, or in the public interest. In *R. v. Bray*, the Ontario Court of Appeal held that *Criminal Code* provisions requiring an accused murderer to show that his detention in custody does not infringe s. 11(e) and that even if it did, the infringement would be justified as a reasonable limit under s. 1 of the *Charter*. Conversely, in *R. v. Pearson*, the Quebec Court of Appeal struck down *Criminal Code* provisions that require persons accused of importing or trafficking under the *Narcotic Control Act* to be detained in custody unless they show cause why such detention is not justified. While acknowledging that the struggle against drug trafficking is a sufficiently important objective to justify overriding a constitutional right, the Court of Appeal found that the law failed the proportionality test because it was discriminatory and arbitrary and did not constitute a minimum impairment of *Charter* rights.

The *Pearson* decision was subsequently overturned by a majority of the Supreme Court of Canada, who found that section 515(6)(d) of the *Criminal Code* does not infringe an accused's right to reasonable bail. The Court accepted that the lucrative nature of drug trafficking and importation can create incentives to continue criminal behaviour after arrest and, furthermore, that traffickers and importers may pose a greater risk than other accused of absconding before trial. The Court also noted that denial of bail under s.515(6)(d) applies only in a narrow set of circumstances, "is necessary to promote the proper functioning of the bail system and is not undertaken for any purpose extraneous to the bail system." Although s. 515(6)(d) would result in denial of bail in certain circumstances, the majority held that it also provides "just cause" for such denial and, thus, does not infringe s.11(e) of the *Charter*.

In the companion case of *R. v. Morales* the Supreme Court of Canada upheld parallel *Criminal Code* provisions placing the onus on the accused to demonstrate that detention is not justified, when charged with an indictable offence allegedly committed while released on bail. In reaching that decision, the Court pointed out that bail is granted "on condition that the accused will cease criminal behaviour;" s. 15(6)(a) "establishes a set of special bail rules where there are reasonable grounds to believe that the accused has already breached this condition." Since the provision is "narrow and carefully tailored to achieve a properly functioning bail system," it constitutes "just cause" to deny bail and does not violate s.11(e) of the *Charter*.

The *Morales* case also involved a challenge to the validity of *Criminal Code* s. 515(10)(b) grounds for detaining an accused in custody. Under that provision, an accused could be held in custody on the grounds that detention is "necessary in the public interest," or "for the protection or safety of the public, having regard to all the circumstances, including any substantial likelihood that the accused will, if he is released from custody, commit a criminal offence or interfere with the administration of justice." Although the Court had no trouble upholding the "public safety" reasons, the "public interest" criterion was struck down for being too vague and imprecise to constitute just cause for denial of bail within the meaning of s. 11(e) of the *Charter*. The majority found that the term gave the courts "unrestricted latitude to define any circumstances as sufficient to justify pre-trial detention."

Although preventing offences or interference with the administration of justice are sufficiently pressing objectives, the resulting limitation on s. 11(e) could not be justified under s. 1 of the *Charter*; there was no rational connection between the objectives and the legislative measure, there was more than a minimal impairment of rights and the effects of the limit far exceeded the objectives of the law. In order to minimize the Court's interference with the legislative function, the offending words "in the public interest or" were severed and struck down, allowing the remaining constitutionally valid portion of s. 515(10)(b) to stand.

8. Right to Trial by Judge and Jury—Section 11(f)

In the *Lee* case, the Supreme Court of Canada ruled upon the constitutionality of the provision in the *Criminal Code* that denies a jury trial to an accused person who would otherwise be entitled to one but who, for no good reason, fails to attend for trial or to remain there once the trial has begun. The Court, in holding that the provision is not unconstitutional, said that the Code provision went beyond merely punishing the accused who fails to appear or to remain for his jury trial. It had been enacted for the valid legislative purpose of protecting "the administration of justice from delay, inconvenience, expense and abuse, and to secure the respect of the public for the criminal trial process." As the challenged Code section impairs the right to a jury trial "as little as possible in order to achieve that legislative objective," it is, therefore, "proportionate to the objective of maintaining respect for the system."

9. Right Not to be Tried Twice for the Same Offence—Section 11(h)

In the *Van Rassel* case, the accused was an R.C.M.P. officer and member of an international drug enforcement team. He was arrested in Florida and charged in the U.S. with soliciting and accepting bribes in exchange for information given to him by the American authorities. He was acquitted at trial but was subsequently charged in Canada with breach of trust under the *Criminal Code*.

The Supreme Court of Canada said that the *Charter* provision "applies only in circumstances where the two offences with which an accused is charged are the same." Since these two offences related to different activities, they were not the same and it was not objectionable, therefore, for the accused to be prosecuted in Canada after being acquitted in the U.S.

Section 11(h) has a common origin with the long-established defences of "autrefois acquit" and "autrefois convict," "issue estoppel" and the rule enunciated by the Supreme Court in 1975 in the *Kienapple* case. The defences, or pleas, of autrefois acquit and autrefois convict are contained in the *Criminal Code*. In order for either defence to succeed the accused must show that the current matter and the one of which he or she was previously acquitted or convicted are the same; the new charge must be the same as the charge at the first trial, or have been included implicitly in that charge. The charges need not be absolutely identical; all that must be shown is that the accused could have been convicted of the current charge at the first trial.

The defence of issue estoppel is based on the principle that the court should not rule on an issue that has already been decided by another court. This principle was recognized by the Supreme Court of Canada in the *Gushue* case.

The rule in the *Kienapple* case provides that a conviction cannot be registered on the second charge if there has been a conviction on a first charge arising out of the same cause. Thus, in a shoplifting case where a person is charged simultaneously with one charge of theft and one of possession of stolen goods, a conviction may be entered on only one or the other where the same goods form the subject of both charges. This is true as well where a person whose breathalyser reading exceeds the legal limit is charged with both exceeding the legal limit and impaired driving. This principle was most recently reviewed by the Supreme Court of Canada in its decision in the *Prince* case, where the Court held that the rule does not apply where there is more than one victim, even if the same facts apply.

In *Shubley* v. *The Queen,* the Supreme Court of Canada held that a finding of guilt in prison disciplinary proceedings does not preclude a subsequent prosecution for the same action under the *Criminal Code*. Since the disciplinary proceedings carried no real penal consequences and were not meant to account to society for crimes against the public interest, s. 11(h) would not apply.

Similarly, criminal prosecution for assault, following conviction for a "major service offence" under the *Royal Canadian Mounted Police Act,* does not offend section 11(h) because the "offences" involved are not the same. In *R.* v. *Wigglesworth,* the Supreme Court of Canada found that an R.C.M.P. officer could be answerable to both his profession and to society at large, for the same act or conduct. Notwithstanding possible penal consequences, a conviction in service court would not answer the criminal charge of assault.

C. Cruel and Unusual Treatment or Punishment: Section 12

This section states:

> 12. Everyone has the right not to be subjected to any cruel and unusual treatment or punishment.

While this section has not been used to set aside the dangerous offender sections of the *Criminal Code* as unconstitutional, it has provided the courts with an opportunity to review indeterminate sentencing under the *Criminal Code*. In *Re Mitchell* and the *Queen*, Mr. Justice Allan Linden of the Ontario Supreme Court held that indefinitely detaining someone who is not a menace to society would be cruel and unusual treatment or punishment, in violation of the *Charter of Rights and Freedoms*. However, where it could be shown that the accused posed a real danger to other persons if his behaviour was not restrained, s. 12 of the *Charter* would not be violated.

In the *Mitchell* case, in attempting to devise a standard that could be applied when determining whether treatment or punishment was cruel and unusual, the Ontario Supreme Court found that the treatment or punishment would have to be so excessive as to outrage standards of decency and surpass all rational bounds of treatment or punishment. "The test is one of disproportionality: is the treatment or punishment disproportionate to the offence and the offender? Evidence that the treatment or punishment is unusually severe and excessive in the sense of not serving a valid penal purpose more effectively than a less severe treatment or punishment will suffice to satisfy the test of disproportionality."

This test was further subdivided and amplified in the *Soenan* case, which dealt with the complaints of a prisoner in pre-trial custody. The court here defined the meaning of "cruel and unusual treatment." It determined that the relevant factors are whether the treatment is in accordance with public standards of decency and propriety; whether it is unnecessary because of the existence of adequate alternatives; and whether or not it can be applied upon a rational basis and in accordance with ascertained or ascertainable standards.

Using these tests and applying some new ones (such as "does the treatment have a social purpose and can it be applied upon a rational basis in accordance with ascertainable standards?") the Federal Court, Trial Division, in the

Belliveau (No. 2) case held that the mandatory supervision program does not authorize cruel and unusual treatment or punishment.

In the *Smith* case, the Supreme Court of Canada was called upon to decide whether the mandatory seven-year minimum sentence for importing narcotics, contrary to s. 5(2) of the *Narcotic Control Act,* breached this section of the *Charter.* The Court, with one dissenting judgment, held that the section did not breach section 12 and was not justified under s. 1 as a reasonable limit.

The fact that the purpose of the legislation, to deter the drug trade and punish importers of drugs, was clearly valid did not prevent the Court from ruling on the validity of the section. Mr. Justice Lamer (writing also for Chief Justice Dickson) discussed the Charter limits on "treatment or punishment." He said that it is generally accepted in a society such as ours that the state has the power to impose a "treatment or punishment" on an individual where it is necessary to do so to attain some legitimate end and where the requisite procedure has been followed.

The protection in s. 12 governs the quality of punishment, and its effect on the person. The words "cruel and unusual" are to be read together as a "compendious expression of a norm." The criterion to be applied is "whether the punishment prescribed is so excessive as to outrage standards of decency"; the effect of punishment must not be grossly disproportionate to what would have been appropriate. This reasoning is very similar to that found in the *Mitchell* case.

In assessing whether a sentence is grossly disproportionate, the court must first consider the gravity of the offence, the personal characteristics of the offender and the particular circumstances of the case in order to determine what range of sentences would have been appropriate to punish, rehabilitate or deter this particular offender or to protect the public from him or her. The other goals that may be pursued by imposing punishment, in particular the deterrence of other potential offenders, are thus not relevant at this stage of the inquiry. This does not mean that in determining a sentence the judge or the legislator can no longer consider general deterrence or other penological purposes that go beyond the particular offender; it means only that the resulting sentence must not be grossly disproportionate to what that offender deserves.

Noting that there was no suggestion that the eight-year sentence imposed on this appellant was cruel and unusual, Lamer J. went on to find that a seven-year minimum prison term was, nevertheless, disproportionate "in light of the wide net cast by s. 5(1)." Because both the offence of importing and the mandatory minimum sentence totally disregarded the quantity of drugs involved, the purpose of importation and the existence or absence of previous convictions of a similar nature, the court found that it was inevitable that, in some cases, a verdict of guilt would lead to the imposition of a "grossly disproportionate" term of imprisonment. Although the legislative objective was sufficient to warrant overriding a constitutionally protected right, the means chosen were not proportionate since there was no need to sentence "small offenders" to seven years in order to deter the serious offender. Therefore, the legislation could not be justified as a reasonable limit under s. 1 of the *Charter*.

On 14 November 1991, the Supreme Court of Canada held that a mandatory minimum seven-day jail term for driving while suspended did not offend s. 12. The facts of the particular case involved a provision of the *Motor Vehicle Act*, R.S.B.C. 1979, c. 288, which allowed the superintendent of motor vehicles to prohibit persons with an unsatisfactory driving record from driving a motor vehicle. Conceding its obligation to examine the statutory provision in light of reasonable hypothetical circumstances, the Court nevertheless maintained that it did not have a licence to invalidate "on the basis of remote or extreme examples." However, the six to three majority decision in *R.* v. *Goltz* left open the possibility of a different result if the mandatory jail term were imposed for driving while suspended for administrative infractions or other reasons of a "relatively minor nature," as also contemplated under the Act.

Relying on the Supreme Court of Canada's reasoning in *Smith* and *Goltz*, the Manitoba Court of Appeal subsequently held a portion of s. 85 of the *Criminal Code* to be of no force and effect because it infringed s. 12. Section 85 mandates both minimum and consecutive sentences for the use of firearms during the commission of an indictable offence. In *R.* v. *Brown*, the defence had conceded that the 13-year sentence imposed "for these offences and this offender" did not result in a *prima facia* determination that his s. 12 rights had been breached. However, the wording of s. 85 is "broad enough to include what has been described as the small or innocent offender," and the Court held that it could result in a violation of s. 12 of the *Charter* in such a case. Since it was the requirement that "jail terms be imposed and that they be served consecutively both to the sentences imposed on the indictable offence or offences and to each other that results in the violation of s. 12," the Court chose to delete the words "or series of events" in s. 85(2). Thus, only the requirement that sentences imposed for a series of firearms offences be served consecutively to each other was removed.

The Supreme Court of Canada subsequently overturned the Court of Appeal decision in *Brown*, finding no violation of s. 12 "when the underlying offence is robbery." Relying on their reasons in *Goltz*, the Court specifically declined to consider the validity of s. 85 "in conjunction with other potential underlying indictable offences."

In *Lyons* v. *The Queen,* the Supreme Court has held that imposition of an indeterminate sentence, upon finding that an accused is a "dangerous offender," does not offend the protection against cruel and unusual punishment because of the availability of parole. However, in *Warden of Mountain Institution* v. *Steele,* the Supreme Court later held that section 12 could be violated where misapplication or disregard of review criteria (for dangerous offenders) resulted in a period of incarceration far beyond the time when an offender should have been paroled. In that case, the National Parole Board was found to have erred in the application of criteria for release.

In *Kindler* v. *Canada (Minister of Justice),* a majority of the Supreme Court held that extraditing fugitives to countries where the death penalty might be imposed did not offend the *Charter,* but three dissenting judges argued that imposition of the death penalty would constitute a violation of s. 12.

In the subsequent case of *Chiarelli* v. *Canada (Minister of Employment and Immigration),* the Supreme Court of Canada examined *Immigration Act* provisions calling for the deportation of non-citizens convicted of an offence punishable by a period of imprisonment of five years or more. The Court held that although it might be considered a "treatment," deportation of "a permanent resident who has deliberately violated an essential condition of his or her being permitted to remain in Canada..., cannot be said to outrage standards of decency" and would not constitute cruel and unusual treatment or punishment.

Other cases dealing with the application of this section have concentrated mainly on such matters as solitary confinement and the double-celling of inmates in penitentiaries.

D. Self-incrimination: Section 13
This section provides that:

13. A witness who testifies in any proceedings has the right not to have any incriminating evidence so given used to incriminate that witness in any other proceedings, except in a prosecution for perjury or for the giving of contradictory evidence.

This is similar to s. 5(1) of the *Canada Evidence Act* with one important exception: the Act contemplates that an objection must be made by the witness, whereas the Charter does not. Also the *Charter* allows a later prosecution for the giving of contradictory evidence (evidence dissimilar to that previously given) as well as for perjury. This change was necessary because the *Canada Evidence Act* has been interpreted as not encompassing a contradictory evidence charge within the word "perjury."

Section 13, which is obviously linked to s. 11(c), affords protection against testimonial compulsion. This protection is better than that which existed before the *Charter* came into force, in that the witness no longer needs expressly to claim protection in order to receive it; however, there is no absolute right to refuse to answer questions. This was the position taken in the *Thomson Newspapers Ltd.* case, where the Supreme of Canada Court upheld the authority of the Restrictive Trade Practices Commission to examine under oath representatives of corporations suspected of violating the federal *Combines Investigation Act.* Since this was an "inquisitorial" (rather than an "adversarial") proceeding, so that no final determination as to criminal liability was reached, there was no absolute right to refuse to answer questions. Otherwise, there would be a "dangerous and unnecessary imbalance between the rights of the individual and the community's legitimate interest in discovering the truth about the existence of practices against which the Act was designed to protect the public." In any case, said the Court, the individual's right to prevent the subsequent use of compelled self-incriminatory testimony continues unchanged by this requirement; hence, the individual's rights and those of the state are kept in proper balance.

An interesting situation developed in the *Dubois* case, where the Alberta Court of Appeal held that the Crown, in an attempt to incriminate an individual who had successfully appealed a conviction, could use the first-trial testimony of the individual in a new trial ordered by the Court of Appeal. It was determined that the second trial of an accused for the same offence is not an "other proceeding" within the meaning of this section; therefore the previous testimony can be used. The Supreme Court of Canada reversed the decision of the Alberta Court of Appeal in this case, however; it determined that an accused's incriminating testimony given in the initial trial could not be used against him in a subsequent retrial ordered by the Court of Appeal. The Supreme Court also felt that allowing the prosecution to use the accused's previous testimony would amount to compelling the accused to testify, thus contradicting the right to remain silent and to be presumed innocent. However, the Court did not say whether it would rule out the use of previous testimony during cross-examination in the re-trial.

This issue was resolved in two later decisions. In *R. v. Mannion*, the Supreme Court held s. 13 was violated when the accused's testimony from a prior trial was used in cross-examination to contradict the accused's testimony, and thereby establish guilt. In the *Kuldip* case, however, the Supreme Court held that the use of such testimony in cross-examination in order to attack the accused's credibility was not contrary to s. 13; in such a case the testimony is not specifically used to "incriminate" the accused, but only to undermine the truth of the accused's testimony.

PARLIAMENTARY ACTION

A. Bill C-70: An Act to Amend the Criminal Code (Jury) S.C. 1992, c. 41

This statute abolished the Crown's right to stand by prospective jurors. It also granted the Crown and the accused an equal number of peremptory challenges and changed the order in which they are declared.

B. Bill C-77: An Act to Amend the National Defence Act, S.C. 1992, c. 16

This statute changed the process for appointing the president and other members of a court martial. It also gave the president authority to exclude the public from a trial or part of a trial and granted the judge advocate authority to determine questions of law or mixed law and fact.

Human Rights and the Courts in Canada

Susan Alter and Nancy Holmes

INTRODUCTION

Although universally embraced in principle, the concept of "human rights" evades a precise definition and is subject to a general lack of consensus on how it should be approached. Certainly, the term "right", in and of itself, is ambiguous. It is sometimes applied in its strictest legal sense, where the right-holder is entitled to something which another has a corresponding duty to provide. In other cases, a "right" indicates an immunity from interference. To speak of human rights, then, requires a conception of rights possessed simply by virtue of being human. Some generalizations can be made in this regard. Human rights tend to represent individual and group demands for access to wealth and power and for mutual respect. These rights are both legally and morally justifiable, and they apply to all persons simply because they are human beings. Most rights are qualified or limited in some way, usually on the basis that with the privilege of rights comes the responsibility to tolerate the rights of others. Finally, human rights are commonly prioritized as either fundamental or non-fundamental.

It is important to understand that the protection of human rights is a field of public policy, although it is not always recognized as such. Controversies about human rights usually involve the question of whether priority should be

Alter, S. and Holmes, N. (1996). *Human rights and the courts in Canada*—Background Paper BP-279E. Ottawa: Research Branch Library of Parliament.

given to individuals' personal claims or to their responsibilities to others. These issues are rarely resolved by applying traditional legal principles. Rather, what is really involved is policy-making. Protecting human rights requires ongoing comparisons of legitimate objectives. The public policy of human rights has tended to divide these rights into four broad categories: (1) political rights, which traditionally include freedom of association, assembly, expression, the press, conscience and religion; (2) legal rights, which include equality before the law, due process of the law, freedom from arbitrary arrest, right to a fair hearing, and access to counsel; (3) economic rights, which include the right to own property and freedom of contract; and (4) egalitarian rights, which include the rights to employment, education, accommodation, facilities and services without discrimination on the basis of race, origin, age or sex.

How a political system can best protect human rights depends to a large extent on variables specific to time and culture. Canada's particular approach has been a mix of the British liberal tradition of relying on ordinary law and elected parliaments, and the American liberal tradition, which places reliance on a written constitution and judicial review. In order to reflect adequately the different sets of mechanisms used to protect human rights in Canada, it is useful to divide the Canadian experience into three time periods.

During the first period, from Confederation to 1960, the federal and provincial legislatures had the primary responsibility for safeguarding the human rights principles inherited from the United Kingdom. The judiciary played only a minor role through its responsibility for upholding the common law principles that had developed to protect these rights. Despite the existence of legal bases for action, the courts and the legislatures both evidenced a general reluctance to address issues of human rights except as a peripheral matter. The second period began with the advent of the *Canadian Bill of Rights* and the enactment of human rights codes at both the provincial and federal level. During this period, the courts were therefore expressly invited by the legislatures to take on a more active role in settling controversial human rights issues. The invitation was, however, basically rejected. It was not until the third period, beginning in 1982 with the *Canadian Charter of Rights and Freedoms*, that the judiciary was accorded the constitutional mandate it had felt was necessary to rule on the substantive validity of legislation, which it now does to ensure compliance with the rights and freedoms granted by the *Charter*.

FROM CONFEDERATION TO THE BILL OF RIGHTS

At the time of Confederation, it was decided that Canada would adopt the parliamentary form of government that had evolved in the United Kingdom.

One of the dominant principles underlying that system was the doctrine of parliamentary supremacy, which held that the legislative branch of the government could determine the powers of the other two branches: the executive and the judiciary. Canada inherited this principle of legislative supremacy by way of the preamble to the *British North America Act,* now referred to as the *Constitution Act, 1867.* This stated that Canada would have a constitution "similar in principle to that of the United Kingdom." This meant that the Canadian constitution embraced the elements of the unwritten British constitution, including the notions of the rule of law and parliamentary supremacy. Legislative supremacy could not, however, apply in Canada exactly as it did in the United Kingdom; as Canada was a federal country, no single legislature was supreme. Instead, the federal and provincial legislatures were supreme only within constitutionally designated areas of jurisdiction.

The *Constitution Act, 1867* also made provision for the establishment of a federally appointed judiciary charged not only with the traditional judicial tasks of settling disputes between individuals and interpreting statutes with a view to the intent of the legislators, but with a third task arising out of the new country's federal nature—adjudication on the constitutional division of powers between the federal and provincial legislatures. Thus, at the time of Confederation, the relationship between the courts and the other branches of government was clearly defined. The federal and provincial legislatures made the law, the executive implemented and enforced the law and the judiciary was responsible only for interpreting the law that the others had made and enforced. Moreover, until 1949, the Judicial Committee of the Privy Council in England, rather than the Supreme Court of Canada, served as Canada's final court of appeal.

The *Constitution Act, 1867* makes no specific reference to human rights or fundamental liberties. While s. 92(13) accords the provincial legislatures the power to make laws affecting "property and civil rights," there is no reference to any civil rights of individuals. The Act does guarantee some group rights with respect to the establishment and operation of schools by Roman Catholic or Protestant minorities and with respect to the use of the English and French languages; however, it is fair to say that these guarantees saw little in the way of judicial enforcement until quite recently. It was the opinion of some jurists by the beginning of the twentieth century that the preamble to the Act bestowed on Canadians the benefits of the tradition of civil liberties that had developed in the United Kingdom before 1867 and which formed part of that country's unwritten constitution. As will be seen, however, the courts were reluctant to interpret the Constitution in this way when it was not clear that such had been the intent of its framers and when the principle of parliamentary supremacy had by that time taken on almost sacred proportions.

As a rule then, judges in this period felt that they were powerless to prevent legislative violations of human rights unless the law that caused the violation offended the federal division of powers. In 1899, for example, the Judicial Committee of the Privy Council in London struck down a British Columbia law that prohibited anyone of Chinese origin from working in mines on the basis that the provincial law interfered with federal jurisdiction over "naturalization and aliens." On the other hand, the Judicial Committee upheld British Columbia legislation that denied the vote to Canadians of Asiatic origin as being within the proper bounds of provincial jurisdiction. In both instances, the Judicial Committee noted that, in accordance with the principle of legislative supremacy, judges could not consider the policy or impolicy of such enactments.

The courts were more than content to leave all policy decisions to the legislatures, even in those areas untouched by Parliament and which had been subject to purely judge-made, or so-called "common law". Without express legislative direction, the courts were not prepared to find human rights violations to be either immoral or illegal. Thus, in the area of race discrimination, the Supreme Court of Canada consistently advanced the principles of freedom of commerce and contract, no matter how flagrant the discriminatory result. In *Christie* v. *York Corporation,* [1940] S.C.R. 139, a black man who had been refused service in a tavern claimed damages for humiliation on the basis of the common law of tort. The Supreme Court dismissed the man's claim and held that, on the basis of the principle of freedom of commerce, merchants are free to deal as they choose with an individual member of the public. In that same year, the British Columbia Court of Appeal also held that anyone "may conduct a business in the manner best suited to advance his own interests", even if that meant discriminating against patrons solely because of their race or colour.

Beginning in the 1930s, however, some judges attempted to use the preamble to the Constitution as a means of establishing a new route, over and above the established common law, for protecting human rights in Canada. In the *Alberta Press Bill* case, the Supreme Court of Canada was asked by the federal government to determine the validity of a package of legislation enacted by the Social Credit government of Alberta to bring the province out of the Depression. Part of the legislation granted a government agency, the Social Credit Board, the power to prohibit the publication of a newspaper, to force a newspaper to print corrections of articles that the Board considered inaccurate, and to prohibit newspapers from publishing articles written by certain blacklisted persons. The rationale behind this portion of the legislation was that the monetary reforms of the legislation as a package would work only if the people believed in them. The Supreme Court unanimously determined the matter on a jurisdictional or division-of-powers basis, finding the legislation to be outside the powers of the provincial legislature because it invaded the federal government's jurisdiction over banking, interest and legal tender. What is significant about the Court's decision, however, is that three of the justices also perceived the legislation as being contrary to the constitutional guarantee of freedom of the press.

Chief Justice Duff based his civil liberties argument on the fact that the preamble to the *Constitution Act, 1867* implanted in Canada the civil liberties principles of the United Kingdom, including freedom of the press and freedom of speech. Moreover, because the Constitution establishes the House of Commons as an elected and representative body, intended to work under the influence of public opinion and discussion, freedom of the press is an essential component of the principle of democracy.

The problem with the so-called "Duff Doctrine" was it could not be squared with the doctrine of legislative supremacy. As a result, it was not endorsed by the majority of the Court. The acceptance of a legally enforceable implied bill of rights would have meant a major restructuring of the Canadian political system. It would have meant recognizing constitutional principles of the United Kingdom, as enforced by judges. Such a judicial enforcement of civil liberties could ultimately have limited the powers of the legislatures and called into question the whole notion of legislative supremacy. Moreover, because an implied bill of rights would consist of abstract principles and judicial decisions about the nature of these abstractions, it would be even less clear than a written bill of rights. The Canadian judiciary at this time was naturally reluctant to embark on such a bold and uncharted course. Instead, the Supreme Court of Canada, even as the final court of appeal in Canada after 1949, ruled in favour of civil liberties claims only on the basis of the division of legislative powers.

THE BILL OF RIGHTS ERA

In the aftermath of the Second World War, human rights became a central issue of concern both at the international and the domestic level. Not only had Canadians witnessed atrocities abroad, but the suspension of human rights for Canadians of Japanese origin, the confiscation of their property and their forced internment during the war had had a profound consciousness-raising effect on the people of Canada with respect to the issue of human rights. It is worth looking at the more important international human rights documents that developed after the war, because their impact on domestic legislation and practice in this area cannot be overstated.

The reality of the crimes committed by the Nazi regime during the course of World War II was a catalyst for the United Nations adoption of the *Universal Declaration of Human Rights* in 1948. The principal aim of the document was to set out, in general language, the basic rights to which all human beings ought to be entitled. Among the rights proclaimed are the right to life, liberty and security of the person, the right to privacy, the right to own property, and the freedoms of expression, religion, movement, conscience, and peaceful assembly. Although, as its name indicates, the Universal Declaration was intended simply as a declaratory document not binding on members of the United Nations, it has achieved the status of customary international law and, as such, it has served to provide both the inspiration and starting point for the numerous international human rights documents that have followed.

In 1966, the United Nations General Assembly supplemented the Universal Declaration with three additional documents: the *International Covenant on Economic, Social and Cultural Rights,* the *International Covenant on Civil and Political Rights,* and the *Optional Protocol to the International Covenant on Civil and Political Rights.* Together, these documents are collectively known as the International Bill of Human Rights. The primary effect of the 1966 instruments was to elaborate and extend the rights expressed in the Universal Declaration and to establish machinery for their enforcement through the United Nations. Canada was an active leader in these human rights developments at the international level, and it has since made serious efforts to ensure that such rights are protected domestically.

As a result of the emerging public awareness of the need for human rights safeguards in Canada, and the judiciary's obvious reluctance to take a stand on these issues, it fell to the legislatures of the federal and provincial governments to bring the country's domestic law into line with its recent international commitments. As noted earlier, the area of human rights was not specifically catalogued under the division of legislative powers set out in the *Constitution Act, 1867.* The closest the Act came to providing for this area seems to be the federal power with respect to "peace, order and good government" in s. 91, and the provincial power over "property and civil rights" in s. 92. In view of this overlapping jurisdiction, both levels of government entered the field of human rights, although the initiative was principally taken at the provincial level.

The first human rights statute of the contemporary era was the Ontario *Racial Discrimination Act* of 1944, which prohibited the publication, display or broadcast of anything indicating an intention to discriminate on the basis of race or creed. The significance of this pioneering statute is that, for the first time, a legislature explicitly declared that racial and religious discrimination was against public policy, so that the judiciary could not simply subordinate human rights to the interests of commerce, contract or property. In 1947, the Province of Saskatchewan enacted the first bill of rights in Canada, which, in addition to anti-discrimination provisions, also proclaimed such political liberties as the right to vote, freedom of religion, speech and press, assembly and association, and freedom from arbitrary arrest or detention. The major drawback to this ambitious statute, however, was the lack of an effective enforcement procedure. The *Saskatchewan Bill of Rights* was followed by the enactment in various provinces of fair employment and fair practices legislation, which contained enforcement mechanisms, though not full-time staff to administer them. The combined effect of this legislation was to serve as the prototype for modern provincial human rights codes.

At the federal level, Prime Minister John Diefenbaker, a civil liberties advocate, was convinced that Canada needed a national bill of rights that would have a superior status to other laws. Unfortunately, he was unable to obtain the broad provincial consensus required to entrench such a bill in the Constitution. Instead, he was forced to settle for a bill that was an ordinary enactment of Parliament and which applied only to matters under the jurisdiction of the federal government. Diefenbaker believed, however, that because of its very nature the courts would use such a bill to nullify federal legislation that conflicted with its provisions.

The *Bill of Rights,* which was enacted in 1960, is a relatively straightforward document. Section 1 guarantees the right to life, liberty, security of the person and enjoyment of property, unless deprived thereof by due process of the law; the equality before the law and the protection of the law; and the freedoms of religion, speech, assembly, association and the press. Moreover, it provides that these rights and freedoms are to exist without discrimination by reason of race, national origin, colour, religion or sex.

Section 2 of the *Bill of Rights* guarantees a number of rights that had already been developed by judges through the common law to protect the civil liberties of an individual when confronted with the judicial system. For example, all Canadians have the right not to be arbitrarily detained or imprisoned. No one can be arrested or detained without knowing the reason, and detainees have the right to retain a lawyer without delay. Section 2 also confirms the right to a fair hearing in accordance with the principles of fundamental justice. Finally, the section contains a notwithstanding clause, which provides that every law of Canada shall, unless expressly declared otherwise, be construed and applied so as not to abrogate any of the rights or freedoms recognized in the *Bill of Rights.*

The problem faced by the judiciary was how, in a system of legislative supremacy, an ordinary statute like the *Bill of Rights* could take precedence over other ordinary statutes, particularly those enacted after it. Indeed, the judiciary made it quite clear that it felt a great deal of uncertainty about applying the statute because it did not constitute a constitutional mandate to make judicial decisions with the effect of limiting the traditional sovereignty of Parliament. In fact, with only one notable exception, the courts consistently rendered the *Bill of Rights* ineffective in the promotion and protection of human rights in Canada. Often, it was determined that the *Bill of Rights* did not apply to a particular case on the basis that the rights it could protect were only those that had existed at the time of its enactment. In other words, the courts gave an extremely narrow interpretation, often referred to as the "frozen rights concept," to the rights set out in the *Bill of Rights.* In some cases, the courts simply refused to find any inconsistency between its provisions and discriminatory provisions in federal legislation, particularly as the legislation at issue was usually based on a valid federal objective with which the courts felt they had no right to interfere.

It is not surprising, then, that at the same time as the courts were giving short shrift to the federal *Bill of Rights,* there was a flourishing of provincial human rights legislation, the administration and application of which was largely taken out of the hands of the courts and confined to administrative agencies in the form of human rights commissions and tribunals. The first human rights code to consolidate various anti-discrimination provisions was adopted by Ontario in 1962. The Act prohibited discrimination on the grounds of race, creed, colour, nationality, ancestry or place of origin, and it established a commission and a full-time staff to administer and enforce the law. The other nine provinces and two territories soon enacted similar legislation. In 1977, the federal government enacted the *Canadian Human Rights Act,* which had strictly federal jurisdiction.

While there is today some diversity among jurisdictions, the principles and enforcement mechanisms of human rights legislation in Canada are essentially the same. Each Act prohibits discrimination on specified grounds (such as race, sex, age and religion) in respect of employment, accommodation and publicly available services. The system is complaint-based in that a complaint must be lodged with a human rights commission or council either by a person who believes that he or she has been discriminated against, or by the commission itself on the basis of its own investigation. If a complaint is determined to be well founded, the commission generally attempts to conciliate the difference between the complainant and the respondent. Where conciliation fails, a tribunal may be formed to hear the case and make a binding decision.

Despite the tremendous success of human rights commissions in dealing with cases of discrimination, there are some areas of concern. For example, human rights institutions were developed on the premise that discrimination is the direct result of individual acts of bigotry. As a result, procedures set out in the legislation are complaint-driven and individually focused in terms of dispute resolution. Not only does this place a heavy burden on the individual to bring forward and pursue an allegation of discrimination, a process which can take years and exact a significant emotional toll, but it has resulted in commissions that are overburdened by an ever-growing caseload. More important, however, is the fact that the current system does not adequately address what today is considered to be a more pervasive and possibly more detrimental form of discrimination—that resulting from the unintended effects of ordinary practices or systems. Since conscious bias causes only part of the discrimination and inequality in this country, it remains to be seen whether the commission model can adapt to meet the challenge of changing times.

The jurisdiction of human rights commissions is also severely limited in at least two respects. First, human rights legislation expressly deals only with inequality in the workplace and in the provision of public goods and services. Given that international human rights instruments to which Canada is a signatory do not limit guarantees of equality to any particular area of activity, some concern has been expressed about whether commissions can be an effective vehicle for the full realization of the rights and freedoms to which our society is committed. In particular, domestic human rights laws do not address the fact that human rights deprivations occur with respect to the ability to access such basic needs as food, shelter, social security and health care.

Secondly, human rights commissions are essentially self-contained in the sense that their findings are enforceable only by means of special procedures and remedies set out in the legislation itself, and not by ordinary recourse through the court system. As recently as 1981, the Supreme Court of Canada, still conditioned to looking to the legislature for the ultimate answer, affirmed this restrictive nature of human rights codes and thereby continued to lay the burden of policy-making on the legislature. In the case of *Board of Governors of Seneca College of Applied Arts and Technology* v. *Bhadauria* (1981), 124 D.L.R. (3d) 193, the Court held that the *Ontario Human Rights Code* must be interpreted as having been intended to restrict the enforcement of its discrimination prohibitions to the measures established by the Code itself, and not to vest any supplementary enforcement responsibility in the courts. The decision effectively eliminated the argument that the very existence of anti-discrimination legislation meant that discrimination, in and of itself, could constitute a civil action for damages before the courts.

Therefore, despite the tremendous legislative initiative dealing with rights violations, the system of human rights law in Canada developed in a peculiarly de-centralized manner. Even with the establishment of a national *Bill of Rights,* the refusal by the courts in any way to weaken the political principle of legislative supremacy, effectively denied Canadians the benefit of a universally applicable human rights statute.

THE ADVENT OF THE *CHARTER*

By virtue of the *Constitution Act, 1982,* the British Parliament ceased to have authority to legislate for Canada; however, perhaps the most significant element of this historic document is the *Canadian Charter of Rights and Freedoms,* which guarantees Canadians fundamental rights and freedoms. While the *Charter* represents a culmination of the Canadian trend away from the British approach of an unwritten constitution as the preferred method of protecting fundamental freedoms, a trend which began with the adoption of the statutory *Bill of Rights,* it is important to note that most of the *Charter* rights were already protected by statute or common law prior to 1982. What is significant, then, is the enhanced legal status which the *Charter* accords these rights simply by placing them in an entrenched constitution. Moreover, s. 52 of the *Constitution Act, 1982* expressly states that "The Constitution of Canada is the supreme law of Canada and any law that is inconsistent with the provisions of the Constitution is, to the extent of the inconsistency, of no force or effect." Thus, the *Charter* expressly modified the tradition of parliamentary supremacy with the principle of constitutional supremacy and thereby ushered in a whole new era of judicial review.

Thus, in 1982, the Canadian courts finally received a clear mandate not only to determine whether the laws passed by federal and provincial legislative bodies violate the rights and freedoms granted by the *Charter,* but to strike down those which do not conform to the *Charter*'s precepts. The question remains, however, to what extent the courts will use their new role to alter the doctrine of parliamentary supremacy and even the structure of federalism itself. In order to answer this question properly, it is useful to study the rulings of the

Supreme Court of Canada, as it is this court that generally sets the tone for the entire judicial system.

During the first years of the Court's treatment of the *Charter*, a clear signal was sent out that the *Charter* was to be given a large and liberal interpretation. The Court emphasized that the task of interpreting a constitution was crucially different from that of construing a statute such as the *Bill of Rights*. In *Hunter v. Southam Inc.*, [1984] 2 S.C.R. 145, Chief Justice Dickson urged his fellow judges "not to read the provisions of the Constitution like a last will and testament lest it become one." *Charter* interpretation, according to the Chief Justice, must be generous rather than legalistic. These words were equally matched by a boldness of decision-making. For example, while section 32 of the *Charter* declared that its provisions applied to all matters within the authority of Parliament and the legislatures of the provinces, the Court in the 1985 *Operation Dismantle* case embraced a broad concept of judicial review in its scrutiny of the federal Cabinet's decision to allow the testing of the cruise missile over Canadian territory. While the Court held that the executive branch of the Canadian government has a duty to act in accordance with the dictates of the *Charter*, no violation of *Charter* rights was established in this case. As well, in the area of legal rights, the Court used the *Charter* to alter the Canadian criminal process away from a "crime control" model to a more "due process" approach that protected the rights of the accused.

Perhaps the height of the broad interpretive approach adopted by the Court in the first years of the *Charter* was reached in the case of *Reference Re Section 94(2) of the Motor Vehicle Act, [1985]* 2 S.C.R. 486. In that case, the Court dealt with s. 7 of the *Charter*, which guarantees the right to life, liberty and security of the person, and the right not to be deprived thereof except in accordance with the principles of fundamental justice. The Court held that the principles of fundamental justice embraced a substantive as well as a procedural due process requirement. Thus, an element of mental intent is constitutionally required for any offence for which the accused could be liable to the punishment of imprisonment. This meant that punishment of an offence automatically on the basis of the act alone, without evidence of intent, was unconstitutional. This decision ultimately had broad implications for the crime of murder, which had traditionally included acts wherein the accused must either have foreseen, or ought to have foreseen, death as a probable, though unintentional, result.

Finally, it is worth noting that the Court's initial nullification of 19 pieces of legislation by way of the *Charter* is in sharp contrast with the Court's prior exercise of deferential judicial review under the *Bill of Rights*, pursuant to which the Court struck down only part of one statute, in fact an obscure section of the *Indian Act*. In addition, not only were the judges of the Supreme Court strongly activist in the first few years of the *Charter*, but in virtually all cases they were also unanimous.

After about 1985, the Court appeared to divide into two wings. The activist wing continued to give broad and generous interpretations to *Charter* rights, while the other wing adhered to the philosophy of deferring to the legislators and, therefore, tended to limit the overall reach of the *Charter*. With the considerable change in the composition of the Court after 1989, a growing sense of caution and judicial self-restraint has appeared to permeate the Court. A good illustration of this emerging trend is found in the Court's 1992 decision in the case of *Her Majesty the Queen and Canada Employment and Immigration Commission* v. *Schachter*. In that case, the issue was the extent to which the courts have the power to rewrite discriminatory laws so as to bring them into line with the requirements of the *Charter*. Prior to November 1990, the *Unemployment Insurance Act* provided parental benefits for men who were adoptive parents but not for natural fathers. Mr. Schachter, a natural father, challenged the law as being contrary to the s. 15 equality guarantees of the *Charter*. In a unique decision, the Federal Court of Canada, Trial Division addressed the problem by reading the words "natural parent" into the relevant section of the Act. The Court felt that to declare the offending provision of the statute unconstitutional, and thus of no force or effect, would take a benefit away from others but would not guarantee the positive right to equality envisioned by section 15 of the *Charter*.

On appeal, the Supreme Court considered the appropriateness of judicial lawmaking. The Court made it clear that judges who rule that laws violate *Charter* guarantees must always be careful not to overstep their bounds and intrude into the legislative sphere. While it may be possible for the courts to remedy legislation that is otherwise under-inclusive, this should be done only where it will clearly not substantially alter the nature of the social program at issue. In most instances, however, it is preferable to allow Parliament or a provincial legislature to formulate the solution to these constitutional problems, particularly where, as in this case, the appropriation of public funds is involved. Therefore, the Court decided that, without a mandate based on a clear legislative objective, it would be inappropriate to read in the excluded class of persons under the *Unemployment Insurance Act*. The better course would be to declare the provision invalid but suspend that declaration to allow the relevant legislative body to weigh all the factors in amending the statute so as to meet its constitutional obligations. Such a declaration was unnecessary in this case, however, given that Parliament had amended the legislation in 1990 to provide equal benefits to natural fathers, before the Supreme Court rendered its decision in the matter.

In assessing the recent changes in the Court, it is useful to keep in mind the nature of judicial policy-making that is involved under the *Charter*. Essentially the courts make human rights policies in two ways. The first is to define the specific content of the rights and freedoms enshrined in the *Charter*. For example, it must be determined whether the "right to life" covers a fetus and whether equality encompasses economic and social rights. Secondly, the courts must decide whether a government objective that violates a right, once it is defined, can be considered justified pursuant to s. 1 of the *Charter*. Section 1 applies to all rights and freedoms under the *Charter* and subjects them to "such reasonable limitations prescribed by law as can be demonstrably justified in a free and democratic society." Therefore, section 1 involves a highly discretionary balancing test between the policy interests of government and the interest in the *Charter* litigant in having his or her rights upheld. It is important to recognize that s. 1 represents one of two concessions to parliamentary sovereignty under the *Charter*. The second is s. 33 ("the notwithstanding clause"), which permits the federal and provincial legislatures to enact laws which violate some, but not all, of the rights and freedoms enumerated by the *Charter*, but only for a maximum period of five years.

It is with respect to the balancing test under s. 1 of the *Charter* that the judicial ideology of the Court has changed most. Initially, a rather strict approach was taken whereby the government had to prove that the law or government action at issue was sufficiently important to override a *Charter* right and that the means adopted to attain that objective was reasonable and demonstrably justified. Members of the Court have now moved towards a more flexible approach requiring a less stringent fulfilment of the section 1 requirement in certain cases. Some would even argue that in recent equality cases the Court has seemed to withdraw from its activist approach to interpreting the substantive content of rights proclaimed under the *Charter*. Indeed, it would appear that some justices are even applying section 1 analyses while determining whether a *Charter* right has been infringed in the first instance. As a result, it has been contended that the scope of rights and freedoms under the *Charter* has been watered down and that the burden on government to defend its actions has lessened significantly.

A number of explanations have been advanced for the Court's shift away from its more aggressive approach to the application of the *Charter*. Some contend that the Court is simply being careful not to tread on what it sees as clear exercises of legislative power. According to this view, innovative and creative change, particularly in the social and economic fields, should come not from the judiciary but from elected legislators who are better equipped to assess the full gamut of policy alternatives. This may explain then why the Court now appears to uphold *Charter* rights more often in areas where it feels most comfortable, such as cases involving the criminal trial process. Others, however, argue that members of the Court have simply come to the realization that the balancing of individual and societal interests in a rapidly changing world does not lend itself easily to the application of neutral judicial principles. Thus, individual justices are being forced to rely on their own reasoning processes rather than conventional judicial wisdom. This may explain why the Court has tended to split on its most recent equality cases, with decisions being rendered by very slim majorities.

The role of government and the legislators has also changed with the arrival of the *Charter*. The Minister of Justice must now examine all government bills introduced in the House of Commons to ensure they are consistent with the *Charter*. Furthermore, even before the bills reach the House, at the policy development stage of legislating, government lawyers are now routinely involved in identifying and assessing the *Charter* implications of any proposed law. Legislation that may seem to run counter to the rights and freedoms protected by the *Charter* must be carefully rationalized and backed by solid policy arguments and evidence. Thus, the struggle to weigh and balance policy interests is an evolving skill in the legislative, as well as the judicial, realm.

CONCLUSION

As a result of a federal structure with a division of legislative powers, plus a constitutional revision in 1982, human rights in Canada are both entrenched in the Constitution and safeguarded in legislation at the federal, provincial and territorial levels. The creation of the *Charter* did not eliminate existing human rights legislation or diminish its importance. To the contrary, not only does the *Charter* itself in s. 26 guarantee the continuation of existing rights and freedoms in Canada, but the advent of the *Charter* also had the profound effect of freeing the courts from the constraint of the doctrine of parliamentary supremacy in the interpretation and enforcement of human rights statutes. In the post-*Charter* era, both the *Bill of Rights* and federal and provincial human rights legislation were given "quasi-constitutional" status by the Supreme Court and this has served to place them above ordinary legislation.

Thus, the *Bill of Rights* continues in force in Canada and its importance lies in those provisions that the *Charter* does not duplicate—for example, the right to the enjoyment of property (s. 1(a)). Federal and provincial human rights statutes also continue to play a significant role in the promotion and protection of human rights because they are concerned with private acts of discrimination, whereas the application of the *Charter* is limited to governmental action. However, because human rights legislation is law, the reach of the *Charter* may well extend to private acts of discrimination through judicial interpretations of the prohibited grounds of discrimination and any statutory exceptions to such prohibitions found in these statutes. Moreover, just as decisions rendered under the *Charter* will be used in human rights hearings, so too will human rights decisions be used in interpreting the *Charter*. While it may seem odd to speak of the effect of a federal or provincial statute on a constitutional instrument such as the *Charter*, human rights legislation in Canada has a history of significant decisions that can be useful tools in *Charter* interpretation.

The *Charter*, the *Bill of Rights* and federal and provincial human rights laws, in conjunction with the legislators' duty to comply with the *Charter* and the courts' role in ensuring such compliance, all combine to provide Canadians with a comprehensive scheme of human rights promotion and protection.

It's Time...It's Time...
Is it Time for Restorative Justice?

John Winterdyk

Whether it is the general public, academics, or practitioners working within the criminal justice system, few would disagree that the system is in a state of crisis. Crime rates rise; police resources are heavily taxed; criminal courts are chronically backlogged; and prisons are overcrowded. After adjusting for inflation, Canadians have gone from paying $4.38 per capita in 1961, to $16.85 in 1980, and to $340 in 1994/95 to maintain our criminal justice system! Can we say we are getting our money's worth? The stage seems ripe for a major shift in how we respond to crime.

ONCE UPON A TIME

Our current Canadian justice system owes much to two schools of thought that emerged in the eighteenth and nineteenth centuries when social justice was somewhat less than equitable: the *classical* and the *positivist* models.

On the one hand, the *classical model* emphasizes such concepts as criminal intent, due process, equity, civil rights, and the rules of evidence. Further, it advocates that punishment should be swift, certain, and proportionately severe. These fundamental principles are still evident in the manner in which the police enforce law and in how the judicial process attempts to assess guilt or innocence.

Winterdyk, J. (1998). It's time, its time .... is it time for restorative justice? *Law Now,* (22): 20-22. Reprinted with permission from the Legal Studies Program, Faculty of Extension, University of Alberta.

On the other, the *positivist model* attempts to recognize individuality and the need to exact some kind of compensation for society when someone is found guilty of a crime. In a very general sense, recent sentencing amendments exemplify some of these elements. The sentencing and the correctional response is designed to find the *treatment* (a medical model) *or punishment* (a retributive model) that best fits the crime committed by the offender. Consequently, the sentencing process has always presented a challenge to the courts. How does one administer justice, in the legal sense, while at the same time balancing justice in the social sense? Nevertheless, our legal system has served us well. The social reforms through the Age of Enlightenment did much to bring us out of the Dark Ages of self-help justice and barbarism. Yet, much has changed since then.

Punishment—Is there ever a Time for It?

The notion of retribution and revenge has had a very long history. In antiquity, justice was based on the Mosaic principle of "an eye for an eye". When there were no formal systems to mediate disputes, we simply took justice into our own hands—*self-help* justice (clan warfare). Such mentality has been the cause of numerous family, clan, and national wars. I was recently told that in 3,400 years of recorded history we have had only about 265 war-free years! Has our preoccupation with punishing offenders done any good?

One of the champions for an alternative form of justice is Ezzat Fattah, founder of the criminology program at Simon Fraser University and a former chief prosecutor in his native land, Egypt. In a recent article, Fattah presented a list of reasons why punishment does not, and never will work. I will list but a few of his reasons.

- *Punishment is ineffective:* The United States sends more people per capita to prison than any other Western country yet their crime problem shows no signs of reversing. China has been executing offenders liberally in an attempt to stem the tide of crime. Singapore's zero tolerance for many crimes is showing signs of faltering. Do we want to embrace such concepts?
- *Punishment is costly:* The financial costs have been escalating as a result of inflation, more legal cases to process, and growing prison populations. What social and financial good has ever come of placing an offender in prison? Recidivism rates remain a reality. What good does locking someone up do the victim?

- *Punishment treats human beings as a means to an end:* While punishing someone can have a cathartic effect on the victim and general public, it does little for the individual being punished. The few souls that reform are a far cry from the many who feel degraded, humiliated, and stigmatized, and who exit prison ready to reoffend. Is there not a better solution?
- *Punitive penal sanctions amount to punishing the victim:* When someone falls from grace, we want to put him or her out of sight. The outcome is the offender loses *and the victim has no real recourse to heal.* Is this true justice? The common link as to why punishment does not work is that the legal system has tended to ignore the victim's right to heal. Virtually every religion has long since recognized this oversight in the legal system.

BORROWING FROM THE PAST FOR THE FUTURE— RESTORATIVE JUSTICE

Restorative justice is a new craze that resembles a movement rather than a particular practice. However, its principles are far from novel. In their own way, the North American First Nations people practise restorative justice as do the Aborigines and the Maori. The philosophy of the ancient *healing circles* embody many of the principles espoused by the *new* restorative model.

When a First Nations community member committed a wrong, the community held a healing circle to repair the damage. Through open discussion and supportive interaction, the offender had to repair his or her wrongdoing by meeting with the victim and members of the community. A mutually acceptable resolution was sought so that harmony (e.g., physical, mental, emotional, and spiritual) could be restored. Healing took place within the community.

WHAT IS RESTORATIVE JUSTICE?

The key principles and philosophy of restorative justice include the following:

- When a wrong (crime) is committed, the offender is obliged to restore the victim, and by extension the community. This involves a shift from moral responsibility to social responsibility;
- The process has strong psychological and sociological underpinnings. Research has shown that publicly *shaming* an offender can serve as a powerful tool to re-integrate the individual;

- Retribution focuses on the crime as being a violation of the state while restoration focuses on the crime as being a violation of people. This involves a shift from a guilt orientation to a consequence orientation. Existing programs that use this approach include the Victim Offender Reconciliation Program, Victim Offender Mediation, and in New South Wales and Australia—*Reintegrative shaming;*
- Crime is not an abstraction but an injury and violation to a person and a community that should be repaired. This involves a shift from revenge and retribution to social, emotional, physical, and spiritual restitution;
- The process should respect all parties—victim, offender, and justice colleagues. Thus, we have taken something from the past, given it a new name and are trying to fit it into an old legal system from a different tradition! How can the legal system incorporate this new philosophy of restorative justice into the legal arena?

CONDITIONAL SENTENCING—JUST IN TIME!?

In September 1996, Bill C-41 came into force. This legislation provides for new sentencing options and the use of alternative measures. It is the administrative legal answer to providing restorative justice.

Judge Heino Lilles has provided an insightful and cogent analysis of the new amendments. First, the notion of providing alternative measures to incarceration will not only require some judges and lawyers to re-align their thinking but require some public educative efforts. This must dispel the myth that the criminal justice system would become even softer on criminals.

All parties need to understand that the central focus of sentencing in the *Criminal Code* stresses the safety of the community. This has not been compromised by the new legislation. For example, Bill C-41 limits the use of conditional sentencing to certain summary type offences and requires mandatory and optional conditions.

Secondly, judges and lawyers will need to be sensitive to the availability of community correctional resources to accommodate the use of conditional sentencing. For example, it has been suggested that in Alberta conditional sentences only be sought for cases where traditionally a custodial sentence of three months or less would be imposed. Peter Teasdale, Regional Director of General Prosecution for Alberta Justice, points out that those who have "committed driving-related offences, break and enter of a dwelling house, domestic violence or other offences involving violence will not be eligible." In other words, the sentencing option would be limited to those who pose minimal risk.

Finally, conditional sentencing might well represent a constructive alternative to our current punitive practices of dispensing justice. It empowers the legal profession with a wider range of options for attaining just solutions.

IS IT TIME? A WORD OF CAUTION

Bill C-41 on sentencing reform appears to represent the legal tool by which to *reengineer* the criminal justice system toward restorative justice. The legislation has been met with considerable enthusiasm. However, I would like to share a few observations of issues that should be addressed before the legal community embraces it further.

- The majority of charges disposed of in adult provincial court are impaired driving, fraud/forgery, failure to appear, and failure to comply with probation. Together they make up nearly 50% of all charges in provincial court. Given my reading of Bill C-41 and Mr. Teasdale's comments along with court statistics, only about 15% of cases might be eligible for conditional sentencing. The criminologist, James Q. Wilson, observed a few years ago that four to six percent of the criminal population is responsible for 50% of all crimes. However, since this four to six percent are not eligible, where should we be directing our justice resources?
- Currently, approximately 36% of adult criminal cases result in fines, 31% in probation, 30.5% in prison sentences (of which nearly 70% serve 3 months or less), and 2.4% in restitution. Given Judge Lilies' observation that "great care must be taken to ensure that conditional sentences are not used *in lieu* of fines, suspended sentences, and orders of probation," how will the legal system avoid widening the net of social control?
- Where is the money to support conditional sentencing programs going to come from? For 1994/95, police continue to receive the largest proportion of justice spending ($5.78 billion or $152 per capita—based on constant dollar figures) while youth corrections receives the lowest allotment ($.49 billion in 94/95 or $14 per capita). Our current focus of spending does not appear to reflect a philosophy of restorative justice.
- Should restorative justice be associated with the legal system and other elements of the criminal justice system? Other countries (e.g.,

New Zealand, Australia, and several European countries) have chosen not to embed the movement within criminal justice.

- As yet restorative justice cannot be considered an empirically tested model or theory of justice. Anecdotal accounts should not be seen as demonstrable proof.
- Under Bill C-41, conditional sentencing requires that intervention occur between conviction and sentencing and serve not as a replacement but as an option available to the court system. Will this add to the cost as cases are diverted into a new infrastructure?
- Does Bill C-41 provide sufficient interpretation to enable sentencing judges to achieve some restorative element by *satisfying* the needs of all parties concerned even when the offender is uncooperative? The Bill does not foist this on the accused.
- Whether we call it *shaming* or restoration, we need to be able to answer whether such concepts can work in our heterogeneous and highly urbanized communities.
- Is the legal system capable of shifting its focus from procedure (establishing guilt/innocence) to one of process?
- Will it be necessary to screen individuals as to their ability to learn from the process?
- Are the victims' rights being superimposed on the offender?
- Will practices that are restorative in nature be compromised once defined within a larger legal/court-based system and its traditions and processes?
- Finally, will restorative justice as administered by the legal system promote a better quality of justice?

A FINAL WORD

The past has been filled with many great ideas about crime control, few of which have lived up to their promises. We should take heart and welcome the opportunity to explore the restorative philosophy as made available through Bill C-41, but there is a need to tread lightly. Criminological research and new criminological theory suggest that constructive reform will not occur until the legal community (and the criminal justice system in general) adopts an integrated and interdisciplinary approach to the crime problem. This requires viewing crime as a human behavior issue not just a legal matter.

A Balanced-Approach Mission in a Restorative Framework

Gordon Bazemore and Mark Umbreit

Previous efforts to reform the juvenile justice system have brought about positive changes including increased due process protections for juveniles, improved classification and risk assessment, and smaller, less crowded residential facilities. These reforms in the structure and process of offender treatment have done little however to change the content of intervention. New programs such as those focused on creative service, work experience, and decision-making skills have occasionally provided innovation and suggested directions for altering the context of intervention. Unfortunately, however, most new programs follow trends and fads in juvenile justice and are typically added without attention to needs or goals. Moreover, even when effective, such programs often serve relatively few clients and thus have little impact on improving the system as a whole.

To meet basic needs, juvenile justice professionals must develop different system priorities for intervention based on clearly stated outcomes directed at the clients or "customers" of the system. They must also change the context of intervention by defining new, more active roles for citizens, offenders, and crime victims in the justice process. An effective mission is needed to guide rational reform and help justice professionals and communities restructure

Bazemore, G. and Umbreit, M. (1997). A balanced approach mission in a restorative framework. In *Balanced and restorative justice for juveniles*. St. Paul, Minnesota: University of Minnesota. (pp. 11-19). Reprinted with permission.

their systems in a meaningful way while avoiding fads and "quick fix" solutions. As suggested in Figure 1, the mission must be used actively in daily decision-making to guide reform and ensure effective management.

Figure 1:   What is a mission and what does it do?

A mission is a statement of the role or function of an agency or system which:	**A mission helps agencies:**
Identifies "customers" of the system	Avoid "fad" programs and "ad hoc" practices
Specifies performance objectives and outcomes	Build consensus with other agencies and other professionals
Prioritizes practices and programs Identifies roles of staff, youth, and community	Engage the support of community agencies and clarify responsibilities
Affirms the underlying values of an agency	Plan for the future and serve as blueprint for implementing systematic reforms

Source: Bazemore and Washington. (1995). Charting the Future for the Juvenile Justice System: Reinventing Mission and Management. *Spectrum, The Journal of State Government*, 68(2): 51-66.

THE BALANCED APPROACH

The Balanced Approach mission addresses the public need for: 1) sanctioning based on accountability measures which attempt to restore victims and clearly denounce and provide meaningful consequences for offensive behavior; 2) offender rehabilitation and reintegration; and 3) enhanced community safety and security. It does this by articulating three system goals directed toward the three primary "client/customers" of the system—the victim, the offender, and the community (see Figure 2). These system goals, which also govern the response to each offense, are: accountability; competency development; community protection.

- If the source of the problem of delinquency is in the community, family, schools, why do all casework strategies target only individual offenders for change and why are these other institutions so seldom involved in the change process?

- If the problem is really that an offender has harmed some person and/or the community, why are victims and community representatives not directly involved in the sanctioning and the rehabilitation process and why isn't restoration of victims the primary focus of sanctioning?

- If the problem is a lack of integration, rehabilitation, and habilitation, why do correctional strategies focus on isolation of offenders?

- If the goal of sanctioning is to send messages to offenders about the consequences and harm caused to others by crime, why are sanctions so unrelated to the offense itself and why is the sanctioning and rehabilitative process so detached from victims and the offender's community?

- If public support is needed to ensure juvenile justice effectiveness (and the continued survival of juvenile justice), why do we continue to send messages to the public that offenders are getting off easy or even being rewarded by the system for their crime (e.g., by referring them to recreational programs and giving low priority to victim and community restoration)?

- If the goal is to ensure public safety while offenders are on community supervision, why do we seem to utilize so few options for structuring the offender's time in productive activity and why do we focus only on offender surveillance rather than promoting strategies for developing safer communities?

- If the goal is to make offenders more responsible and accountable, why do we place them in positions (e.g., in most residential centers and treatment programs) where others assume responsibility for them?

- If juvenile justice professionals are experts in delinquent behavior, why are juvenile justice agencies treated only as a receptacle for dumping problem youth rather than a resource for resolving problems in schools and communities?

Source: Bazemore and Washington. (1995). Charting the Future of the Juvenile Justice System: Reinventing Mission and Management. *Spectrum, The Journal of State Government*, 68 (2): 51-66.

Figure 2: The balanced approach

Restorative Justice

Client/Customers	Goal	Values
Victims	Accountability	When an offense occurs, an obligation to victims and community incurs;
Youth	Competency Development	Offenders who enter the juvenile justice system should exit more capable than what they entered;
Community	Community Protection	Juvenile justice has a responsibility to protect the public from juveniles in the system.

Source: Adapted from Maloney, D., Romig, D., & Armstrong, T. (1988). NV: National Council of Juvenile and Family Court Judges. "Juvenile probation: The balanced approach." Reno, NV: National Council of Juvenile and Family Court Judges.

The overarching goal of "balance" suggests that policies and programs should seek to address each of the three goals in each case and that system balance should be pursued as managers seek to allocate resources to meet needs and achieve goals associated with each client/customer. Balance suggests that no one objective can take precedence over any other without creating a system that is "out of balance" and implies that efforts to achieve one goal (e.g., community protection) should not hinder efforts to achieve other goals. Values associated with each customer and each goal are shown in Figure 2.

As the primary sanctioning goal in the Balanced Approach, accountability refers specifically to the requirement that offenders "make amends" for the harm resulting from their crimes by repaying or restoring losses to victims and the community. Competency development, the rehabilitative goal for intervention, requires that youth who enter the juvenile justice system should exit the system more capable of being productive and responsible in the community. The community protection goal explicitly acknowledges and endorses a long time public expectation that juvenile justice must place equal emphasis on promoting public safety and security at the lowest possible cost. Finally, the mission is founded on the belief that justice is best served when the victim, community, and youth are viewed as equal clients of the justice system who will receive fair and balanced attention, be actively involved in the justice process, and gain tangible benefits from their interactions with the juvenile justice system.

The Balanced Approach mission is rooted in and responsive to traditional values in American communities (e.g., making amends to victims and the public; the work ethic). As a result, it provides a strong basis for engaging the support and participation of the community. To be successful in meeting the needs of the three customers, however, the Balanced Approach mission must be implemented within a value framework which recognizes crime as harm done to victims and the community, values the participation of victims and community in resolving the crime, and prioritizes restoration as a goal of the justice process. Restorative justice provides such a framework.

THE RESTORATIVE JUSTICE FRAMEWORK

Restorative justice offers a coherent alternative to the increasingly retributive philosophical focus of the juvenile court sanctioning process and moves beyond the limits of individual treatment based on the "medical model". While retributive justice is focused on public vengeance and provision of punishment through an adversarial process, restorative justice is concerned with the broader relationship between offender, victim, and community, and gives priority to repairing the damage or harm done to victims and victimized communities. Restorative justice differs most clearly from retributive justice (see Table 1 in its view of crime as more than simply lawbreaking—or a violation of government authority). Rather, what is most significant about criminal

Table 1:   Retributive and restorative assumptions

Retributive Justice	Restorative Justice
Crime is an act against the state, a violation of a law, an abstract idea	Crime is an act against another person and the community
The criminal justice system controls crime	Crime control lies primarily in the community
Offender accountability defined as taking punishment	Accountability defined as assuming responsibility and taking action to repair harm
Crime is an individual act with individual responsibility	Crime has both individual and social dimensions of responsibility

Punishment is effective
  a. threat of punishment deters crime
  b. punishment changes behavior
	Punishment alone is not effective in changing behavior and is disruptive to community harmony and good relationships

Victims are peripheral to the process	Victims are central to the process of resolving a crime
The offender is defined by deficits	The offender is defined by capacity to make reparation
Focus on establishing blame or guilt, on the past (did he/she do it?)	Focus on problem solving, on liabilities/obligations, on the future (what should be done?)
Emphasis on adversarial relationship	Emphasis on dialogue and negotiation
Imposition of pain to punish and deter/prevent	Restitution as a means of restoring both parties; goal of reconciliation/restoration
Community on sideline, represented abstractly by state	Community as facilitator in restorative process
Response focused on offender's past behavior	Response focused on harmful consequences of offender's behavior; emphasis on the future
Dependence upon proxy professionals	Direct involvement by participants

Source: Adapted from Zehr, 1990.

behavior is the harm to victims, communities and offenders that is its result. The most important function of justice is to ensure that this harm is repaired.

The interest in restorative justice has been fueled by the crime victims' movement, the positive experience with reparative sanctions for juvenile offenders, the rise of informal neighborhood justice and dispute resolution processes, and new thinking on equity and human relationships. Support for restorative justice has also benefited from increasing skepticism about the supposed preventive and deterrent effects of the current system and a general sense of frustration with the retributive paradigm and its detachment from the real problems of victims, offenders and communities (see Table 2).

Restorative justice offers a different "lens" for viewing the problem of crime and provides a new outlook on the appropriate public response to the harm that results when an offense is committed. As an overall philosophy for the juvenile justice system, restorative justice provides critical guidance to managers and policy makers in rethinking the traditional sanctioning, rehabilitative, and public safety functions of juvenile justice—and adding the new concern with making victims whole and involving them in the justice process. Neither punitive nor lenient in its focus, restorative justice has as its primary objectives reparation of harm done to victims, recognition by the offender of harm caused by the offense, conciliation and (if appropriate) reconciliation between victim, offender, and community, offender reintegration whenever possible, and the maintenance of safe and secure communities in which conflicts are peacefully resolved.

A Three-Dimensional Focus: Balancing Victim, Offender, and Community Needs

Viewing victims, communities, and offenders as "customers" implies a different way of thinking for juvenile justice professionals. As used in this document, a "customer" is someone who receives a service from the system and whose needs are therefore important. In addition, from a restorative justice perspective, the term customer implies an individual or group that should be actively involved as a participant in the system rather than simply a passive recipient of service or an object of system intervention. Ultimately, system outcomes and performance measures should also be linked to measurable change in the situation and quality of life of these customers.

Restoring Victims. Why victims? Isn't it too much to ask of juvenile justice professionals to be concerned with the needs of victims and to seek and

---

Table 2:   Why restorative justice?—problems in retributive justice and the
           restorative response

---

1. *Lack of clarity about the purpose of the criminal justice system*—
   Restorative justice says the primary purpose of the justice system is to
   repair harm done—to the victim and the community.

2. *Contrary impulses between punishment and rehabilitation*—Restorative
   justice replaces the focus on punishment (as measured by pain inflicted)
   with a focus on accountability, as measured by taking responsibility. Such
   accountability is not in conflict with, and in fact supports, rehabilitation.

3. *Victim frustration and alienation*—Restorative justice provides for victim
   involvement and victim focus.

4. *Public expectation that the criminal justice system will control crime*—
   Restorative justice has a goal of reparation and would measure outcomes
   based on the question: To what degree has the harm been repaired?
   Restorative justice would reject the assumption that sanctions can or
   should be a major influence in crime control; a restorative policy would
   force a rethinking of crime reduction strategies."

5. *Failure of increasing punishment to change behavior*—Restorative justice
   is not premised on an assumption that punishment will change behavior
   and therefore will not fail to deliver on that promise.

6. *Skyrocketing cost of punishment*—Restorative justice would require fewer
   investments in punishment since the system would be measured not by
   how much punishment was inflicted, but by how much reparation was
   achieved.

7. *Failure to integrate social justice with criminal justice*—Restorative
   justice clearly defines a relationship between social justice and criminal
   justice. While individuals are held responsible for their behavior, the
   community is held accountable for promoting community peace, or
   "shalom," which includes social justice. For example, the community has a
   responsibility to enable offenders to make reparation and is not allowed to
   simply banish people.

8. *Widespread system overload*—The conflict resolution approach is likely
   to reduce the number of cases that must be handled in the formal system
   and would allow for more effective use of non-criminal justice community
   resources. A reduction in dependence on punishment would free up
   resources to be used in other parts of the system.

Source: Pranis, K. (1993). "Restorative justice: Back to the future in criminal justice."
Working paper, Minnesota Citizens Council, Minneapolis, MN.

---

encourage their involvement in the justice process? In a restorative justice model, the answers to these questions are based on principle and theory, as well as immediate practical concerns.

First, if it seems that restorative justice advocates give too much emphasis to the victim, this must be viewed as a practical reaction to the current state of affairs. In most juvenile justice systems, the quality and quantity of victim involvement is low and driven by retributive rather than restorative priorities. Although "victims rights" has become the watchword of many prosecutors and politicians, victim needs have not been a major concern. Rather, the concerns and interests of prosecutors, judges, defense attorneys, and rehabilitation programs all appear to take precedence over the needs of victims. To redress the imbalance of an exclusive focus on the offender, a restorative juvenile justice would thus devote primary, initial attention to the needs of victims. These include the need to have their victimization acknowledged; to be allowed to participate in the justice process; and to be given a decision-making role within this process.

Second, it is a matter of principle in restorative justice that the needs of victims receive attention and that those harmed by crime have a primary role in the justice process. But does victim involvement and the emphasis on victim reparation weaken or dilute the capacity of juvenile justice to meet other needs and accomplish other goals? A core assumption of restorative justice theory is that neither public safety, sanctioning, nor rehabilitative goals can be effectively achieved without the involvement of victims and the community.

From a restorative perspective, true rehabilitation cannot be achieved until the offender acknowledges the harm caused to victims and communities and makes amends. Likewise, achieving safe and secure communities will require attention to victims' needs and ultimately the adoption of effective community dispute resolution and mediation processes. Victims, as well as communities and offenders, also have an essential role to play in sanctioning offenders by defining the harm and identifying ways to repair this harm, and also in preventing future harm (public safety). As criminologist Leslie Wilkins has observed, "the problem of crime cannot be simplified to the problem of the criminal." Therefore, the needs of victims, offenders and communities cannot be effectively addressed in isolation from one another.

Restoring Offenders. While giving primary focus to repairing harm to victims, restorative justice also speaks directly to the need for societies to make allowances for offender repentance and to make possible and encourage offender reintegration following appropriate sanctioning. After reinforcing the offender's obligation to redress harm to victims and monitoring and facilitating reparation of harm, members of the offender's community should create conditions to facilitate the offender's reentry into the community. However, restorative justice does not imply that serious and violent offenders who present significant risks to themselves or others should be released into the community. Restorative justice advocates would argue that less reliance on incarceration strictly as a punitive tool, coupled with better strategies and more resources to strengthen the prevention capacity of communities, would be likely to increase use and efficiency of community-based programs. They would recognize the need, on the other hand, for secure facilities to protect the public from those offenders who represent significant risks to public safety. Moreover, restorative justice policies and practices would be employed as part of a systemic response to even the most serious offenders as well as in response to first offenses. On the front-end, restorative justice would demand a sanction requiring the offender to make amends to victims and the community, as well as a reintegrative and/or habilitative response. For the most serious offenders in secure institutions, responses such as victim awareness education may be appropriate. The competency development goal ... more directly addresses the needs of offenders for habilitation and reintegration from a restorative perspective.

Restoring Communities. Daniel Van Ness has written that restorative justice responds to crime at the micro level by addressing the harm that results when a specific offense is committed, through sanctioning focused on victim reparation. At the macro level, restorative justice addresses the need to build safer communities in which most conflicts which lead to crime can be peacefully resolved and the cycle of violence broken. The juvenile justice system and the community should play collaborative and complementary roles in both micro and macro responses to crime; the justice system should be assigned the responsibility for order, and the community the responsibility for restoring and maintaining peace. Restorative justice, through reparative sanctions and processes such as restitution, victim offender mediation, and community service fulfills a fundamental need of communities to denounce criminal behavior, provide meaningful consequences, and send a message to the offender and others that such behaviors are unacceptable. In addition, achieving safe and secure communities cannot be accomplished simply by locking up—or by treating—individual offenders. Citizens and victims must be actively involved in preventative processes such as alternative dispute resolution, as well as in offender rehabilitation and risk management. In an important sense, restorative justice is a *community* solution since as Braithwaite notes:

Crime is best controlled when members of the community are the primary controllers through active participation in shaming offenders, and having shamed them, through concerted participation in ... integrating the offender back in to the community.... Low Crime societies are societies where people do not mind their own business, where tolerance of deviance has definite limits, where communities prefer to handle their own crime problems rather than hand them over to professionals.